PRAISE

"A high-water mark in river r⸻⸻⸻⸻⸻⸻⸻⸻⸻⸻⸻⸻⸻ ⸳⸳ided."
— **Tim Cahill**, author of ⸻⸻⸻⸻⸻⸻ ⸳ks

"*Hell's Half Mile* is the perfect book to read aloud around a campfire with rapids roaring in the background. Full of great tales, funny stories, and river lore, it will make some river runners eager to get back into the boats—and some wishing they had stayed home."
— **Peter Stark**, author of *Last Breath* and *Driving to Greenland*

"This collection lets you live your fantasy: you are on a wild river with a gang of cynical, wide-eyed, honest, and mordantly hilarious companions. The light is ever-shifting; the rock and desert as you hope—or remember; and you are laughing so hard you can't breathe. Rock 'n' roll, river rats, rock 'n' roll."
— **Mary Sojourner**, author of *Solace* and *Bonelight*

"Just when you thought whitewater mayhem was no laughing matter, Michael Engelhard serves up *Hell's Half Mile*, a potpourri of ticklish adventures and misadventures. Find out what happens when bears, bad boats, bureaucracy, bad runs, bees, big holes, and overdoses of boyish enthusiasm are stirred until lumpy with a paddle or oars."
— **Michael P. Ghiglieri**, author of *Canyon*, *Over the Edge*, and *First Through Grand Canyon*

"Rolling with puns and surging with wit. Each author's irresistible writing captures the epic tales logged on the United States' wild Western rivers."
— **Lucia Stewart**, Outdoor Writers Association of America, editor of *Reflections of the Middle Fork*

"From the Arctic to the Grand Canyon, from the first story by R. M. Patterson to Engelhard's colorful glossary—this collection should be enjoyed and appreciated by every river runner."
— **Verne Huser**, author of *On the River with Lewis and Clark* and *Rivers of Texas*

"*Hell's Half Mile* represents the best in humorous outdoors writing and the lowest in guide culture."
— **John Weisheit**, co-founder of Colorado River Guides, co-author of *Cataract Canyon*, and Conservation Director of Living Rivers

hell's half mile

RIVER RUNNERS' TALES OF HILARITY AND MISADVENTURE

Edited by Michael Engelhard

BREAKAWAY BOOKS
HALCOTTSVILLE, NEW YORK
2004

Hell's Half Mile: River Runners' Tales of Hilarity and Misadventure

Compilation copyright by Michael Engelhard 2004

ISBN: 1-891369-47-4

Library of Congress Control Number: 2004106533

Published by Breakaway Books

P.O. Box 24

Halcottsville, NY 12438

(800) 548-4348

www.breakawaybooks.com

FIRST EDITION

In memory of Edward Abbey, Bill Beer, and R. M. Patterson.
Their spirit lives on.

acknowledgments

I FINALLY REALIZED why people use the growth and birth of a baby as a metaphor for doing a book: It hurts and makes you feel like throwing up every morning.

Had I even had a vague idea how much work this anthology entailed, I would have chosen a different project. The worst part was picking essays from a flood of first-class (and some not-so-great) material, to avoid ending up with a fifteen-hundred-page volume. The best part by far was that I got to read scores of riotous stories that I did not even know existed. But wrestling or wheedling these pieces from writers or the "license holders" of their tales frequently resembled hostage negotiations. If nothing else, this enterprise has deepened my admiration of, and empathy with, editors and their tight runs between the Scylla of authors and the Charybdis of publishers.

The people who helped me unearth hidden treasures, or to establish contact with reclusive wordsmiths, are too numerous to be thanked individually. My best wishes and thanks go to them, as well as to the agents and contributors of original essays, who—forever overcommitted and underpaid—often parted with precious words for a pittance (or less). A few people, nevertheless, need to be singled out here: Pete Gross, landlord and ventriloquist extraordinaire; Sue Beer, who entrusted a stranger with the writings of her late husband; Cristina Concepcion (I *didn't* pay anybody more); Scott Thiele, for naming names; computer whiz Carrie Valdez, patient and ever-helpful; Samantha Mitchell, for being reasonable; John Nichols and Lynne Bluestein of the University of New Mexico Press, and Stephen Topping of Johnson Books, for having a heart for the underdog; Verne Huser, who brought R. M. Patterson's timeless story to my attention; Lynn "Track-'em-down" Hamilton of Grand Canyon River Guides; Dirk Vaugan of Tex's Riverways, for pleading my case; José Knighton at Back-of-Beyond Books; Rodger Touchie and Vivian Sinclair of Heritage House Publishing; and David James Duncan, who helped me get in touch with a few more writing river rogues and in redrawing the line between fiction and nonfiction. I am grateful for all their efforts and encouragement.

Thanks also go to Garth Battista of Breakaway Books, for believing in humor as an antidote to daily routine, for believing in my ability to pull this off.

Lastly, I appreciate all readers who, in spending hard-earned dollars for this, not only support starving writers, but simultaneously validate e. e. cummings' most reasonable demand: "To hell with literature, we want something red-blooded."

First Publication Credits

"The Bear Voyageur" from *Far Pastures*; "Wilderness Temperament" from *The Telling Distance*; "River Rats" from *Downriver*; "High Water" from *There's This River*; "River Music" from *O.A.R.S. catalogue 1995*; "Zero Heroes" from *Canoe & Kayak*; "Das Marlboro Abenteurer Team" from *Car Camping*; "Frozen Ro-tundra" from *Sandstone Seductions*; "Games" from *What the River Says*; "Tempting the River Gods" from *Threading the Currents*; "Rafting? Schmafting: I Want My River Back!" from *Dancing on the Stones*; "This River Is Out to Get Me" from *We Swam the Grand Canyon*; "Hapless Is as Hapless Does" from *Paddler Magazine*; "Jug Not Jig" from *Fly Rod and Reel*; "The Mother of All Takeouts" from *The Hibernacle News*; "The Best 'True Tourist Tale' Ever" from *Aspen Times*.

contents

preface

THERE IS A joke nearly as ancient as the sandstone canyons enfolding my desert domicile, Moab. Q: How can you tell when a river guide lies? A: When he (or she) opens his (or her) mouth.

Whether in bars or around campfires, on boat ramps, at trade shows, weddings, or wakes—wherever two or more specimens of *Rattus aquatus* (the common river rat) come together, they will reminisce and swap tales. It is true, with each telling the waves get higher, the holes more gnarly, and the boat smaller. More than likely, the epic account opens with "No shit, there I was," a phrase, that by now has become formulaic and as typical of this genre as "Once upon a time . . ." of another. And yet, like the cowpoke, fly fisherperson, huntress, and mountaineer, this hardy breed has developed a repertoire of fact-based stories that are as hair-raising as they are hilarious. Theirs is largely an oral tradition. When strapped for cash, however—which they almost always are—boat people have been known to pick up paper and pen, attempting to finance their next adventure (or bar crawl) through the selling of yarns to obscure publications. These hidden and scattered treasures not only deserve to be collected and preserved; they ought to be discovered and cherished by the world at large.

The book you hold in your hands is destined to become a minor classic in the under-represented and overlooked body of revisionist adventure writing. It is the long-overdue chronicle of Monty Python's meetings with Lewis & Clark. I do not hesitate at all to call it "timeless." The following excerpt shows not only that such work can indeed sparkle with wit and eloquence, but beyond that shine with enduring value and greatness. It also reminds us that even the living legends of this métier often started out bungling rather than brilliant.

For me this floating began near home on Crooked Crick in the Allegheny Mountains of western Pennsylvania. (The wrong side of the mountains.) My brother Hoots and I built a boat. He was nine years old, I was ten. To be honest, we didn't build it, we stole it. From my father. Nor was it exactly a boat. Actually it was a rectangular wooden box, about four feet by three and one foot deep, used for mixing cement in. In the words of singer Katie Lee, another river rat, our boat "had no stern and had no bow / It looked just like a garbage scow." The bottom was flat, the insides well caulked with dried concrete. To my brother and me it resembled a boat. With immense effort we dragged, pushed and weaseled this thing down through the woods to the creek, a labor of several hours. It was very heavy. We slid it down a muskrat slide and shoved it into the water, climbing aboard. There was room for us both; we were small. We clung to the gunwales as our scow sank peacefully and immediately to the bottom of the creek, leaving us sitting in water up to our necks.

That was very long ago.

LIKE EDWARD ABBEY, many of us survived to tell of similar formative events, experiences we would not want to relive, but not to forget either. River wisdom postulates that there are two kinds of boaters: those who *have* flipped and those who *will*. Most of the contributors to this anthology fall into the former category.

Between these covers, you will find assembled the crème de la crème of western river writers, people who wield paddle and oar as deftly as the Delete button on their PC. They are all here: the misfits and misanthropes; the dreamers and daredevils; weekend warriors and professional guides; nataphobes and bibliophiles; "established voices" and undiscovered gems. Each one of these incredible tales is true—at least to the degree any river runner is able to distinguish reality from whisperings of his or her sun-addled and river-pounded brain. The discerning reader will, however, notice the occasional pseudonym. Yet even the perpetrators of these essays assure me that their short biographies, as well as the events and characters described, are factual.

It will come to the same reader's attention that I have applied the term *river runners* loosely. Some of our protagonists ride strange craft, others—none at all.

A few more words regarding the title may be in order here. Initially, I had my heart set on *Hell to Pay*, in commemoration of the notorious rapid in Cataract Canyon, named by the Best expedition of 1891. Then my phone rang. A friend informed me that there already was a book with that title. A quick search on the Internet yielded not one, but half a dozen, including *A Thriller; A Novel of Responsibility;* and *The Unfolding Story of Hillary Rodham Clinton.* I could already hear the clamoring of people who had purchased *this* book by mistake. I also feared it would grow mold in the dark recesses of the "Celebrity Biography" section of Barnes & Noble. My next choice was *Hell or High Water*. But alas, this euphonious line had also been snatched, for a book about James White's much-disputed first passage through the Grand Canyon (during which he passed out on a raft of crudely tied logs).

In utter desperation, I turned to John Wesley Powell. This one-armed Civil War veteran first recorded the name of the boulder-strewn, thunderous stretch of whitewater in Lodore Canyon that now graces the cover. If not necessarily known for his sense of humor, the great explorer at least deserves credit for his doggedness and can-do attitude.

As with so many writing projects, the roots of this one are deeply personal. A humorous river story I submitted to various adventure glossies was rejected repeatedly. Eventually, one editor agreed to publish it—grudgingly—butchered and buried somewhere between "A Buyer's Guide to Flotation Devices," and a column called "Outtakes from above the Takeout." I decided that Art deserves better. Thus, in addition to many other things, *Hell's Half Mile* (which easily could have become a book about getting published) is one river runner's sweet revenge.

the bear voyageur

R. M. Patterson

THE RAIN WAS getting heavier and the first muddy drops were starting to soak through the sod-and-pole roof and fall on the table of the old trapping cabin. Oscar had been holding forth to me on the subject of bears and the horrible jackpots they got people into, but he cut himself short and rose hastily. "Give me a hand to stack this grub on my bed," he said. "There's rocks and spruce-bark over the sod in that corner and maybe it'll stay dry. We can tarp up the rest of the stuff on the floor."

Oscar's life had been a varied one. He had been cowpuncher, packer, and prospector in his time, and now, this summer, he was cooking for NWX in the Mackenzie Mountains of the North-West Territories. On this dismal afternoon Oscar and I were sitting in Faille's cabin, feeding wood into the stove and trying to keep things dry.

Outside the rain lashed down on the sod roof and on the hissing surface of the lake. The helicopter was grounded, and out in the mountains, in four lonely, scattered camps, above timberline and by the shores of alpine lakes, the field parties would be cowering in their shelters or beneath overhanging rocks, cursing this storm—which might well be snow for some of them. Streamlined modern prospecting had skidded wetly to a standstill.

Oscar put two fresh-made pies into the oven of the cookstove and shut the door on them. "There's supper," he said. "That is, if we can keep the oven from floodin'. And there goes that bear with the twin cubs again—she must have a regular round that way." And he pointed through the open door and across the lake to the distant shore. He had eyes like twin telescopes: all I could see was a dim movement through the blueness of the storm.

"I figure there's two reasons why Faille built his cabin on this island," Oscar went on. "One—there's hardly any mosquitoes on it; and that's a queer thing for July in this Flat River country. And, two—maybe it's kind of off the trail a bit for bears and wolverines. Though that's only my guess. The way a bear'll swim if he ever winds anything, a bit of water's no protection."

"Not much," I said. "I remember one time I was fishing in a big eddy below the Long Canyon on the Finlay. There was a bunch of fresh-caught fish in the canoe. I was sitting quite still and just drifting round and round—and paying no attention to what I thought was a bit of old burnt log floating round with me. And, believe it or not, it was a black bear, and I just woke up in time or he'd have been into the canoe with me. I grabbed a paddle and flicked that canoe down the rapid below the eddy—a grayling couldn't have moved quicker. A seventeen-foot prospector canoe is just not big enough for a man and a bear."

"No," Oscar said. "But a twenty-foot freight is—and for *two* men and a bear. I'll tell you a tale—"

"A bear in a canoe? Do I *have* to believe that?"

"Now just hold your horses a minute. Give me a chance. This is a true tale and I had it from Big Paul himself: the first time I heard it was when we was workin' a prospect together in the Coast Range. Big Paul was no liar and I've heard him tell about that bear a good half-dozen times, and he never varied a word. Put a couple of sticks in the stove and I'll take a look at my pies. And then I'll tell you about Big Paul and Axel and the bear."

So we fixed the stove and the pies, and then I sat myself down to listen ...

The time, Oscar said, was around 1900. Late for the main Klondike rush, Big Paul and his partner had found a streak of rich pay gravel on a bench a little way up a creek that was tributary to the Stewart River. They brought a grubstake up from Dawson by canoe, enough to last them over a year with any luck—and that meant, with a moose or two added. They worked their claims through that first summer, and then all through the winter—burning and thawing and bringing the gravel to the surface. Now and then they took a panful of dirt over to the cabin they had built on the larger flat beyond the creek where the building timber grew. They panned it out there, in the warmth where they could keep water unfrozen, just to see how they were getting on; and what they saw encouraged them.

Spring came to the Yukon; the Stewart River ice went out and Big Paul's creek ran free. To cross it, in order to get to the claims, he and his partner fixed up the same rigging that they had used the previous summer—a line across the creek, stretched between two trees, and a block of wood with a well-rounded and polished hole in it through which the line was passed. The block slipped easily to and fro on the line; to it the canoe was attached by a short length of trackline that could be adjusted to suit the height of water. The whole thing made a sort of a cable ferry and a stroke or two of the paddle was enough to get the canoe across.

The pay-streak seemed to be easing off a bit, and the dump was thawing. The two partners started in to clean up, and they shoveled and sluiced and sluiced and shoveled, and all went well. Occasionally they took a day off and did some more prospecting across the creek—sinking one more shaft—and it was on these occasions that a she-bear with a good-sized yearling cub in tow began to do some prospecting around the main camp on her own account. The men were running low in grub and they couldn't afford to take chances— so they shot the mother bear and added her to the larder. They shot at, and missed, the yearling.

But the yearling didn't go clear away. He would come back from time to time, and then he would hang around looking lonely and forlorn and pretty sorry for himself. Sometimes he would disappear for a day or two, probably on a log-bashing expedition in search of grubs, but he always returned. Big Paul felt a bit remorseful about knocking off the yearling's mother, and the yearling didn't seem to want to do any harm or bother anybody. Finally, to cut a long story short, they tamed him and he became a part of the outfit. He even learnt to cross the creek in the canoe with them, sitting gently down amidships on his behind like a civilized Christian . . .

Summer dipped towards autumn and the wild berries ripened on the hills beyond the creek. The bear rarely crossed over on his own account, but he always thoroughly enjoyed the days when the men worked down the shaft on the bench. He would cross with them in the canoe and then wander off on his own—and he became bigger and fatter, and his coat was getting a most wonderful shine to it.

Finally it became time to break camp and get going, down the Stewart to the Yukon and down the Yukon to Dawson. The clean-up had been good but the pay-streak seemed to have petered out. There was no reason to stay longer.

The partners were worried about the bear. He was a personal friend by now and they felt responsible for him. To take him down to Dawson was out of the question—they might as well shoot him here and now and have done with it. Then they got an idea.

"We'll break camp," they said, "and have everything packed, ready to load up and go. Then we'll take a pick and shovel and cross the creek as if we were going to put in a day on the bench. We'll start work as usual and he'll mosey off up the creek. When he's well out of sight we'll beat it back to the canoe, load the outfit, and hit for the Stewart . . ."

They couldn't think of anything better, so they did that and all went smoothly. The bear headed happily for his favorite berry patch, upstream and out of sight, and the two men went quietly down the hill and crossed the creek, feeling rather shamefaced at deserting a friend.

They needn't have worried. Before they could load more than a piece or two into the big canoe, they heard frantic shouts from across the creek. They looked up and, by God, it was Axel and he had come this way after all!

Axel and his partners were working some claims over the divide to Indian River. Axel had been over on a visit in the wintertime and it had been arranged then that, if he didn't go in to Dawson with some Indian River outfit when the fall came, he would come over and go down the Stewart with Big Paul. He was a couple of days overdue but they had waited . . . And now, there he was—making wonderful time over the deadfall and round the rocks with a nice, slick, shiny bear close on his heels! You had to hand it to that bear—his routine had been upset, there was no canoe available, and a complete stranger was loping along just ahead of him, raising hell about God knows what—and still he behaved like a Christian and a gentleman.

"Damn it," said the bear's foster fathers, "here this silly something goes and turns up at the last something minute and now we got the whole something job to do again!" And Big Paul got into the canoe and flipped it across the creek with the paddle.

Axel wasted no time getting into that canoe. He got into the fore end of it, knelt down, eased his heavy pack off his shoulders, and swung it round in front of him. And all the time he was talking hard—or rather, shouting, after the manner of the Swedes when something has excited them. But Big Paul wasn't paying much attention; he just sat on his bedroll in the stern and laughed like a loon at the quiet, assured way in which the bear got into the canoe and sat down close behind Axel. And at intervals he thanked God Axel hadn't got a rifle.

"Ja, by golly," Axel was shouting as he bent over his pack, "dot vos yust a piece of luck for me you fellows vos not gone." They were in midstream now and Axel was feeling happier. "Ay tank dot damn bear has beat it," he went on, casting a glance at the deserted bank; then he turned his head round, the more easily to bellow at Big Paul. He found himself looking practically down the bear's throat, and with a wild yell of "Yesus!" he hurled himself straight over the nose of the canoe and was swept away down the stream.

The canoe fetched up against the bank. Sobbing with laughter, Paul and his partner tore across the point to try to intercept Axel, who, they knew, was in grave danger of drowning. They found him in deep water, under a cutbank and held down by the spiky branches of a big spruce that had fallen into the creek. They had a devil of a time getting him out of there, and every time they thought of Axel's face in the canoe when he saw the bear they laughed till they cried.

First they got Axel free of the branches and then they got a line down to him—a line with a loop in the end of it. The Swede had been a longish time in the water, and the cold and his first panic fear seemed to have numbed his wits; however, he managed to get the loop under his armpits and Big Paul drew the line tight. Then they hauled him up, Paul on the brink heaving and lifting, and his partner behind taking up the slack and snubbing round a tree. It was just as well they played it that way because, when Big Paul heaved Axel's head and shoulders over the lip of the bank, the bear, who had taken a keen interest in all these wild doings, was right there to give the distinguished stranger a friendly welcome—and the first thing Axel saw was the bear's face grinning at him from about the same range as before. His English vocabulary was not very extensive and he was evidently a man who could quite easily get into a rut: he let a scream of "Yesus!" out of him and did his best to fling himself backwards into the creek.

That finished Big Paul—he just sat down and rolled on the ground. His partner had strength enough to take one extra turn of the line round the tree, "just so as to keep Axel from spoiling the show," and then he sat down and rolled too. They wept and shouted together, and now and then they hit each other—and their insides ached and ached. Most of Axel was still dangling over the water, but his frantic, yellow-whiskered face stuck up over the bank at ground level, roaring out prayers and the most dreadful threats in his mother tongue. Every time the two men felt like sobering down a bit, one sight of that bellowing, rampageous gargoyle was more than enough to set them off again . . . But it worried the bear. All *he* wanted to do was to *understand*, Big Paul said—but they couldn't tell him. They were past telling anybody anything by now.

In the end they managed to stop laughing long enough to drag Axel up and over the edge of the cutbank—with him fighting them every inch of the way. They had one hell of a job calming Axel down and introducing him to the bear—but, as Big Paul saw it, a man couldn't rightly blame the bear for that. Out of the four of them, he alone had minded his manners and behaved like a gentleman . . .

Silence fell on Faille's cabin. Oscar got up, turned his pies in the oven, and took a sight through the open door. The rain was easing off a bit, and blue sky showed in the west behind the Yukon peaks, which were cloud-free now and covered with fresh-fallen snow.

"And *now* maybe you'll believe in canoe-ridin' bears," Oscar said.

Something in the way he spoke told me that there was more to this story of Big Paul. "Well—and how did they get out of there in the end?" I asked. "I mean, without the bear?"

"Oh, they worked the same kind of trick again," Oscar replied. "And Big Paul said the way Axel loaded that canoe a man woulda thought he was headin' in to record a claim on Eldorado! Just crazy to get a-goin', he was, before the bear could get things figured out. He said by Yumping Yiminy *he* wasn't goin' again with no bear in no canoe—no, by Yupiter, not even if he had to hump his pack all the way across the divide again to Indian River!"

"And you think that's a true tale?"

"Well, I do. And I'll tell you, for one thing, why. Big Paul always had trouble finishin' that story. When he came to that bit about where they had Axel snubbed to a tree and his face just showin' above the cutbank, he would bust out laffin' fit to kill himself. He wasn't a young man when I first knew him— and the older he got, the worse he got. Screamin' like a jackass till he was clean out of wind and purple in the face. That was evidence enough for me: you just *knew* that it was Axel he was seein', away north in the Yukon, prayin' to God and cursin' him and his partner and that bear.

"And I'll tell you another thing. Big Paul was in his seventies when he died—not so many years ago, somewhere down Kamloops way. He died sudden, one evening in a friend's house; they figured it was his heart. All I heard was that he died happy—he was laffin' and enjoyin' himself right to the end. It wasn't till some years afterwards that I heard he'd been tellin' a bear story. Then I knew. In his mind he'd gone back in time to 1900 and north a thousand miles. And after all those years, it was that yellow-whiskered, roarin' face of Axel's that killed him."

Born in England in 1898, **R. M. Patterson** was a graduate of Oxford University and worked for the Bank of England, before he decided in 1924— more or less on a whim—to leave the comforts and confines of British society behind. He escaped to Canada, where he found his niche as a logger, trapper, prospector, rancher, and owner of an orchard. Patterson is best known for his explorations of the Northwest Territories' South Nahanni River and countless wilderness escapades described in *Dangerous River* and *Far Pastures*. He died at age eighty-six, a venerable Jack London and Henry David Thoreau of the Canadian West.

wilderness temperament

Bruce Berger

IT IS ONE of our romantic American notions that one can "find oneself" in the wilderness, a self obscured by the entanglements of town. After several decades of journeying in the wild, I find the self is just as elusive as ever, and suspect that as a kind of psychic bedrock it may not even exist. On the way to this nondiscovery, however, I may have run across an aspect of personality that can be pinned down, that varies from person to person, and that expresses one's attitude toward the outdoors. Less grand than one's "self," it might be called one's wilderness temperament.

Thoughts were churned up by a trip I recently made in a party of thirteen down a southwestern river. Only once before had I been on an actual river trip, a two-week float through Glen Canyon before its annihilation by Lake Powell. That experience of Glen Canyon was overwhelming, and a minor drawback comes back only now. Idyllic as it was to float the Colorado River between massive tapestried walls, I felt vaguely imprisoned by our rubber raft. More vivid were the times we worked our way up side canyons, or clambered slickrock to the rim. In retrospect, I realize I was far happier on rock than on water.

On the recent river trip, more than twenty years later, I was given command of a Sportyak, a tiny one-man plastic rowboat, part of an armada that included two more Sportyaks, three kayaks, two rubber pontoons, and a canoe. I was told and then shown how it worked. Childhood rowing instincts came back, and I even enjoyed bobbing over small stationary waves the river folk referred to as "haystacks." On the second morning I was advised to stay close behind a more experienced yakker, for the river would get eventful.

When the yakker yelled "That's it!" over the noise of the water, I figured I was doing it right.

A moment later I realized that what the yakker had yacked was "Rapids!" The little boat I meant to keep facing forward swung magnetically toward a rock midriver, swerved around it, spun into a hole beneath it, emerged backward, and was swamped by the wave below the hole. A series of giant haystacks followed, each trying to pour more water into my full load. The boat was too heavy to spin forward again, and rather than take the waves sideways and overturn, I kept the boat facing backward. Below the rapids the party pulled out to catch its breath. I was congratulated for having come through right side up, and was assured that keeping the boat backward I had exercised control. What I felt, along with adrenaline and a sense of fatalism, was that I'd been wholly at the river's mercy, and that any congratulations were due the makers of the unsinkable Sportyak. And past the postmortem loomed a broader issue: What had all this frantic nautical activity to do with the country I'd come to see?

As the trip splashed on, distinctions among water folk emerged. A Sportyakker who did overturn pronounced it the best moment of the trip. Another so loved the act of rowing that he kept a rowing machine in his living room. One pontoon rider felt the river wasn't challenging enough to bother with in a kayak, so why not keep dry and drink beer? Another had tried all forms of craft, and found fulfillment in a canoe. I most enjoyed my hike up a sandstone fin, and was happiest afloat when I could adjust the view with one oar. Our party expressed thirteen attitudes toward travel by water.

I began comparing river travel with the two other unmechanized ways I had entered the wilderness: by foot and by mule. Mules, like boats, make constant demands on your attention. The effort of kicking, yelling, and making fearful noises with a switch seemed far more exhausting than walking, and I remember the look of a friend who jabbed with his heels, swore, and kept yelling back, "Is he moving? Is he moving?" For all our exertion, the animals moved more slowly than we could have on our own, and after the first trip I let the beast haul my gear and walked unencumbered.

As for backpacking, we all know the way it intensifies earthly gravity.

wilderness temperament — bruce berger

Backpacking is awkward, ugly, monotonous, and lacks thrilling bodily sensations. On the other hand, I have never had a breeze spin my backpack the wrong way as I trained my binoculars on a snowy egret. I have never raised my camera, only to have the backpack lurch forward and cause the shutter to click on pure sky as I became tangled in reins, camera strap, hat strap, loose glasses, riding crop, and rage. Disengage from a backpack and it will not bolt or float away. It asks only that you haul it from here to there, and leaves you free to pick up rocks, stalk birds, compose pictures or paragraphs, finger lichen, or let your thoughts seep into the ground. Devoid of glamour, it is pure access.

If wilderness is a place where one can blur, for a time, the confines of the ego, the modes of wilderness travel would seem to offer a general choice between dissolving into the fabric of nature or into sensations of the body. River running, mountain climbing, and cross-country skiing, at one extreme, nerve the traveler toward challenge, endurance, and physical excitement, and wilderness offers full scope for pushing flesh to the limit. The attitudes on our recent trip, for all their variety, tended to regard the sinews of water as the chief attraction, and the surrounding strata as pleasant background. Pack animals occupy a cumbersome middle ground, while backpacking represents the opposite extreme: transportation one withstands simply to get there. The mode one prefers—one's wilderness temperament—is no more logical than a preference for black forest cake or hot peppers, but river runners savor the kinks of tumbling water and alternate craft, while backpackers plan one plod after another. Without regretting a trip I have taken, I know that I am, at heart, a servile backpacker.

As self-knowledge, the determination of one's wilderness temperament may fall short of enlightenment. But if one does not truly find oneself, at least one will not find oneself on the wrong trip.

Another transplant from the East, **Bruce Berger** attended Yale University until realizing that graduate school was interfering with his education. Consequently, he worked for three years as a nightclub pianist in Spain, where he also turned into a compulsive wanderer of deserts. His prose and poetry have appeared in *The New York Times, Barron's, Best Nature Writing 1999,* and *The Glen Canyon Reader.* His books include *There Was a River, Almost an Island,* and *The Telling Distance,* which won the 1990 Western States Book Award. Since 1968 Bruce's home has been a three-room log cabin in Aspen, Colorado.

river rats

Edward Abbey

ONE COLD EVENING in February I checked into the Tri-Arc Travelodge in Salt Lake City, a respectable-type hotel in a decent, law-abiding town. I was dismayed to find the place swarming with hairy ruffians in cowboy hats, greasy down vests, wool shirts, boots. It looked like a bronc riders' convention, an assembly of lumberjacks, an upsurge from the rural underclass.

I adjusted my necktie. Nervously I consulted the desk clerk: Should I give up my reservation, find a safer place to spend the night?

The clerk smiled a reassuring smile. Don't be alarmed, he said, it's only another boatmen's jamboree. They'll all be in jail by midnight.

The clerk exaggerated. By twelve that night only one boatman had been arrested. The police caught him committing a public nuisance in the Tri-Arc parking lot. When they shone a spotlight in his face he gave them the finger, then ran for cover back into the bar. Forgot to button his fly. He was caught, charged with "Lewd and Obscene Conduct," and locked in the city slammer. His friends bailed him out—for a hundred dollars—at two in the morning, letting him rot in a cell long enough to sober up.

Thus began, in traditional form, another annual meeting of the Western River Guides' Association, an organization of professional whitewater boatmen and outfitters. These are the people—including some women—who, for a price, will take you by rubber raft, pontoon boat, Sportyak, kayak, dory, or canoe down the remaining free-flowing rivers of the American West: the Snake, the Salmon, the Owyhee, the Dolores, the Yampa, the Rio Grande, the San Juan, the Green, a few others, and—climax of them all—the Colorado in its thunderous course through Cataract Canyon in Utah and the

Grand Canyon in Arizona.

The length of a river trip can range from one day up to twenty-two; the cost to the customer from a hundred dollars to two thousand. Most of these commercial river operators provide a complete service: transportation to and from the points of embarkation and debarkation; the boats, motors, oars; the special equipment, such as rubberized bags, life jackets, and waterproof storage cans, usually considered essential; food, cooks, and cooking gear; emergency first aid; and most important, the skill, experience, and knowledge of the boatmen themselves. It is no trifling matter to row a boatload of passengers through Satan's Gut in Cataract, through the Green River's Gates of Lodore (a canyon that might have been named, as well as imagined, by Edgar Allan Poe), or into and out of the rocks, whirlpools, and twelve-foot waves of Crystal Rapids and Lava Falls in the Grand Canyon.

You might think, all the same, that despite the hazards you would prefer to do a river trip entirely on your own, alone or with a few friends, rather than pay some expert a profit-making fee to do all the work—and have most of the fun—for you. A natural and wholesome feeling. For myself, I would rather paddle a washtub through the storm sewers of Los Angeles than merely ride along, one among a huddled pack of hapless passengers, on a thirty-three-foot motorized neoprene jumbo rig wallowing down the corridors of Grand Canyon. There'd be more satisfaction in it; greater spiritual rewards. But nature, commerce, and officialdom have placed obstacles in the course of self-reliance.

First you must buy the minimum equipment. Expensive. Then you must find the time to acquire the experience necessary if you wish to run the wild rivers successfully, without a series of upsets. Finally, and for the popular runs most difficult, you have to get a permit. A *permit*? Of course; you didn't think the rivers were there, free, public, and waiting for any damn fool who thinks he can float in a plastic tub from Lees Ferry to Hoover Dam's Lake Merde, did you? There are rules, restrictions, regulations, most of them desirable, some of them unavoidable, that come inevitably into effect whenever too many people crowd upon a limited resource.

I detest the word *resource*. How could a wild river, part of nature's bloodstream, ever come to be regarded primarily as a damn *resource?* As if it were no more than a vein of coal, a field of cabbages, a truckload of cow manure?

Rhetorical question: We know how it happened. Human needs, human demands, human greed—alas, we must say it—have so expanded during the past half century that we are compelled, like it or not, to look upon the world as a meat pie, to be divvied up according to the will of the strongest. No particular race or nation can be blamed for this sorry situation; it has arisen naturally; human beings, like other animals, obey the reproductive regulations: Be fruitful, multiply, replenish and overplenish the defenseless earth. In a newly founded, relatively still rich society like the American, that which is not needed for food and survival is utilized for entertainment; a river becomes a "recreational resource" and fun, play, sport become among other things a business enterprise. An *industry*, in accordance with the carefully instilled belief that you can't have fun unless you pay for it.

As most everyone knows, the Colorado River was first followed for most of its length by Major Wesley Powell and his men in the year 1869. In the eighty years afterward no more than a few dozen others repeated their daring journey. Then in the 1940s and 1950s a few experienced river runners, such as Norm Nevills, Ted Hatch, Don Harris, Albert Quist, hired themselves and their boats out to those willing to pay for the experience of a whitewater float trip. Commercial river running was born. The business grew rapidly as more and more boatmen set themselves up as outfitters; by 1972 they were taking some fifteen thousand customers per season through the Grand Canyon alone.

At this point the National Park Service, charged with the responsibility for preserving Grand Canyon in its supposedly wild and natural state, finally stepped in—too late—and set maximum limits to the volume of this new and burgeoning commerce, licensing boatmen and outfitters, and limiting use of the river to those permittees already established there. Ninety-two percent of the river traffic was allotted, in various proportions, to the twenty-one commercial outfitters, leaving only 8 percent for everybody else, for those private citizens who preferred to do it on their own.

In 1972 this seemed fair enough; the demand for river-running permits by private parties was small. But this is no longer the case. As whitewater boating becomes a more and more popular sport, the conflict between freelance boaters and the commercial outfits has grown intense, creating a legal and political issue still unresolved by the courts or the Park Service.

However the issue is finally settled, if it is, somebody is going to get hurt; when the demand for something far exceeds the supply there is obviously not enough for everyone. Attacked from all sides, as usual, the Park Service proposed a compromise that satisfied no one: doubling the annual visitor-day use of the river over a longer season and increasing the private-party allotment from 8 to 33 percent. The catch to this is that the river is a cold and difficult environment during most of the year; the water emerges from the depths behind Glen Canyon Dam at a temperature of forty degrees. If the commercial operators are forced to share the three summer months (the favored season for a river trip) with a larger proportion of noncommercial boatmen, then they, the commercials, fear that they will lose customers, lose business, lose money.

Another sensitive question is that of motorized boating in the national parks. Under pressure from conservation organizations like the Sierra Club, the Park Service has been trying for over a decade to include its portion of the Colorado River in an official wilderness system. Wilderness entails a ban on motors. Any proposal to ban motors in the Grand Canyon stirs up the wrath of the larger commercial outfitters, whose prosperity (a gross of half a million dollars per year in some cases) depends on the quickie trip—the rapid transport by motorized rubber raft of a large volume of paying passengers. Pack them in at Lees Ferry, rush them through the Grand Canyon, hustle them out by helicopter. What should, by traditional standards, be a two-to-three-week adventure can be condensed by such means to a four- or five-day whirlwind tour. The passengers don't object; they don't know what they're missing; they don't know any better; and the operator becomes modestly rich. (One of these quickie-tour outfits was sold a few years ago to a group of investors for over a million dollars.) So far the large commercial outfitters have been able, through political finagling, to forestall wilderness designation for the interior Grand Canyon and thus defeat every attempt by the Park Service to manage the river in the general public interest.

But in the long run the big outfitters are on the losing side. As should be apparent to everyone by now, we are approaching a new age of frugality in the national economy; motorized recreation in its many forms (snowmobiles, trailbikes, dune buggies, off-road vehicles, motorboats, etc.) must sooner or later be phased out of existence. The commercial river outfitters will be forced by economics, if not by the Park Service, to junk their outboard motors, dispose of their giant rafts, use smaller boats and—sharing the profits—employ more oarsmen. They'll learn to live with it. All concerned will be better off because of it—the big outfitter, whose business will be reduced to the family-size enterprise that it should be; the boatmen, who will find more jobs available; and last and not of least importance, the paying passengers, who will see the Grand Canyon as it should be seen, at a leisurely pace, in quietude, as members of small groups.

Private river runners versus commercial river runners; motors versus oars; these are two of the hairiest, prickliest issues that boatmen and outfitters, the government, the politicians, and the general public must somehow deal with. But why should emotions be involved? the reader may ask; surely these things can be settled on the basis of common sense and equity, with the aid of an ordinary desktop calculator. Not so; these are questions of profitability, of money, in some cases of big money—and therefore, quite naturally and understandably, blood is stirred and passions rise. (Some people get very emotional about money.)

Take the impossible question of fairness, for example: Is it fair that the small outfitter should be forced out of business by the big outfitter? Or fair that superior managerial ability should be penalized in some way so as to allow the small outfitter (perhaps less hard-driving as an entrepreneur but a *nicer* guy, offering his customers a more enjoyable experience, who knows?) to remain in business? Is it fair that currently established outfitters be allowed to keep a virtual monopoly, through the government's permit-franchise system, of the use of what is supposed to be a *public* river flowing through public property such as a *national* park? But would it be fair to open the rivers wide to one and all, on a first-come first-served basis, perhaps driving into bankruptcy some of the established river outfitters who may have invested not only money but thirty years of their lives in the business?

What is fair? Life is not fair, said ex-president Carter in one of his more brilliant unrehearsed spontaneous public statements. His answer was satisfactory to the winners but infuriated those who saw themselves as unjustified losers.

The river outfitters complain bitterly about the various agencies—Park Service, Forest Service, Bureau of Land Management, state boating commissions, even the U.S. Coast Guard, and of course the IRS—that they must deal with, and of the maze of red tape and regulations they must grope their way through in pursuit of an honest dollar. (The pursuit of happiness.) And indeed the constraints are many and complicated: the permits, the safety requirements, the sanitation and disposal requirements, restrictions on wood fires, user-day quotas, number of passengers per boat, minimum and maximum allowable days per trip, campsite restrictions, scheduling restrictions, allowable charge per customer, user-day fees payable to the agency, and other variables create a nightmare of paperwork, logistics, penalties, and dubious rewards.

And yet the outfitters need these regulations, or most of them, now that their well-advertised operations have attracted such enormous numbers of people. Without regulation a few unscrupulous operators could soon make a mess of things, fouling the campgrounds, drowning an occasional passenger, overwhelming the river with crowds so large that a river trip would lose what vestiges still remain of an actual "wilderness" experience. More important, from the outfitters' point of view, is that unregulated river use, without the protection of the permit system, would expose them to unlimited competition. Any muscular young fellow with a couple of Canyon trips to his credit, a boat and a pair of oars, could then offer to take you or me down the river for a fee much below that charged by the commercial operators—and be glad to do it. Might even do it for nothing, if he was a friend, and make more of an adventure of it all to boot, since you'd be a participating member of the trip and not a mere passive passenger. And save all participants a lot of money besides. (In 1979, for example, I took part in a twenty-two-day share-the-expense trip through Grand Canyon for $350. A commercial trip of equivalent value would have cost me at least a thousand dollars.)

These are the hot issues in the river-running business, and should be discussed at every opportunity. I was surprised to discover, therefore, when I sat in on some of the river guides' meetings at the Tri-Arc Travelodge, that they were mostly busy in wrangling with representatives of the Park Service and the BLM about matters of secondary interest: amount of user-day fees, the sale and transfer of outfitter permits, safety regulations, sewage disposal, etc.

Well-meaning but innocuous resolutions were passed, urging the federal government to designate this or that stretch of river as an official Wild and Scenic River, thus protecting it to some extent from the dam builders, power plant promoters, oil shale developers, and other good-intentioned but wicked people. But when Howard Brown, director of an organization called American Rivers Conservation Council, suggested that the outfitters impose a five-dollar surcharge on each river-boating passenger to help finance wild river lobbying in Washington I could detect no support for the idea. (It should be said that the WRGA does contribute a thousand dollars per year to Mr. Brown's efforts, and that individual members of the group contribute more on their own.)

One of my favorite old-timers among the outfitters, Martin Litton, owner of Grand Canyon Dories, Inc., worked in a combined attack on the Bureau of Reclamation and the metric system:

> BE IT RESOLVED, That the Western River Guides' Association deplores the costly, misleading, confusing, and dangerous trend on the part of the Bureau of Reclamation to report river flows in unfamiliar, nontraditional, unintelligible, unusable terms of cubic meters per second and calls upon the Bureau of Reclamation to stop it.

Passed, with only three dissenting voices. When I asked one of the dissenters if he really cared all that much for the metric system he admitted that he didn't, he just wanted to vote "against Martin." Why? "Oh—I always vote against Martin. Keeps him honest."

One BLM official introduced another with the careless remark that "maybe you fellas would like to bounce a few questions off him." Voices in the crowd replied: "Questions? How about beer cans? How about rocks?"

The official, clutching the rostrum with tense hands, immediately got himself in more trouble with the rivermen by announcing that the BLM was going to make it "tough" and "hard" for outsiders to sell or transfer river-running permits; those permits, he said, with incredible lack of tact, are not private property but the property of the U.S. government. He should have said "of the public" or "of the American people." But he didn't. More angry outcries: "Whose government? Who owns the goddamned government?"

Again Martin Litton rose to state the case for the outfitters. Litton, a former journalist, is a forceful speaker, not at all shy in public, always ready with well-thought-out opinions on any subject. "River-running permits," he argued, "like grazing permits in the cattle business, are essential business property. Possession of them gives us a legal right, established by custom and common law, to buy and sell them as we see fit." And he pointed out the obvious fact that a river-running business without the franchise to take paying customers down the river is worthless.

Ken Sleight, another veteran river guide, who has been operating a family-sized outfit for thirty years, stood up to make a plea for both a floor and a ceiling on the size of any one river-guiding enterprise. A floor is needed, he said, a certain minimum amount of user-day and passenger permits guaranteed by the government on a long-term basis, in order to provide an economic base sufficient to keep the small outfits (like his) in business. The ceiling is needed to prevent the large outfits from getting too large, stifling competition, buying out the small guide services, and establishing a complete monopoly. Many small outfits, said Sleight, can provide a more varied and therefore better service for the public than a few big ones.

The meeting concluded with the election of officers. Boatman Stewart Reeder seconded the nomination of boatman-outfitter Clair Quist for the board of directors. Reeder's speech consisted of one sentence: "Clair's been running rivers since he was a bucket-ass kid." Reeder paused for thought, said nothing more, and sat down. Clair Quist, "from the underworld of river guides," as another boatman told me, was elected by universal acclamation.

What is a bucket-ass kid? I asked. Anyone not big enough to sit on a chair, I was told.

The best thing about the river-running business is the people in it. The worst thing is the business. I find it saddening to see good honest boatmen forced to become accountants, clerks, advertisers, lobbyists, managers, and executives in order to survive in what used to be, before the roads were paved, half the rivers dammed, and the crowds came, not a business but an adventurous trade.

Fourteen years ago a seasonal park ranger stood on the beach at Lees Ferry, Arizona, on the Colorado River, watching an outfit called Grand Canyon Expeditions preparing to launch on a twelve-day river trip. The ranger had never been down the Grand Canyon himself. The wistful expression on his face must have been apparent to the owner and head boatman Ron Smith. "For chrissake, Abbey," says Smith, "don't just stand there like a sick calf. We need a number two nigger. Somebody to wash the pots. Go get your bedroll and come along."

"I'll get fired."

"Who cares?" Smith says, opening a can of beer with the pliers on his belt. So I gave my boss due notice—thirty minutes—and went along. Nor was I fired. When I came back two weeks later my job was waiting for me—only the boss was gone; the Park Service had transferred him to some cannonball park in Virginia. (A little mix-up in the paperwork.)

Good men, these boatmen. Generous, vigorous, competent types. The exasperating kind of people who can and do well most anything: hunt and fish, naturally. Build a boat, a house, or a hogan. Repair an outboard motor in rapids or fix a truck engine in a sandstorm. Pitch tents, build fires, cook meals in driving rain. Great lovers? Of course. Truthful? Undoubtedly—drink you under the table any day. Sporting men? You name the game—poker, pool, craps, Frisbee, backgammon, macramé, Monopoly—they'll play it.

For instance:

A boatman named Hall is watching a couple of sharp California dudes playing eight-ball at a table in Flagstaff. They are good. Hall challenges the winner. The dude looks at him: Man, you're no pool player. Well, says Hall, I ain't too good with these here skinny *cuesticks* you got but if somebody'll bring me a long-handled shovel, why, I'll take you on. The dude sneers, the bets are laid, another boatman brings in a garden spade. Hall chalks the tip of the handle, breaks the rack, runs the table. (Of course he then had the problem of getting out of the poolroom with his winnings—always the hardest part of the game.)

There could be an element of bullshit in some of the stories. Boatman Al Harris tells me this one:

"We took this kayaker from Vermont along down the Grand. He done pretty good till we got to that Hance Rapid. There he tried to run the hole, ate it, got sucked under, came back up about half a mile downriver. After we pumped the water out of him and sewed up his head and he commences to come around, he says, Jesus, I'll never do that again; it hurts—you got any drugs? So I open the old first-aid kit and look over the pharmacy. Well, I says, we got morphine, Demerol, Amytal, codeine, Percodan, Thorazine, Valium, Librium, lithium, ether, methadone, mescaline, LSD, peyote, and some of that what they call wacky tobaccy—you know, *mary-hoona*. Homegrown. I'll take them all, the kayaker says, and he did; he passed out for ten days but said he felt just fine when we got to the takeout at Diamond Crick."

In this story even the accent is suspect: Harris can talk like a Harvard graduate when he's not putting you on. Or when he is. As for vigor, I remember the time a friend and I were going through Cataract Canyon with Ken Sleight and Bob Quist (Clair Quist's brother). At the worst possible moment, entering a hellhole of rock and waves called the Big Drop, the outboard motor failed. (A Johnson Sea Horse.) Grab oars! yells Sleight, grabbing the spare oar on the right. Bob Quist—a very powerful man—grabs the one on the left, jams it in the oarlock. A fang of limestone menaces the port bow. Bob takes a deep bite in the water and gives a mighty, a superhuman heave. The oar, brand-new, never before used, snaps apart in the middle. We make it through the rapids anyway, right side up, pinballing off the rocks. One oar or two, one boatman or none, it didn't seem to make any significant difference. The true function of a boatman, on a river trip, is to provide *moral* leadership. Ask any boatman.

When a passenger, confused by the terms *upstream* and *downstream*, asked a boatman I know to explain the distinction, he tied a length of string to a cork and gave it to this—this—this person. Throw the cork in the river, he said, and hold on to the string; whichever way the cork goes, that's downstream, probably; unless you're in a eddy. The other way is upstream. But keep ahold of the string. What's the string for? the passenger asked. For the next time, he said; it'll last you for years.

One day Clair Quist was telling me about some rancher friends of his—these jolly cowboys climbing into his thin-skinned rubber boat with big spurs on their boots. I imagined I heard a note of envy in his tone. "Don't you wish," I said, "your father had left *you* a working cattle ranch?" (Certainly I was familiar with the wish.)

"No," Clair said, after a moment; "our old man left us something a lot better—Glen Canyon." (His father had been the first to operate a guide service there.) "But the politicians took it away from us."

Ah yes, that dam. That Glen Canyon Dam, and the 180-mile lake behind it that boatman call Lake Foul. In all of the Rocky Mountain, Inter-Mountain West, no man-made object has been hated so much, by so many, for so long, with such good reason, as that seven-hundred-thousand-ton plug of gray cement, blocking our river.

Final anecdote. Ken Sleight and a few others are sitting around a campfire, on a beach, by a river that still flows. We're talking about *that dam*.

"Listen," says Ken. "It's not enough to talk about it. Let's do something about it." He holds out his hands to those on either side of him. "Grab hands. Tie in. Form a circle." We join hands around the fire. Ken closes his eyes and leans back a little. "Now concentrate," he says. "Concentrate real hard, all together, and let's see if we can't lift that dam. Just a few inches. Let the water out." Eyes closed, we concentrate and strain, visualizing the huge dam, trying to make it rise. "Oh," groans Ken, "it's so . . . heavy. It's so . . . goddamn . . ." *sigh*—"heavy . . ."

On the evening of the last day of the guides' meeting, about to leave for the Salt Lake airport, I went into a bar for a final drink with some of these river rats. Through the smoke and whiskey fumes (this bar was the kind known, in Mormon Utah, as a "private club"), I saw a mob of them jammed around a long table. Sleight was there, of course, and the Quist brothers, and Al Harris, and

Steve Reeder, and Dave Kloepfer, and Kim Crumbo, a few others, and Grant Gray with his wife Millet and Pamela Davis, and the parking lot nuisance of course, I'll not mention his name, and Frogg Stewart—collectively the worst element, the most disgusting and disreputable crew in the whole river-running clan.

Naturally I hesitated a moment inside the door, then decided to chance it. What the hell, I was leaving in an hour. So I stayed for a bourbon or two, and listened to the talk. Feeling relaxed, happy, foolishly sentimental, I began saying good-bye to these great people, shaking hands one by one around the table. My necktie, worn for prevention of disease only, was dangling in the drinks. Halfway through the process I started to feel a bit silly. Bob Quist, roaring above the babble, confirmed the feeling: "God, Ed," he yelled, "you look like a politician." Grinning at me through the smoke.

I stopped, turned, gave him the big finger. He jeered at me again, an unspeakable epithet, which, nevertheless, he spoke. I slammed my left palm against the crook of my right elbow and sprang *two* rigid fingers on him—the deadly Neapolitano *double prong*, thrust right in to the hilt. Again, I turned and had almost reached the safety of the exit when I heard an augmented roar of clapping, laughter, and screaming in my rear. I looked back. Bob Quist had climbed on his chair and pulled down his pants. The son of a bitch was mooning me.

I fled at once. Never turn your back on a boatman.

Lauded by many and feared by quite a few for his novel *The Monkey Wrench Gang*, and his essay collection *Desert Solitaire*, **Edward Abbey** wrote over twenty books of fiction and nonfiction. Before finding his true calling, this part-time river runner and full-time curmudgeon also took turns as a seasonal park ranger, fire lookout, social worker, and student of anarchist theory. The bearded trickster from Pennsylvania passed away in 1989 and was laid to rest—in his ratty old sleeping bag—somewhere in his beloved Sonoran Desert. Sources of dubious reputation and questionable sobriety have sighted him repeatedly—soaring above Utah's redrock canyons, in the form of a turkey vulture.

there's no safe way down the selway

Richard Bangs

WHITEWATER RAFTING . . . SUCH a tantalizing pairing of words, wet with contour and risk. The *w*'s and the *t*'s slide over and around one another like intertwined snakes. And then there are the layers of resonance, managing to evoke temptation and fear at once.

IDAHO'S SELWAY IS America's most restricted river, with only sixty-two private rafting permits issued each year and only one group—maximum sixteen participants—allowed to launch per day. The odds of winning the lottery for a permit are about one in thirty. Of the winners, only about 50 percent actually make it on the river, often because the unpredictable water level during the seventy-five-day season is too high or too low. Cited by cognoscenti as the wildest river in the lower forty-eight states, the Selway is also considered one of the toughest, with forty-five named rapids in its forty-seven-mile run, and a reputation for swallowing rafters as though they were pills. Some claim Lord Grizzly still roams here; nobody disputes the corridor boasts rattlesnakes, wolves, black bears, mountain lions, bighorns, cutthroat trout, blackflies, and mosquitoes. Its weather is notorious, with snow and freezing rain possible anytime through June. Even Lewis and Clark were daunted here. When they crossed what is now the Montana-Idaho border in 1805, and considered the cruel country surrounding the Selway, they turned north for Lolo Pass instead.

So it was all the more remarkable that we were halfway down this humming, pine-cloaked river, at the brink of several nasty Class IV rapids, and standing around the campfire sipping bourbon was the brain trust of *Slate*, an online policy magazine: Michael Kinsley, its editor; Scott Moore, publisher; Scott Shuger, creator and writer of "Today's Papers"; and Cyrus Krohn, associate publisher. Don't these guys have some sort of keyman insurance that requires not traveling together on the same conveyance? Publisher Scott Moore, a plucky outdoorsman who lived in Boise for many years, was the lucky man who drew the Forest Service lottery-win for a Selway permit, and who organized this expedition. And he ensorcelled several people into joining the trip who had never before been rafting, including Michael Kinsley, a man who, though an enthusiastic camper, tells me he simply does not possess the adrenaline gene.

"HOW DID SCOTT get you on the Selway?" someone asks Michael.
"I thought he said 'Safeway.'"
Even I was a tough sell. I had been a professional western river guide for several seasons, and had unsuccessfully entered the Selway lottery half a dozen times, but that was some two decades ago, when in youthful arrogance I refused to be dissuaded by the thought of my own demise. I'd long ago lost the raft in which I ran the 1970s. I wasn't sure I had the white stuff to guide an "expert" river at age forty-nine, especially after spending the last four years rowing a desk at the travel agency Expedia. I even contacted my friend Snake Hughes, who owns an Idaho rafting outfit, and asked about the launch date Scott was awarded in late June ... His reply: "*June 19 can be a stinking high water date, and you do not want to boat the Selway in extreme high flows! The nature of the river is to go from high to low water rapidly in a big flush. Feast/famine. June 19 is a potentially problematic launch date.*"
Was Scott Moore hauling us to some whitewater-rafting abattoir?

NONETHELESS, WE GATHER by the river at a place called Paradise, 3,067 feet above the sea, about eighty miles south of Missoula in the heart of the 1.3-million-acre Selway-Bitterroot Wilderness. The Selway is the sui generis American river, one of the charter designees in the National Wild and Scenic Rivers Act of 1968, and farthest from any roads, concrete, or neon.

Here, at the put-in, its currents are a bewildering skein of fluid dynamics. So much water rippling along at different speeds, displaying a glittering richness of surface texture, gives the Selway a parlous, puzzling, vibrant look—the same look I see in my face as I lean over to pull a cooling Icehouse beer from the river.

At 1:12 P.M., our Seattle-based rent-a-guide Cliff Valentine, smiling like Torquemada, calls us all to the river. He has the team put its hands on the neck of a paddle and do a joint locker-room-like crescendoing cheer. It seems half-hearted, but in minutes we launch, the water level gauge at Lowell reading 3, a thankfully reasonable level. A year ago on this date the river was in flood, and it would have been suicide to attempt.

We have four Avon self-bailing inflatables: one paddle boat in which all participants wield a paddle in command of a captain, and three oar boats maneuvered by a single guide. There is also a hard-shell Dagger kayak, our safety boat, and a couple of self-bailing Hyside inflatable kayaks. Because the river has *Giardia lamblia* (the protozoan that causes Beaver Fever), we carry our own water, which is rationed; but we also have sixteen cases of beer. Among the eleven of us, only one has ever seen this river (Scott Moore, who ran it ten years earlier, after the permit season, in very low water), and only two have ever run wild rivers as guides, Cliff and myself. I am concerned with the overall lack of experience, and at last minute try to recruit two experts. One declines, but the other, Steve Marks, a Hollywood agent and part-time wild river hound, says yes. But Alaska Airlines delays out of Burbank make it impossible to make his connection to Missoula the day of departure. So he will try to hire a private plane and fly in and meet us at first night's camp.

So downstream we purl. The river, clear as gin, makes popping sounds like ice cubes in a drink. The clouds slam shut across the sky, like the door of an observatory dome, and it begins to rain, a cold drizzle. After the first wave everyone is shivering, teeth are chattering.

The day is packed with technical Class II and III rapids (rapids are ranked on a I to VI scale, the latter being a deathtrap waterfall). I feel like a character in a Ron Shelton film, an aging athlete finding the zone one last time as I dance the boat through the labyrinthine course. It is great fun, and I am buoyed by this trippy blitz of rapids, and by a sense of collaborating with the forces behind this river wild. But I am also uneasy as I watch the paddle boat, with Michael in it, make crablike runs down straight shots, bumping and slopping, out of control. "Someone will dump this trip," I tell Scott Shuger who is riding on my boat. I wince as the paddle boat misses an entry and slews sideways into a rock. We need Steve Marks if the paddle boat is going to make it through the really tough stuff that begins on day three. Even Scott Moore, an active hobbyist rafter, loses his hat and draws blood in these first rapids. Jon Nehring, a Montana native and river enthusiast, paddling a Hyside inflatable kayak, twice pops out into the river.

Scott Shuger is now shivering mightily, and so for distraction, we take to talking movies—manufactured realities usually coveted for offering more adventure than real life; but, here, the celluloid editions serve the opposite, and seem respites from the harshness of the Selway.

Late in the afternoon we pull into camp at Shearer, where Steve is supposed to meet us, but he's not here. I hike the overgrown airfield, stepping over bear scat, and trek down river about a mile, hoping Steve might be somewhere, but there is no sign of him.

Back at camp, Michael fiddles with his GPS and determines we are right where the map says we are; Cliff, a connoisseur of ecdysiasts, shares his pre-trip review of Missoula's finest; spatula jockey Dave Wood (one of two of Scott Moore's uncles on the trip), along with Cliff, cooks up a storm, mussels, baby back ribs, and Albertson's potatoes au gratin, complemented with a bottle of Marilyn Merlot. Someone shows up with a handful of ripe huckleberries, and a lively horseshoe game is tossed. All with an ear to the sky, hoping at the last minute Steve Marks will arrive. But finally the shutter of darkness closes, and hope is gone. I stumble to bed, and see that a roll of toilet paper I had left by the side of the tent has been chewed to shreds by some animal. I zip up the tent, and slip to sleep.

I AWAKE WITH the sound of a mosquito buzzing my ear, and slap at it, but the sound only gets louder. Then I realize it's a plane, a plane, and bust out of the tent and run to the airfield. Sure enough a four-seater Cessna 172 drops out of the sky, and bounces along the grassy strip. Out steps Steve, dressed in black fleece, looking like Harvey Keitel's Vincent The Cleaner, here to make things right.

After a buttermilk pancake and rasher of bacon breakfast, a wallop of Starbucks, we load the boats and roll downstream. Scott Shuger, hearing that paddling keeps the body warmer than riding in the oar boat, trades with Michael, who now rides with me.

Overhead four hawks ride the eddies of the wind; an osprey dives, surfacing with a fish. A hermit thrush calls from the shade of an ancient cedar tree, and a gaggle of red-breasted mergansers paddles around an eddy. We pull into a beach rimmed with arrowleaf balsamroot across from the Selway Lodge, first homesteaded in 1898, and now the only lived-in structure on this stretch of river. My friend Tom Peirce and his family owned and operated the lodge for many years, and when they put it up for sale in the early 1990s, I fancied buying it, but couldn't afford it. Now it is someone else's own private Idaho. A log bridge spans the river, and Scott Moore promptly struts to its middle, strips off his shirt, and jumps in. The man has balsamroots. If Michelin awarded stars for fearlessness, Scott Moore would collect three of them.

Not far downstream we approach our first Class IV rapid of the trip, Ham. Already, Steve has whipped his paddle crew into shape, and they're ready for the test.

Ham is a giant rock in the middle of the river with a surface smooth as monument stone. The main current shatters against its middle, and does a fissiparous bop down the sides. Scott says he wants to follow my run, so as I launch he pushes out as well, a few yards behind. I popple down the right side, a clean run, but then look back to watch Scott's run, and he's not there. We wait an interminable time, and then see Scott come caroming through, with one oar bent in the middle like a broken bird wing. Turns out Scott had turned to watch the boat upstream, and had crashed into a rock above Ham, smashing his oar. He made it to shore, where he switched with his spare, and made a decent run through Ham. Steve and Cliff make the run as though whistling through a rifle barrel.

The evening is a somber one. We're camped just above Moose Creek, a tributary that disembogues enough to nearly double the volume of the Selway. For most of its course the Selway drops an average of twenty-eight feet per mile, more than triple the gradient of the Colorado River through the Grand Canyon. But the section just downstream jumps off a bridge, falling 150 feet and tearing through ten rapids in just three miles. It's here the eschatologists ponder our attraction to the flame of risk: Most of the Selway's drownings occur in this stretch.

A few of us hike downstream to view the hydrotechnics, and even from the path a hundred feet above the river we can see the grotesque mushroom boils, the sharp falls, the keeper holes. The river seems to go insane, liquid chaos frothing, twisting, skibbling around and doubling back on itself like rogue fireworks. We can hear the rapids' thunder pealing through the burled gorge. We spend the waning light scouting the cataracts, trying to pick out routes, and I'm seized with a *feeling of horripilation*. Things could go very wrong tomorrow. Back at camp, conversation and dinner are spare; spaghetti, halibut, and Franzia wine in a box. Dyspepsia hangs in the air. Everyone heads to bed early; Steve Marks takes a Valium.

AT BREAKFAST, AS the peaks unravel themselves from the morning fog, Michael announces he will take the Forest Service trail around the big rapids today, rendezvousing with us at Meeker Creek, five miles downstream. He doesn't get a thrill from riding close to the edge in big whitewater, and confides: "It's important for someone to have the courage of my cowardice." And he adds he wouldn't mind experiencing a little wilderness solitude. It seems a smart idea, and I am a bit envious, knowing I can't take this option, as I have to row one of the rafts. And now I will row it without a passenger, which is a loss of needed ballast and bowline handling.

After Michael takes off, someone wonders aloud: "Will Michael be safe from the wildlife trekking alone?"

"Are you kidding?" Cyrus rejoins. "With the Northwest Kinsley's razor-sharp wit, I fear for the animals."

It's a perfect day to get wet, sunny and cloudless. Cliff has us perform another group whoop, and suggests another river ritual, whereby we scoop up a handful of the *Giardia*-laden water and swoosh it around the inside of our mouths asking for favor from the river gods; then we spit it back to the river. Never superstitious, I do the ritual regardless. Scott Moore does not. By eleven we're off into the rapids. Scott gets swept into Double Dip without scouting, and comes close to the tipping point, washing through, emerging to the eddy looking like a crustacean with its shell off.

We come to Ladle, considered the toughest rapid on the river, and make a long scout. There is no logic to Ladle—the river takes sudden tours around rocks, splits off in two or three erratic directions at once, then convenes again, as though in a square dance of the mad. On the far right there seems a passage, but then I see that spars of fallen fir bristle at the final drop like a cheval-de-frise. Only through close study can I see if a route will play, or veer off into an illusion, or a rock, or worse, into the craterlike fissure of a souse hole with its twisted, churning mouth waiting for a catch. I'm tempted to plot my course on paper, analyzing the hydraulics, factoring the weight distribution on my boat. But anatomizing rapids is like translating a poem: It risks missing the unanalyzable spirit of the thing, its beautiful and hazardous play upon freedom. So I finally just walk back upstream, tug my life jacket tight, and head into the maelstrom, where I make a pretty run. Jack Visco, who is paddling the safety kayak, decides to portage halfway down the rapid. Steve, whose crack crew is not-quite ready for Olympic competition, makes a rowdy run, hanging up for long minutes on a rock midstream toward the end. Cliff ricochets down the course like a pinball. Scott, going last, though, slams into the wall at the end, and almost flips again. He shouldn't have ignored Cliff's ritual.

Downstream, I sweep by an overhanging branch, and a grist of bees buzzes out. Two sting me on the back of the neck as I'm entering Little Niagara Rapids, and it feels like someone has applied a poultice of broken glass above my shoulders. But I grit my teeth, keep my focus, and make the run with the flair of a figure skater, as well as subsequent runs down Puzzle Creek, No Slouch, Halfway Creek, and Miranda Jane. And, when we pull in at the appointed tributary creek on the right bank (where else?) to pick up Michael, the beach is crowded with butterflies. Michael saunters down to the river's edge and mock-scowls, "I called for this taxi two hours ago."

Later, though, as we nosh on peanut butter sandwiches, and watch a deer swim across the river, Michael shares his psychic valence: "That was the most beautiful hike I have ever done. I'm very glad, though, I was up on the path, and you were down there."

As we pull into camp, a snake slithers out of the root around which I tie the bowline. But fear is history now, so I ignore the snake and go about business, setting up camp, bathing in the cold river, uncorking bottles. In the furbelows and folderol of the chat between the first swig of Chilean Pisco and the puff of a Cuban cigar, Doug and Dave Wood walk down the beach wearing specially made DEPARTMENT OF JUSTICE, ANTI-TRUST DIVISION black T-shirts, and Michael plays taps on a kazoo. The worst is behind us, and we celebrate deep into the night.

"I KNOW I had a good night when I wake up with my sunglasses on," Cliff greets the group the last morning. The sky squeezes the lemons of dawn, and I slip on my wetsuit booties, and start doing a barmy hop, as some stinging bug is at my heel.

Finally, we're on the last few miles of river. There is one last Class IV rapid, Wolf Creek, and Michael chooses to walk around, even though there is no path so it requires some aggressive bouldering and bushwhacking through vegetation with claws. The run has two routes; the right is a relatively easy straight line that ends in a piling wave. Steve, Scott, and Cliff all make fine runs. I eye the left side, a serpentine set of maneuvers around a series of exposed rocks, stepping down toward a funnel that disappears between two boulders that turn the air between them white. The worst obstacle is a rock shaped like a peacock tail near the end of the rapid, where a current hoses into it, then plumes out like a parachute. A missed stroke would almost certainly spell trouble. But I've been dancing my whole way down the river, stitching the current like a needleman. So I decide to go for it. I'm performing every bit as well as when I was half my age, and the past now seems real, attainable, like a fish shimmering beneath the surface of shallow water.

Overflowing with hubris, I pitch the boat towards Wolf Creek Rapids. The entry is perfect, and I make the tight pull past the first boulder, and glissade through the top parts of the rapids. But as any moviegoer knows, this is a ritual scene rich in peripety: It is always the cop about to retire, the thief out for one more score, the lover promising the adventure will be his last, the guide running the final big rapid, who has the fatal reversal of fortune. For an instant, heady with my success, I let my guard down, and suddenly slam into the rock, the rock radiating water like a fan. I hit it square, and the raft thrums, like a tree struck by an ax. Then the boat buckles in half, yanking my right oar from my grip, and rears as if bent on catapulting me into the roiling soup. Suddenly, a deep silence sweeps in and hovers around for an endless second. I seem stuck in a horologic hole. Then the sound pours in again, as into a bowl, and the buzz of the river's prop slices through me ear to ear. Against the river's will, I manage to hang on. I snatch the flying oar from the air, push its throat back into its lock as the boat skids—out of control—on a crackling surge of foam through the last part of the rapid. At the egress, I spin the raft around, and miraculously land at the beach at Michael Kinsley's waiting feet. "I was almost up the creek without a paddler," he chides as he crawls into my boat, knowing well there are no more big rapids downstream.

There is only one more moment of terror, when I mistakenly inform Scott Moore there are only twenty cans of beer left; his draw drops, his face whitens like a balloon about to burst, and he looks more frightened than at any of the rapids. "Ooops . . . my mistake," I correct as I open a cooler on my boat and find at least a hundred more cans.

The last miles of the day are relatively smooth, and Michael asks to take over the oars. He's not bad, though when he misses a current and gets swooped into an eddy, he comments that his boating skills confirm his wisdom in walking the day before. Still, with some pointers, he makes good runs down some Class II rapids. He could be a guide someday.

The paddle boat sneaks up on us as Michael is making some final strokes, and breaks out into a chorus, "Michael row your boat ashore."

"Not like I never heard that in summer camp," he grins. And steers the raft to the takeout.

Richard Bangs is one of the founders of Sobek Expeditions, a pioneering adventure travel company offering trips in over sixty countries on six continents. A former Outward Bound president and author of fourteen adventure travel books, he is also chief editor and founder of various online adventure magazines. Richard has recounted his numerous adventures in Africa, China, Indonesia, and other off-the-beaten-path locations in *The Lost River*, *Whitewater Adventures*, and a dozen coauthored books.

binkler's butterball

Michele Murray

THERE IS A tribe of underfed (and probably intoxicated), good-humored River People who have been camping together along the banks of the Colorado River between the frothy throat of Gore Canyon's sluice-box below Kremmling and its eventual confluence with the Eagle River above Glenwood Canyon for tens of thousands of years. This ancient tribe evolved over time into a unique family, as they became isolated from their mainstream origins. Their culture encompassed a microcosm within a unique ecological niche of Mountain and River, below the angular unconformity of yellow and red sedimentary rocks of the "State Bridge Formation," where it juts into the basaltic base of mystical Mount Yarmony: spiritual redoubt of Ute Indian Chiefs.

In the last hundred years, this tribe has shared the banks with an influx of newcomers, "River-Virgins" toting a variety of luggage for portage, which originally included beaver pelts, industrial novelties such as apple-corers and automated washing machines, railroad timbers, and other stuff desired by turn-of-the-century society. Today, on summer weekends, the tribe portages apparati for kayaking, fly fishing, rafting, and other wet hullabaloo-ing. One summer weekend last century, a River-Virgin named Cory Binkler arrived at the undulating lip of the Colorado River with a frozen turkey in his possession. Cory was a plasma physicist visiting from Seattle, Washington; he was known for his charisma.

Cory had arrived at a place on The River, where a structure referred to in his driving directions as "Uncle Charlie's Blue-Tarp City on the banks of the Colorado, across the river from State Bridge Lodge" was set up over a circle of tents and backpacks. He reread the handwritten invitation from his childhood friend Katie, who was still on The River, slowly float fishing in a dory between

Rancho del Rio and Dot Zero. Uncle Charlie—a zesty, cantankerous river guide with a wild, white ponytail under a very beat-up Stetson cowboy hat—had constructed the enormous, crazily dipping canopy out of a thirty-foot-by-thirty-foot blue tarp (as only an ex-denizen of the Vietnam jungle can).

The tarp covered a large area in a campground across The River from State Bridge Lodge, which is an outdoor music venue. Charlie intended Blue-Tarp City as an open stay-over destination for the tribe and people who drove up from Denver to hear the band. The River People knew one only needed to float down the river casually and, at the end of the day, watch for an enormous blue tarp. They knew All People were welcome. That's why Katie invited Cory Binkler to meet her there on his long-overdue vacation to Colorado.

For some reason, Uncle Charlie was fascinated with Cory Binkler—maybe it was the plasma physics, maybe it was Cory's ponytail, but most likely, it was the frozen turkey. Cory Binkler had chauffeured a twenty-pound frozen bird from his apartment in Seattle to The River. Charlie was astounded by the bird as well as by Cory's initial request: "Does anyone have a large grill?" Cory over-estimated the quality of the facilities. He asked kayakers, rafters, and residents of a tepee if anyone had a large grill or other sort of sophisticated cooking device. He was offered a tripod over a stone ring. Charlie balanced the bird atop a conspicuous boulder like an unidentified corpse at the morgue.

Cory wasn't totally unprepared. He had brought necessary items: a sleeping bag, sunglasses, oven mitts, a cooking thermometer, ballpoint pens, charcoal briquettes, and apple-wood branches, all of which formed a nest of debris in the backseat of his car. No grill, though. "Bird-zilla" had traveled all the way from the Great Woods of the Northwest in a large, "thermally dynamic," battery-dependent cooler in the trunk of his car, only to be stared at by all in its solidified state. Cory went about creating a space for himself and looking after his personal hygiene, unbaffled.

Later in the evening, still awaiting Katie's arrival from The River, Cory borrowed Charlie's ax—a professional, logger-sized weapon nearly as big as himself. He staggered backward under the ax head's weight, then muscled it forward in an alarming dive at what everyone assumed to be the iceball of a bird, in order to downsize it into reasonable proportions. However, Cory was only hacking his apple-wood branches into chips. Some of the River People coached him how to avoid chopping his feet off. By the time Katie arrived, he had reduced not only his little branches to shredded slivers, but also one great log that couldn't get away.

"What?" Katie asked Charlie. "He brought a frozen turkey?" She was obviously pleased to see Cory in camp and amazed to see him all grimy and sweaty. But she also seemed a little embarrassed by her friend's bulging bundle of bird on display by the campfire.

"What are you going to do with it?" she asked.

"I didn't know what I should bring. You said there were probably going to be lots of people. I just brought this turkey. I have a special recipe. Can you please help me find an oven or a large grill tomorrow? It's really important. If I don't cook it within a certain amount of time, it won't work."

"We'll see," Katie answered, with doubt in her voice.

In the morning, the River People had shuttled their crafts upriver to Rancho del Rio. The plan for the day was to float back to State Bridge Lodge, in time for the music and campout at Blue-Tarp City. A soiree of native-looking types (for *Gilligan's Island,* maybe) with ragamuffin beaded hair twitches, leather-thong necklaces, Patagonia river shorts, and Teva sandals were seated at KK's BBQ Stand drinking beer. It was nine o'clock, and they were waiting for their river-guests to arrive. KK's BBQ is strategically located in the middle of Rancho's grounds—one has to drive slowly around her stand and be examined by the local professionals before reaching the parking area. By the time the tourists have unloaded, smeared themselves with sunblock, packed purses and pockets with all their valuable possessions (and kissed life-as-they-know-it good-bye), the river guides are mostly sober again.

Cory was becoming frantic. He had to *get the big bald bird a cookin'* by a certain time or else it would not get done. He stressed over this matter even before Katie was awake. By the time they arrived at Rancho, Cory had concocted a backup plan. He immersed the big frozen bird in Charlie's five-gallon plastic bailing bucket, where it soaked in brine laced with the apple-wood chips. The resourceful cook then stowed it in Katie's dory to be shuttled up to Rancho.

When they arrived, Cory hauled the troublesome carcass to KK—a woman who seemed to be the hub of the Universe. He hoped she might let him use part of her huge grill for the next five hours. Though she is one of the most gracious hosts to be found in three counties, Cory had no idea he was dealing with the most focused and intense Bar-B-Q woman on this planet. KK utilizes every inch of her grill to cook up piles of ribs, chicken, brats, burgers, and wieners for the hungry souls of the district.

Katie's tolerance evaporated when Cory attempted to return the rejected bird to her dory. The River was high and she wanted to fish. It would take a strong oarsman to row three people, two fat dogs, and a twenty-pound suckling-sized turkey in a bucket of brine against the current in order to cast into trout lairs without being hurried.

Katie thought she might release the turkey into the river, to have it bob through eddies and rapids like flotsam. A vision of it washing up at the campsite all bloated and *foul* put her off this plan. (Also, river regulations forbid the dumping of solid waste into the stream.) Fortunately for Cory, whose composure was cracking, Charlie responded. He put the bucket of frozen-bird-and-brine in the storage of his raft.

At KK's BBQ Stand, Katie met one of her regular fishing pals. They put Cory and two dogs in the stern of the dory; Charlie loaded four guests and the *big dead bird* into his raft. Then they pushed off. Both boats were full of beer and food in coolers, too. Charlie knew Katie would be rowing against the current to slow her boat and hover at nice, fishy holes, so he planned to take his people on land expeditions in the meantime. He had places where he tied up his raft for hiking up to Ute Indian ruins, old eagle traps, fur trapper's cabins, and even dinosaur tracks. Katie would do nothing but fish the entire day. She intended to use Cory as her slave at the oars.

Shortly after the current sucked the bow of the dory downstream into a seam of faster-moving water, Cory began fiddling and fussing with a piece of twine he had produced from his shirt pocket. He had put it in a little plastic bag—the kind that zips. In an instant, he fashioned handmade "river-gear" for attaching his glasses and hat to a buttonhole on his shirt. Katie wasn't sure if she should be amazed or annoyed with him.

Cory noticed her inspecting gaze. "Remember that time I almost lost my hat in the wind?" he asked her. "Now I don't have to worry about losing either my hat or my glasses!" He was clearly pleased with his systematic approach.

"Here, Cory. Watch how I hug the bank and keep the boat parallel to the shoreline," Katie said. "Think you can do this?"

Her enlisted man rowed most of the day—certainly through all the big, slow "lakes" where the river widened and offered little current for assistance. It's not an easy job to scoot around in a lake when the water is "greasy" either, as was the case in many of these great pools. "Greasy" water occurs where the current is upwelling from below to the surface and sucking back down again in plumes. There is no orientation or direction to the current, though it can produce a deceitful, strong undertow, which can yank an oar right out of the helmsman's hands. The surface has a glossy, wrinkled texture that literally looks greasy.

In addition, the wind had picked up, making it even more difficult to keep the dory in line.

Cory began raising his arched body into the air, with his pelvis jutted forward, and leaning back on the oars as they slowly dipped and descended into the current. "What *are* you doing, Cory?" Katie asked. " You're scaring me."

"It's the 'love-stroke,' Momma! I'm applying the weight of my body to the torque force of these levers and converting potential energy into kinetic energy, which requires much less muscle energy in addressing the inertia of this ship."

Katie tried hard to freeze her smile. This odd man moved her heart as surely as he moved the dory. The "Charm of Cory" was upon her. She remembered again why she loved him despite the distance and time that separated their lives. She never intended to let the years slip by—it just happened. Now they were both in their thirties and neither had ever been married, though both had been close (not to each other). Whenever she met him, Cory opened her heart and filled it with wonderful, life-enriching sustenance. He was one of her most favorite people in the world. Once, Cory had commenced a self-imposed moratorium on visiting or even contacting her for nearly five years. She felt as if a significant beacon on which she had come to rely for grounding and centering in her chaotic life had been extinguished. (They never talked about the reason why—she just assumed *she* had been an asshole.) A world without Cory was a world with a big, cold hole in it. Katie wondered if he knew how she felt about him, if he knew how valuable he was to her. But she never asked.

"Those 'levers' are called 'oars.' Can you slow us down a bit, Mr. Love-Stroke?" she responded.

When they came to the big, faster water, either Katie or her fellow angler took over the oars. At those times, Cory delighted in hanging one hand over the gunnels while holding on to a beer with the other. He laughed at the mist of whitecapped rapids as they were decapitated by the chine of the dory's hull and sprayed his face. Otherwise, Cory rowed Katie's and her buddy's butt and the turkey's and dogs' all the way downriver, against the wind and with growing prowess at the sticks.

Cory was quickly becoming comfortable with his new role. He spoke and joked in the voice of a pirate. The fishing duo tried not to laugh at everything he said. He was visibly enjoying torturing his captives both with his silly comedy routine and with physical experiments of dexterity at the oars. He quickly realized he could use eddies to return upstream to offer fish-filled riffles to his "shipmates" again and again. No one was thinking about cooking the damn bird anymore. Katie wondered if she could infiltrate a clan of Cory's friends and colleagues as easily as he adapted to the creed of her unsophisticated friends. She knew he envied her lifestyle (everyone in the city did), but she didn't know if he sensed how much she admired him, that she believed him to be the deeper, more developed person.

"Cory, when we get to State Bridge, I'll ask the owners if you can use one of the ovens in their restaurant. They're my friends." But it didn't look like Cory was worried about his bird Buddha anymore. One fine day on The River had transformed him into River Man. He was truly content just rowing them all about, in and out of eddies, slowing only for suspected trout hideouts. He held the dory right on line with the drift—as if he had been doing it all is life.

"Oh, that would be perfect, Katie."

Unfortunately, State Bridge Lodge had a large wedding reception going, and the kitchen was rock-and-rolling with swinging cooks and waitresses who seemed as happy to be working as the guests were to be dancing. Charlie and the other guides had joined their guests, guests already in a high state of alcohol-induced entropy and no longer River-Virgins. Fortunately for Cory, the genuinely friendly bartender (as *all* the bartenders at State Bridge *always* are) offered a two-legged Weber grill without lid or grate from his cabin. It was a true roadside grill—found by the side of the highway. Uncle Charlie briefly left his devoted entourage to devise a third—and much needed—leg from a prolific junk pile behind the lodge. Further rousting in the garbage produced a refrigerator shelf, which, after Charlie bent the corners, made for a grate. Now the plasma physicist was ready to commence the brawn work.

Cory fashioned a chimney from two economy-sized coffee cans. He perforated and filled them with charcoal. Katie was intrigued to observe that, stacked vertically inside this vented reactor, briquettes burned much more efficiently. Next, Cory made Katie's fishing lackey hold three long sheets of aluminum foil at arm's length as he rolled a seam between them and constructed a large astrodome. The engineer-chef then placed his brine-soaked apple-wood chips on the grill as a bed for one magnificently huge turkey—now flabby, and waving its arms about, like a needy chimpanzee. When the wood chips began to smolder, he nestled Big Bird in them and covered her nudity with the foil dome. The gone-camping-and-floating turkey was now beginning to resemble dinner. The scent of Thanksgivings hung in the air, but this congregation of scantily clad, drunken River People reminded Katie more of a bacchanal.

The motley crew danced and carried on to a live band at the lodge for five hours straight, while Cory repeatedly stuck his thermometer in the chest cavity of the turkey, until it reached a critical temperature and had held it long enough. When its transition had satisfied the scientist, he presented the amazing, golden bird to the crowd, with oven mitts and the flourish of a doctor delivering a newborn to its mother. The lodge owners laid out buns, forks, plates, and napkins. Everyone ordered side dishes of potatoes and other tasty morsels from the kitchen and feasted on the moist, smoked turkey as if they had never eaten one before. In the morning, there were even leftovers for next day's regatta.

Weeks after Cory left The River to return to his Seattle life as one of Boeing's project directors or something to that effect, Katie learned of his internet website for smoking turkeys. ("How do you get one into a pipe?" was her initial reaction.) One recipe featured an "Expedition-worthy Tur-Duck-Hen," a Turkey-stuffed-with-duck-stuffed-with-chicken like Russian dolls. She didn't expect to see Cory again for a while—probably a long while. That's just the way it has always been between them.

Katie, however, knew she wouldn't be surprised if one day she came floating around a bend and saw Cory at the "levers" of another dory, demonstrating the "love-stroke" to a duo of fly fishermen trying to hide their mirth from this odd bird.

Michele Murray is a freelance writer and regular contributor to the *Mountain Gazette*. A fine cartoonist, she also created "Belinda Smegler"—a fictitious character who writes a cooking column for the *Summit County Independent* newspaper. When not writing or drawing or rowing, she plays the bassoon. Michele is indebted to Karen Christopherson, Al Marlowe, John Fayhee, and especially Doug White for their encouragement of her writing. She lives on the brink of South Park, Colorado, with a husband who, her editor is convinced, is just another pigment of her inflammation.

the bean

Craig Childs

I AM THE OGRE guarding the gate. I am filthy with sleep and draped in ropes of unfinished dreams. You will have to fight me. You are the gray Elderhostel traveler who always wakes before dawn, who creeps through the dark camp in search of the bean. You are the Grand Canyon client entering the silent kitchen, the river ceaselessly humming and laughing in the distance. Even if you make it to the gate before I do, I will be there soon enough lifting my battered club, my ponderous fist. Even if you somehow decode the locks and latches of ammo boxes and ice chests, even if you sneak into the secret caches of lunch meats, cookies, mustard, and cracker boxes, the bean will be elusive, like a hidden sack of opals. I know what you are up against. I do not need to move quickly.

If I am late in reaching you, and if, as impossible as it seems, you find your precious coffee, if out of the ludicrous bin of ladles and knives you pull the pot and parchment filters, you must still reach the stove. It is a dull metal beast. You do not entirely comprehend the stove. It is as alien as the cockpit of a bush plane. Where is the starter? Which knobs, which valves?

I will catch you there if nowhere else. I will groan from the dim of my cave, "Can I help you with something?"

You will wave your sword in the air, lifting the bag of coffee to show me your intention. Please, you will beg, can you help me? As if that would stop me. As if the ogre would shrug and return to slumber on the deck of a wooden dory or in a sleeping bag wadded on the sand.

"Coffee isn't ready until six thirty."

"Six thirty?"

"I told you yesterday."
"I need some now."

AS IF I would relinquish this movable temple to you. As if I would let you light this stove with a *whumph* of blue-orange flame that kinks your eyebrows and leaves you smelling like a burned cat. As if I would let you crack the delicate crystal of my kitchen. Do you have any idea about the tightrope we walk here, the meticulous strain of carrying an entire restaurant down a river of blowing sand and wells of rapids? You will misplace the sugar, accidentally vent propane into the air, leave an ice chest open for the ravens and the ringtail cats. I cannot allow such things.

Your filthy cravings mean nothing to me. I do not care how surly you become. I will call you an old fuck and order you back to your wilderness if I must. You may erupt. It's not unexpected. Mild-mannered marketing analyst by day, fierce, fire-eyed weasel by morning. You've disarmed lesser guides before, beating them back, or worse: casting your spell of pity until they are doing the dirty work at your command, moving like zombies to prepare your coffee.

But here you will realize the horrible truth. I do not crave the bean.

I have always thought coffee tastes like an infusion of charcoal. I share no sympathy. Look deep into my motionless eyes.

There you will witness stories of dread.

There you will see me long ago, eighteen years old and guiding down on the Green River for the first time, leading a fleet of canoes to the Confluence. You hear the cries of those damned souls who joined me there. Oh yes, they had a magical trip: stars and canyons and days of unimaginable grandeur. But through the sighs and laughter you hear the true terror: Your young guide doesn't even understand coffee . . . and he was the one who planned and packed this eight-day tour. There is nothing to clutch in the morning but weak bags of Lipton's tea.

No coffee . . .
No coffee . . .

YES. I SEE you weakening, the fear sinking into your bones. You hear screams out of the past. The time I gathered the hard brown seeds of palo verde trees, cooked them over the fire, ground them with a stone, and brewed them in a pot. It was a curiosity I offered the hardier Elderhostel folk who had the day before tasted my wretched creosote tea. I told them this new concoction tasted like coffee to me. Wails rise up from the abyss of time, ghosts drinking to this very day cups of burned wood.

You are staggering. You cannot hold your ground. I have seen a troop of rafts pass by in the Grand Canyon, a private trip of people wearing foul expressions, beating the water with their oars. One of them, some furious martyr, called out to us, "We ran out of coffee on day five! How many days you think to Diamond Creek?"

"Nine."

"Nine???"

"Nine."

The oars struck even harder.

I KNOW THE hardships men and women have faced in pursuit of the bean.

You are nothing but a bleary-eyed addict, your hair uncombed and crawling with agitation. Sad to watch, really. The hour you must wait will try your very soul. As I lumber toward you I lament the lazy comfort of modern, civilized people, how tribulations come in such regular and small doses. So used to being shamed every day are you, sent into another waiting line, put on hold again and again, it is easy to drive you away. You will flee my kitchen stripped of honor, but ready to slip it back on like a T-shirt so that we will again enjoy each other's company around the campfire.

MAYBE IT WILL not end this way, though. Maybe you will come back to the river someday with your own coffee, your own tiny stove stuffed in your gear. You may recognize the raw passion of your addiction and act accordingly, rather than expecting twenty-four-hour espresso stands to pop up along the river bends. As I sit in the dawn sand of the river meditating in the slow silence, I will not be the ogre you must fight. I will recognize your movements as you find a solitary place, tinkering with your stove, preparing your coffee in a small French press. Your ravenous fascination will be yours alone. Perhaps you must then become the ogre. The dark smell of your coffee will drift among silent tents, calling the waking dead to life. As they stumble toward you, hoping to beat down the gate and score an early cup of Joe, you will know what to do. I have taught you well.

Guard the gate.
Raise your club.
Chase them back into their dull nightmares.

Craig Childs wrote the first of eight prize winning books of wilderness travel and natural history in Laundromats and libraries—wherever he could plug in a computer—but mostly by hand. His brainchildren were conceived during year-round ramblings between Utah's canyons and Baja California's dunes. An archaeologist, Prescott College instructor, newspaper editor, trombonist, beer bottle flutist, and onetime gas station attendant, Craig's writing has appeared in *Outside, Audubon, Sierra, Backpacker, Arizona Highways, High Country News,* and the *Los Angeles Times.* When he is not chasing flash floods in the desert, he lives with his wife and son in a barely plumbed cabin in western Colorado. On the throne of his wall-less outhouse in the snow, he feels like a true king.

high water

Christa Sadler and Dave Edwards

Editor's Note: In the memories of most Colorado River guides, 1983—the year of unexpected spring runoff, the year Glen Canyon Reservoir almost lost its dam—will always be prominent. The guides involved in this trip told the following tale at a guides' training seminar, where it was recorded by Don Briggs. Don graciously provided a complete transcript of the telling, from which this story was written.

THIS STORY SHOULD really be called The Last Time That Don Was Ever the Head Boatman, and The Last Time Don Will Ever *Be* the Head Boatman. It was a launch on *high* water, the flood of 1983. In fact, there may not have been any trips that left after this one at all. They were running a Lower Canyon oar-powered trip with a guy from California who was sort of a New Age guru; we'll call him Ronald (not his real name). Don met this guy on the Tuolumne River in California, and they had a pretty good time. Ronald asked about other trips, and Don talked him into coming down the Grand Canyon. This was back in, well, who knows when, but long before the spring of '83 when the biggest runoff from the Rocky Mountains in twenty years met with a full Lake Powell.

The trip was scheduled as an eight-day "lower half," and Ronald was going to hike his folks down the Bright Angel Trail; that was supposed to be part of their enlightenment. They were all set to go.

But then the dam started spilling water. Lots of it. Every morning someone would call up the Bureau of Reclamation and ask how much water was coming out of Glen Canyon Dam. Then they'd call up the Park Service and ask

"Can we go or can't we?" The park responded, "Well, we have to talk to the Bureau of Reclamation." The water was rising higher and higher behind the dam, and Don called Ronald in California because he didn't know if the trip was going to happen or not. The Park Service was saying, "Yes, you can," and then "No, you can't." Back and forth. Then the Park Service finally decided, "We're just going to leave it up to the outfitters. It'll be self-regulating."

They were going to run paddle boats originally. But that didn't seem like such a good idea. There was a big meeting. Some said running the canyon at that water level wasn't safe, and others said it was, but only with small boats. And *no* paddle boats. There was some question about snout rigs; but in a snout rig at high water you'd put in at Lees Ferry and be down at Lake Mead before you could blink. There would be no stopping anywhere. So, no snouts.

In the meantime, Don was getting calls from Ronald, who wanted to know if the trip was happening or not. Everyone talked. Somewhere along the line Don realized that because the river was so high and so fast, they could run the entire canyon in the eight days they had planned for the lower half. So he called Ronald and convinced him that this was a good idea. "Not everybody's gonna get to do this, Ronald. You're maybe the only guy that ever gets to. So come on ahead, we're gonna try it." (See, they figured they might not be able to stop at Phantom Ranch to pick anyone up who hiked in.) Ronald agreed, and the group showed up at the Ferry.

Now, Ronald had once been a doctor, a surgeon. Then, in the operating room, he had an epiphany that he shouldn't be cutting people up. Instead he should go out and enlighten them. He recruited people for group energy healing, group meditations, and those sorts of things. He had a little following around the country that he had taken on different trips all over the place, but he had never done a trip like this, on a river, with one of his groups.

He was into something he called Transformation, and the people who were coming on this trip were first attending a Transformation conference. Then they were going down the Grand Canyon. When the guides asked, Ronald could never really explain what Transformation meant. But he he about to find out more about it. Everyone was about to find out . . .

Lees Ferry. The boatmen had no idea what the river would look like at

62,000 cubic feet per second. When they got to the Ferry they were told that the water was now up to 70 or 72,000 cfs. It was huge. Scary. But there was a trip to run, so the group took off. What else could they do? The boats just *flew* downstream. They camped way down, around Mile 40. Got there in about five hours as opposed to two and a half days. The trip was going great. It was the first night on the river, and Ronald called everyone around, including the crew.

Part of the deal was that the guides had to be part of the group. They couldn't go off by themselves; they had to blend in. They couldn't just be with the folks, get to know them, talk to them. They were going to be part of the Transformation. Ronald expected them to hold hands in the circle and all that. And *no* alcohol. That was another part of the deal, very important.

So the group got together that night and everyone sat around, chanting and humming, trying to create a little circle of energy. Well, Don was pretty nervous as head boatman, and he found that all his energy went toward just thinking about how all these people were going to stay alive on that big, fast, *high* river out there. While everyone was chanting their special sounds, Don was therefore humming to himself, *Ohhhh, be good to me, be good to me river.* He wasn't sure what everyone else was thinking, but that's where his thoughts were.

The next day the trip floated down to the Little Colorado. They got there by two o'clock in the afternoon. The water was unbelievable, about fifteen feet deep and turquoise—gorgeous. The flood of the main Colorado had backed up the LC, and it was a lake. It was extraordinary.

A motor rig came toward them from out of sight around the corner, coming *down* the Little Colorado. It had gone so far up because the water was so high, which was surreal enough. Then a helicopter flew over and a guy with goggles threw a bag out of the chopper. Don and another guide ran up the hill to get the bag. Inside was a note, weighted down with gravel. They both read it. Don said, "We're gonna read it in front of the entire group. That's what this is all about, a group experience." They both chuckled.

They went down to join the group by the peaceful blue water. Don sat above the people, and they all looked up at him. He said, "We just got this note and I figured you want to know what it says." He proceeded to read:

ALL TRIPS MUST stop at Phantom Ranch and check in with the ranger. You must leave a copy of your pass, and manifest, including names, with the ranger. Below Phantom Ranch, notice: As set in 36 CFR.6A, Closures and Public Use Limits: The superintendent may close to the public use all or any portion or part of an area when necessary for the protection of the area or for the safety or welfare of persons or property by posting of the appropriate signs indicating the extent and the scope of the closure. All persons shall observe and abide by officially posted signs designating closed areas and visiting areas. Rangers and notices will replace signs. The superintendent has closed Crystal Rapid to all passengers of both private and commercial trips. Passengers must walk around Crystal with only boatmen and swampers to run Crystal.

Don looked down at his people. They were getting a little concerned. They clearly weren't ready for this.

This closure is due to the extreme hazard of Crystal Rapid. Four motor rigs and numerous oar boats have flipped. Ninety people were in the water. There has been one fatality and fifteen injuries. This closure is in effect until further notice. Water levels are expected—

"that's the key word here,"

—to remain at 70,000, with possible increases.

Don looked down at his people again, and the lovely blue water. He could see what they were thinking: *I'm gonna die tomorrow.* He began to wonder if it was such a good idea to read the notice to them. *What the hell,* he thought, *it's a Transformational experience.*

On the way downstream the group passed two Sanderson motor rigs on a beach, whose crew had their stuff spread out all over camp. Don's group waved, but the Sanderson crew seemed very solemn. Don figured, *Hell, they're probably scared to death, too.*

They camped at Carbon Creek. The beach was so tiny that the group had to sit up in the rocks to do the circle that night. The next morning there was a constant stream of helicopters going back and forth. One right after another, all the time from first light. They were cleaning up camp when the Sanderson rigs pulled up. The crew was grim. It turned out that one of them had decided to run the hole at Nankoweap. It was the only piece of water he'd seen, the only significant whitewater, in sixty miles. He'd flipped the motor rig. They called the trip off and decided to fly their people out. The boatman who flipped his boat was in a state of shock and the other boatman quietly told them about the flip.

That didn't do a lot for the confidence of the group. They saw those two huge motor rigs. They looked at their tiny rafts. Don tried to reassure his group. "Hey, everything is going fine, you know?" "Uh-huh." They finished breakfast. The people worked their tails off so that the crew would have to come to the Transformation, and couldn't use breaking down camp as an excuse not to join in. They sat down in a big circle, holding hands. It was a huge trip, around thirty-four people. Ronald finished his monologue and then proceeded. "Well, we have these guides on the boats, and they know about the geology and the natural history and they're great cooks, but we don't have anyone on the boats to make sure the energy is moving into a good direction. Now, we're not even sure the rangers are going to let us through at Phantom, but if they do, we're about to run the whole Gorge, down to the top of Crystal, a place where ninety people have just swum. One fatality. Fifteen people injured. So what I'd like to do today is have an energy monitor on each boat, to make sure the energy is going in the right direction."

So energy motors were appointed for each boat. The crew saw them as informants. Kind of ironic, really, because any boatman's job just naturally involves being an "energy monitor." But with Ronald's energy monitors, you had to be happy. You couldn't be nervous: bad energy. The boats headed downstream. At Hance Rapid, they all got out to scout. Every boatman's heart was way down, deep in his gut, looking at Hance at 75,000 cfs. It was ugly out there, holes the size of condominiums and water moving really fast.

"Everything's gonna be just fine." As they coiled up the lines before casting off, the energy monitors came up to each boat and tried to get the boatmen to hold hands while they sang a song. Right before going into Hance. The song felt more like a dirge. "The river is flowing, flowing and growing. The river is flowing, down to the sea." Over and over again.

Boating-wise, the guides did pretty well through the Gorge. Everything was fast; the eddies were massive whirlpools. They were running on adrenaline and teamwork. The trip stopped at Phantom to get permission to go on down. That night, camp was at Mile 96, Schist Camp. Just two miles above Crystal.

In the morning all the crew wanted to do was go downstream and face Crystal. But three of their boats had holes in the bottom. The water was so high, and there was such a surf, that the boats had all pushed up on sharp rocks that weren't water-worn. So they patched the floors, which took two or three hours. There was no shade and it was really hot out there in those black rocks. The guides were nervous and uptight and beginning to lose it with Ronald. They were thinking, *We're not going to have to Transform today? Ronald's not going to sit everyone down in this 110-degree heat above Crystal and make us all Transform, is he?*

Sure enough, they sat down and held hands in the 110-degree heat above Crystal. People were sweating. After fifteen or twenty minutes of silence, Ronald said, "You know, yesterday was a great day. We ran all those rapids and we had our energy monitors. But you know how we got to the bottom of these rapids and everybody would yell and cheer because we had good runs, and we were really excited to be down at the bottom and safe? Well, what I'd like us to do today is to try and save that energy."

And he started to talk about these Far Eastern Tantric sexual practices. He equated this new idea of boating to a practice where the men don't ejaculate. When they get excited they retain it and are thus inspired from "within." The guides were thinking, *This is right above CRYSTAL, for Godsakes. We're supposed to run this rapid at 70,000. We're supposed to get down below Crystal and crack a TOMATO JUICE? In SILENCE?*

The wave in Crystal was phenomenal—125 feet long, 20 feet high, and 15 feet deep. All the passengers walked around Crystal. The guides ran each boat with two boatmen, one to row and one to bail, one boat at a time. They made it. And at the bottom they cheered out loud and drank beer. They could have been killed.

The next morning there was a big circle in camp. The trip was starting to become fractionalized between Ronald's hard-core followers and the people who were beginning to realize where they were and that what was happening was really special. They were clueing in to the fact that running the river at this water level in such small boats was extraordinary. They wanted to experience the place, let the canyon do its work. So the group discussion started getting a little wild.

Ronald said, "There's something I want to say. I've been noticing that the focus is on the guides and what is happening on the river." The guides were thinking, *We don't even know what's around the next bend, we don't even know if we're all gonna live through this,* when Ronald continued. "People paid to come on this trip with me and they are focusing more attention on the guides, and I'm really upset that this is the case. This is something I would like to correct."

One of the guides lost it. "Ronald," she said, "you told everybody to get involved in this trip, and I've never seen you in the kitchen. I've never seen you lift a hand to do anything."

"Thank you for sharing," Ronald said.

On the trip went, down to Olo Canyon, where they had to pull in and see what it looked like at 85,000. The water had topped the debris fan, and the boats pulled right in to the wall, up to the lip of the first plunge pool. Don thought that the trip should just camp there. It would be a great place to have a circle, above the pools, in the amphitheater.

When Don told the group his plan, Ronald started to get worried. He looked up at the pool and the rope you had to climb to get to the amphitheater, and he couldn't quite figure how they were going to get everyone up there, and all the equipment. The other guides didn't think it was such a good idea. *Ronald* didn't think it was such a good idea. Don could see mutiny about to happen, and he finally just said, "I want to camp here. You'll thank me later."

Everybody clambered up the rope into the bowl. The crew cooked something simple for dinner down in the boats and passed it up, so they wouldn't have to cook up there and could keep the place clean. Everyone was all set to camp, when Ronald decided to do some chanting at night, instead of the next morning, like he usually did. The moonlight was really bright, and the frogs were just going nuts. It was outrageous in there, and Ronald asked them all to close their eyes and chant. They couldn't see the moonlight on the walls, or hear the sounds of the canyon. It was completely incomprehensible to the guides. *This is one of the most amazing places in the Canyon. All these people have to do is shut up and open their eyes and they would be Transformed.* By this time, the boatmen were punchy. They felt like they were drunk. They *wished* they were drunk. So they just got up and left. The crew took their black bags to the lip of the amphitheater and heaved them into the pool with the boats. Laughing hysterically, they jumped down into the pool and climbed into their boats to sleep. And there was Dave, relaxing on his boat with a bottle of Glenlivet scotch.

Downstream, the last night on the river, everyone was supposed to share their favorite part of the trip, or something special that had happened to them. Ronald passed around three bottles of expensive sherry, for thirty-four people. Time to lighten up, finally. Everyone was saying this and that, only Don wasn't saying much of anything because he was thinking about the takeout. He was thinking about how they were all going to stop at Diamond Creek, if there even *was* a Diamond Creek. Maybe the water was too high.

The boatmen felt put on the spot; it was hard to talk. When your turn came with the bottle, you had to say something. The bottle had gone around about two-thirds of the circle when it came to Dave.

Now at some point in the trip, almost every guide had lost it with Ronald and the whole situation, publicly. But Dave hadn't said a word. Oh, he had laughed about things privately, with the guides, on the boats, but never out loud. Dave sort of sat there. He looked at the bottle and turned it in his hands. Then he said, "Well, first of all Ronald, you're an asshole." There was a long pause. Then he talked for a while about the river, the flood they were riding on, the danger, and recognizing the experience for what it was. And when he finished, he said: "And furthermore, Ronald, I will come *every* time!"

Epilogue

WELL, THE RIVER won in the long run, because two years later Don heard that Ronald wanted to do the trip again, but only under the stipulation that none of the guides who were on the first trip would go with him.

He came down the once more in 1992, on a family trip with his kids and wife. A guide on the trip said he was a "really nice guy." Maybe the river really had worked on him back in 1983—just took him ten years to be Transformed.

Christa Sadler has been a river guide since 1986. That alone might call her sanity into question. Add to that her work as a geologist, freelance writer, and educator, and a recent stint as a small-town newspaper reporter in Alaska during the winter, and it's pretty clear she's beyond help. But she has fun. Her own anthology of river stories, *There's This River*, was published in 1994.

Dave Edwards retired from being a Grand Canyon and expedition guide after three decades on the river. He now owns a studio in Flagstaff, Arizona, and works as a photojournalist, mostly in Asia, where the *real* gurus are.

stur-gis had a wet-suit

Brad Dimock

I THINK THE Green River's Desolation Canyon in central Utah may be my favorite of all river trips, but it certainly did not start out that way. My first visit was inauspicious at best, and I swore it would be my last. It was in early April, in the dead of winter.

Normally April is in spring, but not in '74. The wind was screeching when we launched and got worse each day. Occasionally there was snow mixed in with the flying sand—other times just sleet. We had been out about three days, and had still not even gotten to the canyon proper, when the wind decided to really show us its stuff. On a long, wide bend of the river, the waves grew whitecaps.

We were about a dozen in number, all Prescott College students, on an outing. "Intermediate Kayaking Expedition" was, I believe, the name of our course. Our two support rafts' progress went from slow to none to backward. They blew back upstream around the corner. The rest of us, novice kayakers all, fought our way ashore to a broad, wet gumbo mudflat. There were no trees or shelter for miles. We dragged well ashore onto the plain of brown goo and climbed back into our boats, backs to the wind, and waited for the tantrum to subside. Like a flock of seagulls in a storm we sat, each in a yellow kayak, perfectly aligned with the gale, arms hugged tight to our chests, heads bowed, a hundred yards from the nearest water, the frigid wind whipping by.

In those days, the river gear industry had not yet emerged. Rafts and kayaks, such as they were, were slow, heavy, ponderous things. Paddling jackets consisted of cheap raincoats with duct-tape cuffs. Polypropylene and drysuits were not even a twinkle in their creators' eyes. We were cold, wet throughout, and miserable. Well, most of us were.

Sturgis had a wetsuit. I repeat, with a nyah-nyah sneer: Stur-gis had a wet-suit.

And it was Sturgis who first had to pee. Mistakenly electing not to wet his wetsuit, he removed his spraydeck, wriggled out of his boat and squished a few steps downwind. Wetsuits rarely have flies. Sturgis had to take off his jacket, then peel the suspender-like tops of the suit down off his shoulders, and from around his hips, pushing his spraydeck down to his knees, before he could begin to relieve himself. This he did. With little else to amuse us, we watched.

Things were going well enough for him until the next gust came. Huddled in our kayaks, we felt it hit us in the backs, bowing us further forward. And we saw Sturgis's kayak shift, then leap into the air. Sturgis, concentrating on business in hand, had no idea he was about to be hit from behind by a fifty-pound kite. Not that it would have helped. Feet stuck in the mud, wetsuit around his knees, it was now just a matter of acting out the drama. With a *thwack!* it hit him square in the back, felling him like a tree into his fresh, warm puddle in the mud—then cartwheeled down the flats, into the river and upstream around the bend. All but Sturgis laughed hard and long, some of us gasping for air, clutching our cramping sides. Sturgis failed to see the humor, which was a pity, because it was really the high point of the trip.

Things got worse as the expedition went on. Much worse.

I'D BEEN TELLING this story for nearly twenty-five years when, last summer, I saw Sturgis in the grocery store. Now stories, when not written down, develop a life of their own: Details evolve, characters enter and leave the tale, wording changes to best suit the teller's needs. Wondering how my version of the story compared with his after all these years, I parked my shopping cart next to his in the dairy section. I told him something like the version I have written here and asked him if it, indeed, had happened that way. There was a long pause as Sturgis rubbed his chin, nodding slowly and trying to remember just how it went. "Yes," he said, "that's how it went. That really happened. But I'm just not sure it was *me.*"

Brad Dimock was a river guide for thirty years, on the Colorado River system and around the world. Since 1998 he has made his living as a writer, co-authoring *The Doing of the Thing: The Brief, Brilliant Whitewater Career of Buzz Holmstrom*, and writing, in 2001, *Sunk Without a Sound: The Tragic Colorado River Honeymoon of Glen and Bessie Hyde*. Both of these books won the prestigious National Outdoor Book Award. Some of his own boating escapades have been anthologized in *There's This River*. He lives in Flagstaff, Arizona.

river music

Jessica Maxwell

FROM THE BANK, the river looked like a snake, glistening green and sliding through the rocks. I couldn't see its fangs, but I knew they were there, waiting for me just around the next bend, sharp, white, and dangerous. The Rapids. I was scared.

Hell hath no terror like that of those-who-have-almost-drowned, which I had in a river long ago, young, foolish, and in the company of similarly moronic friends, one of whom somehow managed to rescue me at the exact moment I had surrendered to the death-god of the river.

The ordeal left me deeply marked by the power of whitewater, and I had avoided it ever since. But now, I knew, my number was up. After all, I had lived an adventurous life. Being a nature writer by profession, I had been obliged to kayak in deadly storms, hike rattlesnake-ridden ridges, track moose through blizzards, crouch just inches from stampeding buffalo, overcome my fear of flying, fish alongside Alaska brown bear, swim with whales, snorkel with salmon ... why, I had even camped on the steppes of Outer Mongolia with the local pit vipers, one of whom decided to make an unscheduled appearance in my neighbor's bedroll. Clearly, I was out of excuses. The old rookie-in-the-wilderness routine was a leaky canoe without a paddle. It was time to make peace with the grim river reaper.

So there I was, standing in the bleached morning light of an Idaho August with the worst forest fires in a decade breathing dragon breath down on the billion-year-old batholith basalt banks of the famous Salmon River, which, much to my current mortification, I had signed up to float. To make things worse, the Salmon also is called the River of No Return, which meant, of course, that I would never get out alive. I'd never return home, never see my dog again, my French china, the little black dress Nordstrom finally got around to mailing me after it was back-ordered for three months . . . so much for a Gwyneth Paltrow Christmas. I knew my whole life was going down that black snake hole with the great green river reptile that was, at the moment, still slithering past my feet. I cursed myself for putting myself through this.

"Need sunblock?" asked an insufferably cheerful river guide.

"No," I replied. "I need a lobotomy."

We were putting in, as they say in the river-running business, at Corn Creek, a two-hour drive from the already remote town of Salmon, Idaho. At the moment the place looked like an ant farm. Fat yellow rafts and elegant high-sided wooden dory boats waited in the shallows while troops of extremely tan people crawled all over them. They were our fleet of guides—one per guest, I noted—and their mission was to stash the mountains of supplies that now littered the beach into secret compartments deep in the viscera of the vessels that would carry us downstream for the next six days. Coolers, tents, duffel bags, sleeping bags, tables, lanterns, cooking gear, rubber boots, and backpacks . . . the scene looked to me like preparations for war.

"You can stow your ammo can here," offered a quiet dory guide named Lonnie Hutson. We had, indeed, been given genuine government issue metal ammo cans in which to keep the stuff we wanted near us at all times—sunglasses, cameras . . . arsenic. I studied the other guests for similar signs of angst. Nothing. Just smiles and spirited stomping around.

"Hi, I'm Jeanne," announced a pretty woman with an East Coast accent. "That's my husband, Herb." Herb waved and smiled, which made him look exactly like Lorne Greene. They were, it turned out, a bonanza—a psychologist-and-doctor team from Maryland who had already done O.A.R.S.'s seventeen-day Grand Canyon dory trip and lived to tell the tale . . . many times and with *great* enthusiasm. I asked Jeanne if I could ride in her lap.

That is all you have to say to a psychologist to get her undivided attention.

"This your first river trip?" she asked. I told her about Outer Mongolia and the stampeding buffalo, and was relieved to see little spaniels of compassion dogpaddle across her eyes. Jeanne patted my arm.

"Then this is the best thing you can do for yourself," she said. "I was just as scared when we did the Grand Canyon, but by the end of the trip the white-water was like an exciting friend and the walls of the canyon had become my home. Besides, these are the best guides in the world and this is the safest com-pany—we researched it thoroughly before we chose it. You'll be fine."

"I'll be *damned*," I thought. I *was* damned. Lonnie had just given me a front row seat in the upcoming theater of disaster, pointing me to the bow of his dory.

"Keep your life preserver on at all times," he instructed. "And if you *do* go out of the boat, stay on your back and *keep your toes up*. And we'll come and get you."

"Where?" I thought. "In China?" Even though it was high summer in a drought year and the water was stunningly low, the Salmon, as far as I could tell, was moving along at a serious clip. How could someone in a boat behind someone in the water ever hope to catch up? I decided right then and there that I was *never, ever,* under *any* circumstances, going out of the boat. When we pushed off the bank at Corn Creek, I had a death grip on the gunwale with my left hand, the fingers of my right tourniqueted around the handgrip, and my toes jammed under the bow hatch. I looked, I am sure, like Wile E. Coyote trying to hold back yet another Roadrunner boulder, but I didn't care. "Call me Ishmael," I thought. "Call me a chicken. Just *don't* call me a lifeguard because *this* sailor's staying dry come hell *and* high water."

Even from the depths of paranoid dementia I could see that the Salmon River is a beautiful place. Running free its entire four hundred miles, it is one of the longest undammed American rivers left. This triumph occurred largely due to the heroic efforts of a man named Frank Church and of former Idaho governor Cecil D. Andrus, both of whom saw to it that millions of acres of unspoiled wildlands through which we were now floating were kept that way. Idaho's glorious unfettered heart is now called the Frank Church River of No Return Wilderness. Bear, elk, eagle, and bighorn sheep call it home. It is, indeed, a masterwork of rock and pine, river and sky, and very serious white-water.

"What's that?" I asked Lonnie. It sounded like rolling thunder.

"That's our first serious whitewater," he said. "This is a drop-and-pool river," he added, as if abstract analysis could somehow derail the tsunami of panic that was flooding my mind.

I can now proudly say that I personally know how General Lee felt when he heard all those damn Yankees coming up over the draw. How Ralph Branca felt when he heard the crack of Bobby Thompson's bat at the 1951 World Series. How Beryl Markham felt when she heard her plane's engine sputter over Nova Scotia. How the itsy bitsy spider felt when it heard the first raindrops come down the waterspout. Because I am now on a first-name basis with that sense of dread that deep-fries your brain in two seconds flat. You know what's coming and you know there's not a damn thing you can do about it. History has been written in the grease stains of such events.

In my case, the ordeal was more hysteric than historic. Or, rather, hairsteric. The guttural growl of the impending rapids triggered an instantaneous replay of my entire drowning experience, ponytail rescue and all. Adrenaline shot through my body. My hair hurt. I couldn't breathe so I held my breath . . . and assumed Wile E. Coyote position.

Lonnie surveyed the roiling water calmly—you could almost see the logarithms computing in his eyes. He rowed the dory to one side, then let the river do the rest. It did. Suddenly we were flying. Dipping and flying with water spraying out in all directions. Suddenly, my drowning memory was eclipsed by an earlier one, a thing of absolute delight. What was it? Boat. Speed. Water spray. Laughter! Happy squeals and laughter. My sisters. The Matterhorn. *Disneyland!*

There is a time before fear. A time of joy as pure as a bunch of kids running around chasing each other just to do it. A time when you feel in every cell of your body the miracle of your own existence. We are born into it, every one of us, and even though life with adults—and certainly *as* adults—tends to tarnish it, often badly, what I learned on the river that morning is that you can have it back.

"Lonnie," I said with tears in my eyes. "That was *fun.*"

"That was Killum," he replied, smiling. "Killum Rapids."

"Kill 'em?" I repeated, and started to laugh. "Kill 'em Rapids!" I shrieked. For the rest of the trip, the rest of the rapids were a piece of birthday cake.

We were a flotilla of five—two dories and three support rafts—and a crew of ten—five guests and five guides, including a brawny young man named

Colby Hawkinson who was in training and wasn't allowed to row live people. He was, however, entrusted with the beer, which I took as a supreme vote of confidence from the other guides. As for the guests, besides Jeanne and Herb there were Mike, a California businessman, and his beautiful, college-student daughter, Jenny. Like Jeanne and Herb, they, too, had been down the Colorado River. I was the only real river rookie of the bunch.

With the exception of Colby-the-trainee, our guides were all veterans. Curt Chang had actually founded what is now the Idaho dory arm of O.A.R.S. twenty years ago. Lonnie had been a river guide for seventeen years. The two junior guides, Don Rhoades and Brannon Riceci, had six and four years on the water respectively. The water was the only real problem we had, give or take a few raging forest fires. It was lower than anybody had ever seen it. That meant rocks no one had ever navigated were now exposed, and riffles once floated over with ease were now shallow boat-busters. Everyone was worried about getting the dories down the river in one piece. It was going to be a bumpy ride. But first, lunch.

BESIDES SAFETY AND service, O.A.R.S. guides are famous for their cooking. I would add that they should be famous for their kitchens, which are astonishing feats of construction and deconstruction that remind you of the circus coming to town. Once Lonnie, the trip leader, selected a beach, the crew eviscerated the rafts, set up the cook station, and had lunch ready before I had figured out how to undo my life jacket. Et, voilà! We were in Lebanon. There on the sand beach beneath the pines we were served fresh hummus sandwiches, grilled eggplant, and excellent tomato and cucumber salad. If they had trotted out Turkish coffee and fresh-baked baklava I wouldn't have been surprised. The guides' baking skills, as I later learned, definitely could have handled that fantasy.

The lunch kitchen vanished as quickly as it had appeared, and while kingfishers cruised the air above us, we embarked once more. The air above us, in fact, had become somewhat of an issue. It was an opalescent pink, the particle-rich gift of downstream forest fires. After Fear of Rapids, Fear of Smoke had been second on my list of concerns—either one could have made breathing equally uninviting. But even now, with a strong wind whipping down the canyon, the thick, heavy air was pleasant, like the aroma of southwestern incense. Floating through the burning forest itself, I was sure, would have been another story.

"You have to remember that this fire moves about a mile or two an hour," Lonnie explained. "You could outwalk it blindfolded."

That did it. My final fear was foiled. There was only one small, nagging concern left: la toilette.

"First, you have to remember to take this helmet," Lonnie began. We had made camp on a handsome beach, king salmon and Idaho steaks were already popping on the barbecue, and our gear was neatly stowed in cute little igloo tents that kept threatening to turn into Eskimo yo-yos and go cartwheeling across the sand because we happened to be in the middle of a major wind-storm. Nonetheless, it was time for Latrine Captain Lonnie to give his official Toilet Talk. So we all stood in an attentive if squinting circle around him and a little, wooden-seated Sani-Can that looked suspiciously like the one that first coaxed you out of diapers.

Someone, probably Dr. Herb, asked if the helmet was for protecting you if the wind blew you off the throne.

"No," Lonnie replied. "It's so that other campers know if someone's using the head."

"That's using your head," offered Guide and Stand-up Comic Don Rhoades, who wasn't supposed to be at our talk in the first place. Lonnie del-icately ignored him, explained that new toilet paper was in *this* can and used toilet paper in *that* can, then he informed us that for both hygienic and eco-logical purposes we must "separate functions," that is, do #1 in a plastic tub (fit-ted with a wooden seat) and #2 in the Sani-Can. There was a little handheld plastic hospital-looking urinal thing for those who found this rule too physi-cally challenging. Personally, I was beginning to wish I were still in diapers, but thought better of reporting this to Jeanne.

Once we were finished with the Sani-Can, we were to sprinkle the whole business with sweet-smelling lime powder kept in a former herb jar still labeled PARSLEY—nice touch, I thought. Finally, we were obliged under penal-

ty of Death by *E. coli* to *wash our hands* with the antiseptic liquid soap and
water kept beside the commode.

All in all, it was an elegant system, clean, smart, and very private. Once
everyone left, I decided to try it out. Apart from ending up looking like George
Washington thanks to the wind blowing a cloud of lime powder in my hair, I
found my first Sani-Can experience, well, a relief. It also had the best view in
camp, which, we soon learned, is the O.A.R.S. tradition.

Dinner was wonderful, despite the wind. I mean, salmon *and* steak? Fresh
corn on the cob *and* spaghetti? How could they top that? They did . . . with
homemade strawberry shortcake (Curt had baked the biscuits at home), fresh
berries and whipped cream hand-whipped by Brannon in a metal bowl held
in the river for proper chilling. It was as if the Camping Goddess had flown
down on pine-scented wings and gone Zing!—"Thy whitewater fear shall
turn to glee, thy forest fire smoke shall turn to incense, thy wilderness bathroom shall be beauteous and scenic, and thou shalt be fed like Queen Piggy
her Royal Self . . . We just threw in the wind so you wouldn't think you'd died
and gone to heaven."

Actually, once I crawled into my sleeping bag I thought I *had* died . . . and
gone nowhere. Talk about stiff! The pad for which I had paid a fortune felt
maybe two degrees softer than your basic bedrock.

"You should have bought a Paco Pad," Colby said when I dragged myself to
the campfire and complained. "They're the best."

"Instead she got a Snore-No-More," Don replied in a Monty Python soprano.

"A Sleep-Be-Gone," Colby added shrilly.

"A Comfort-Be-Damned," Brannon cried.

I crawled back into my tent and finally fell asleep listening to the lullaby of
the wind and the sweet breathy song of the river . . . and Don shrieking to
Brannon: "You have no arms or legs. I'm not going to fight you anymore." And
Brannon screeching back: "Oh, it's only a flesh wound . . ."

Breakfast was fresh blueberry pancakes, sausage, and Lonnie's excellent coffee, which was so strong that morning that we dubbed it "Rodeo Brew." The
wind had stilled, the day was bright, and the sky was that Tidy-Bowl blue of
those Don Ho cocktails you always end up not drinking in Hawaii. You start

thinking tropical thoughts like that when you're floating along on a hot morning in big sky country . . . until you hear the distant growl of an approaching rapid. Salmon Falls.

Jenny and I rode in Brannon's dory that day—for variety, every day everyone switched guides—and Brannon looked concerned. To the left, water fanned over huge exposed boulders. To the right a narrow chute between two rock walls waited like a cavity in the devil's molar.

"That's the tightest I've ever seen it," Brannon said. "There's no margin for error."

We watched transfixed as Lonnie, carrying Jeanne, Herb, and Mike, navigated the slot without a hitch. Brannon followed his lead and we made it through just fine.

"The rafts aren't gonna make it," he warned. "They're too fat."

Sure enough, Don's raft got stuck halfway. Lonnie and Brannon beached their dories, scrambled back over the rocks, and leaped aboard. Then they all started jumping up and down like demented gorillas. I couldn't hear Don but assumed he was saying something like: "That's *my* banana . . . now give it back or I'll smash you with this paddle."

Suddenly, the raft lurched free and the rest of us cheered. We cheered again and again when Curt's and Colby's rafts made it through. By the time we arrived at Barth Hot Springs for lunch we were in a jovial mood, even though the weather had taken a turn for the worse and everyone was chilled. After a short hike to the hot springs, a rejuvenating communal soak, and another stellar lunch a la playa we pushed off again . . . and swiftly hit rock bottom. Literally. Blam! Blam, blam! The dory bounced off two barely disguised boulders, then snagged on a third. Curt's raft pushed us free.

"We lived," Brannon announced.

"On the next one we might have to get out and wade," Lonnie hollered.

"What we need is the Flintstones' car with a little hole in the bottom," Brannon replied.

By now, the low water made navigation so tricky Lonnie insisted on checking out all rapids before running them. So we would pull over and tie up to a rock. Then the guides would hike downstream, squat like Native American scouts, and discuss the water for about twenty minutes.

"Does this one have a name?" I heard Brannon ask.

"Naw," Lonnie replied. "It's just tight. It'll be hard to be clean on it," he said finally. "You've got permission to bang 'em." And so we did.

For one particularly shallow rapid Lonnie had Jenny and me transfer to Colby's raft. With less weight dories do better in such situations, and being rubber, rafts tend to thwang off rocks, rather than plow into them. So we had an opportunity to find out why rafts are a lot like shampoo—they give your ride more body and bounce, and make it more manageable. Rafts will practically wash your hair for you. Because, without the protective high sides of a dory, you get a lot wetter. It was on that little raft sojourn that I first experienced "The Ice Bra," wherein a five-foot column of icy water leaps out of the river unannounced and dives straight down your shirt. That was the last time I rafted without zipping my jacket up to my nose.

By the time we made camp that evening we all felt as battered as the poor dories. But Lonnie had chosen a beautiful spot called Swimmer's Beach. Chipmunks scolded us from the boulders, a mink dodged out of sight, and a family of river otters paddled by like a very nervous welcoming committee.

"I feel like a kid at summer camp," I announced.

"You are," Lonnie replied.

But no summer camp I ever knew dished up the kind of supper we had that night: Colby's excellent barbecued chicken with rice to absorb the heavenly sauce, Greek salad with green *and* kalamata olives . . . and fresh-baked brownies. There was a wild game of horseshoe after dinner, then Jenny told about five million ghost stories, then Don, Brannon, and Colby had a coal tossing contest . . . barehanded, a sport that rendered their complaints of "rowing blisters" the next day somewhat suspect.

Fun aside, it was a marvelous night, filled with aromatic zephyrs, cricket music, and the haunted cries of the night birds on their evening hunt. Never had the evening sky seemed fairer. Never had the stars shone brighter. Never had I wished more that I hadn't been such a big chicken and arranged to bail out of this trip two days early. That was *before* my whitewater epiphany, of course, but arrangements had been made, the plane was hired, and, like going down a rapid, once you're committed there's no getting out of it. I couldn't remember feeling so blue.

"Tomorrow's my last day," I confessed to Jeanne. Naturally, she understood and was so sympathetic that just to make me feel better she made the quintessential Girl Camper sacrifice: She gave me some of her Baby Wipes.

It was a grand day, that last one. During breakfast a family of seven bighorn sheep marched through the far edge of camp to take a drink in the river. Then we got to go down Big Mallard, rapids so colossal that Curt told everyone to "batten down the hatches."

"We be battened," Brannon answered.

"We're battin' a thousand," Don concurred.

We were. Everyone made it through this tricky whitewater just fine. As well as through Elkhorn, Growler, and Ludwig, famous Salmon River rapids, all. That afternoon we camped beneath a bridge on the far side of an old homestead called Jim Moore's. Black bear were feasting in his orchard, as little hills of oxidized apple scat testified. Colby informed us that—acting as a miner's general store—Moore's place had been quite a going affair during the gold rush.

"Before he died in 1942, he supposedly buried his life savings somewhere on the property," Colby said.

"What if I found it?" Herb asked.

"You do and we split it, buddy," Lonnie commanded. "I got you this far."

Don, Brannon, and Lonnie cooked that night and dinner was perfect again: Caesar salad, fettuccini with fresh shrimp and red and yellow peppers, and Lonnie's amazing fresh cod with bouquets of fresh dill and lemon wheels. It started raining midway, and everyone helped erect a cooking tarp. Then Brannon vanished and reappeared wearing a chrome-yellow rain hat that looked like "The Flying Nun Goes Deep Sea Fishing."

"I can't cook with someone wearing that," Don complained.

"You got a problem with this hat?" Brannon replied. "I got no problem with this hat. The hat stays." It did. And the only thing better that night was Curt's peach cobbler, baked in a Dutch oven right on the campfire.

It was hard to leave the next morning. Besides feeling like a chicken-dweeb, I knew I'd miss everyone terribly. We all hugged and exchanged addresses, then Curt rowed me downriver one hour to the pickup spot. When my plane headed back upriver I pasted my eyes to the window until I found our camp . . . then began waving like an idiot. I reckoned no one could see me up that high, but I kept waving anyway. Then I saw her. A white dot waving back. Jeanne! Tears threw themselves down my unwashed cheeks. Jeanne! Jeanne! Good-bye! Bye! Thanks for the Baby Wipes! Bye!

All that stuff you hear about the deep bonding that occurs on wilderness trips is true—especially if you share feminine hygiene products. Without all the complications of home, the experience is an act of purity. And you remember it that way. Pure terror. Pure joy. Pure air, sky, and river. Pure friendship. The scary parts are really scary, the triumphs are true. You rely on the wisdom of enlightened guides, if you're lucky enough to have any, to get you through— the rest is your own courage. When it comes to adventure, I've come to believe in a motto that's a little twist on a great, old Beatles line: The risk you take is equal to the growth you make.

Looking down at the river from the plane that day, it reminded me of a piece of beautiful dark music, broken at graceful intervals by the white notes of the rapids. An oboe solo, an aural cascade, bridging one piece of the melody to another until, together, they sing the glorious, bittersweet song of one of the last free-flowing rivers in America.

For two decades, editors of magazines such as *Esquire*, *National Geographic Traveler*, and *Forbes* have sent **Jessica Maxwell** on hair-raising international adventure assignments including fly fishing in the Amazon and trying to catch the biggest salmon on earth in Outer Mongolia. Bill Bryson included her *Audubon* feature on Bhutan in his anthology *Best American Travel Writing 2000*. Luckily without photographs, because the photographers discovered wild marijuana and their photos were all blurry. The author of *Femme d'Adventure* and *I Don't Know Why I Swallowed the Fly* lives in Eugene, Oregon with her benevolent predator trial attorney husband, two ultracool stepsons, and their part-bobcat kitty who will sit on command for a wild salmon treat but nothing else.

zero heroes

Auden Schendler

WE PEGGED THE Cour d'Alene guy as a Nazi right off. He was, after all, wearing state trooper shades under a frizzy white mop of hair, and was probably on some survivalist trip. It was just him—in his fifties, and his son, looking sixteen or so, in two rafts, in the spring, in the middle of nowhere. And Cour d'Alene? Come on. Nobody lives in a house there; it's all "compounds." They were clearly on some male bonding and training episode, readying for the "big one," when the Blackhawks come dust off the last of the rebels and they have to hit the desert. We got ready for them to pull out the grenade launchers come sundown, worried they'd be the kind of campers to hike up canyon walls to trundle rocks, yelling things like "fire in the hole" and "Gooks in the wire."

Maybe we were edgy. We met him just above what at high water can be some of the largest rapids in North America, known affectionately to river rats as "The Big Drops." Or we were antisocial. At the time we were scouting the drops, we had been alone for a week. That had been enough time to drink five liters of bag wine, work through a few major life issues and a small bag of mushrooms, set a camping chair on fire (it blew into the coals, then ignited) and build several thirty-foot-high bonfires.

The big fires were not the result of drunkenness, initially. Just before we put on the river at Potash Canyon for an early spring run of the Colorado River's Cataract Canyon, our local congressman had "declared war" on tamarisk, the invasive ornamental weed from Asia that chokes riverbanks throughout the West. We felt we had been given clearance. The big fires were brush clearing. We broke limbs and burned them, then threw entire bushes on the fire, then whole plant systems, ten feet high, then discussed setting the entire riverside wall of tamarisk aflame. It was a classic case of escalation. Had we gone with the last pyrotechnic option, the riverside jungle exploding in flame would have been reminiscent of the opening to *Apocalypse Now*, with us drifting away in our raft, rotating slowly as we floated downriver, illuminated by the flames.

Christ it's hard to break away. You go on these trips to gain some kind of purity, get away from the biases and the pop culture of the daily grind. Why else hit the river at a time when you know, for certain, that there won't be another soul along because the water's too cold and low and the weather's too unsettled? You get out there, then you find yourself making these huge fires because your representative declared war on tamarisk, pegging a perfectly nice man from Cour d'Alene as a Nazi, and the next thing you know you're thinking about reenacting a scene from a movie—with a lighter.

We were a crew of four, with a couple of kayaks and one raft. Mark is a six-foot-seven religion student who had tried his hand as a car dealer (in "the family bidness") but one day thought he was dying on the lot while trying to pitch a Ford Expedition to a grandmother; he felt his heart flutter, and went to divinity school. He ended up at Berkeley only after having been rejected from Harvard despite, or thanks to, the first line of his application essay: "I want to be a car dealer with a soul."

There also were two brothers, Drew and Cador (it's an old family name). Drew is the ruined man: He had virtually dropped off the earth after having two daughters. I hadn't seen him in years. He had negotiated this week off by burning several lifetimes' worth of marital capital, trading away free time he didn't know he had, committing to watch the kids for years of Saturday-night book groups, all negotiated with the tension and anxiety of a hostage situation. In fact, there was a hostage, and it was Drew. Cador and his wife were on the verge of having twins after three years of infertility treatments, finally breaking through to the Promised Land that had, ominously, ruined his brother. A man of God. A ruined man. A man on the verge of being ruined and redeemed all at once. And myself, a chronic trip planner with an office job: limbo man, a guy who can relate to Walker Percy's character in *The Moviegoer*, who is happy to be in a fender bender just because it takes the edge off the monotony of the routine.

Drew had brought along two magazines: the *Sports Illustrated* swimsuit issue, and *Maxim*, the subpornography glossy for men you can buy right under (but not behind) the counter at 7-Eleven. It had articles like: "Ten Ways to Max Out on the Bench and in the Bed." Drew thought it was an appropriate thing to bring along on a guys' liberation trip. Or at least on what was for him a guys' liberation trip. Reading *Maxim* while seated on our two kayaks stacked on the bow of our raft during a long flatwater stretch, Mark wondered out loud if "anyone else feels this terrible, terrible empty feeling every time I pick up these magazines. But I can't stop looking at them. I can't."

None of us could. We referenced the magazines constantly, each time trying to pull something out, as if consulting the I Ching. But there was no soul there, and certainly no truth: *Maxim* country, it turned out, was a pathless land. We knew this from the beginning, of course, but we thought the magazines might add some irony to the trip. The whole point was to get away from that trash, and then to be so flagrantly against protocol as to bring it along, we thought that was just too in your face and counter countercultural. Perhaps we could transcend that stuff by bringing it so close and overdosing—like curing yourself of cigarettes by smoking fifty at once. Burning it out.

But the closest any of us got to transcendence was one day when a couple of our crew ate some mushrooms. On the stacked kayaks, Cador laughed and cried for three hours, and when we tried to reach him, he'd wave us off with a dismissive flick of his hand, as if to say: "You couldn't understand." Drew rubbed his back when he seemed agitated and cried. The kayak stack on the bow became an untenable position for anyone but Cador, because it put you too much in touch with reality, with the Canyon. As the raft slowly spun and we lay there, Cador kept saying, amazed: "Every time it turns, it's a whole new world." He was the only one who could take it. After laughing and crying for several hours out there, he asked for a drink, and Drew handed him a fluorescent Nalgene bottle of water. He waved it away. "I can't drink out of that," he said, and so Drew transferred the water to a plain bottle so Cador could drink it.

As Mark said, "We all need someone to pour our water into a tolerable bottle, rub our back when we cry."

We all had inclinations toward purism in the outdoors, maybe even asceticism in general. Cador had spent some time in India, and when he wasn't curled up in a ball from bad hash, he learned a bit about Buddhism. Mark was a disciple of Ken Wilber, the philosopher who has used meditation to achieve higher states of consciousness. Drew was trying to leave as much baggage behind as he could. As for me, all my life I have wanted to do a "rice trip." The idea is that you'd go out with a bag of rice and a fishing rod, and you could live, really, for a hell of a long time, if you were a good enough outdoorsman. You'd just catch fish and eat them with the rice: protein, carbs. Boom. But we were constrained by time, responsibilities. Instead of the rice trip we got bag wine and lawn chairs. Instead of the endless, open-ended sojourn, we had one week. Instead of liberation from the bonds of pop culture, we got Jiffy Pop from a Cour d'Alene dentist.

Which is what the "Nazi" turned out to be. A dentist with a minivan. He and his son showed up on the second-to-last day of our trip and really bummed us out, since we wanted to be alone. We first saw him scouting some smaller drops above the big ones. We raced to the big sandy beach we knew was the last place to camp. He showed up and asked if he could camp there too. Practicing good river etiquette, I said yes. Practicing bad river etiquette, he camped right next to us. Why did he have to be in our kitchen?

We became less annoyed when he came over to us in a sweat suit with Jiffy Pop and a Budweiser tall boy for each of us. He and his son were both in full sweat suits, like Rocky Balboa. It was endearing but odd garb for the river (they rowed in them too) since when you get wet in it, you stay wet. We charred the Jiffy Pop in our flaming inferno.

THAT AFTERNOON, A ranger in a pig-boat—a snout-nosed pontoon raft with two 260-horsepower engines so powerful the craft can up-run rapids—cruised in to camp. We had a firepan, which is good low-impact practice, but we had gotten in this huge fire mode, and there was so much driftwood around, and it was so early in the spring, that we couldn't help ourselves. The fire was the size of a small car. That wasn't the problem, though. We hadn't been able to get a permit for the river.

The ranger hopped out, partly to check our camp, partly, it turned out, just to chat. "We don't have a permit," I said. "But we applied for one and just couldn't pick it up. The office was closed and we couldn't wait. You can check our names when you get back, you'll see I'm telling the truth."

The ranger took our names, but he did it with a smile, saying: "We do things a little differently down here. This is the longest, wildest, undammed stretch of free-flowing whitewater in the U.S." I asked him if he knew the guy who swam Cataract Canyon in fins, when the river was running at 40,000 cubic feet per second. Just looking around, swimming through wave troughs four stories high, holes the size of subway cars and worse, and hydraulics known to strip a man of his Chuck Taylors and everything else. At that level, even to be knocked from a raft is serious business. "Keeper" holes will recirculate you for minutes. Even if a swimmer is lucky enough to miss the big holes, the waves are so big, the water so turbulent, that "flush drownings" are common from long swims. And this guy *swam* it at 40k, then came back to do it again at 60k, with a diving mask so he could look around. But at that level he disappeared.

IT'S HARD TO balance one's escapes: They can either be too wild, lonely, and dangerous, like the Cataract Swimmer's, or too tame and pedestrian. Even on big rivers the middle ground is hard to find. A friend who is also a chronic expedition planner once joined a two-week trip down the Grand Canyon, probably his twentieth. On this particular run, there was this man, probably the antithesis of the cataract swimmer, who had a different big puffy striped top hat—those clown hats that look like the Cat in the Hat's on steroids—which he brought out every night and pranced around in. And he had a big inflatable man named Stanley that he brought out every night: he thought it was a big joke. My friend thought it was amusing on the surface, but that's not why he'd come to one of the truly breathtaking places in the world. By the end of the trip, if he'd had a .357 he would have had the barrel in his mouth most of the time. Instead he went on long walks, considered hiking out at Matkatameba Canyon, showed up late for dinner, came off as a total ass.

YES, IT TURNED OUT the ranger who stopped at our beach knew the swimmer. "This section got so big last year, we just parked this rig at the bottom and fished people out all day. We filmed to show we needed better rescue gear. There were people above the Big Drops crying because they knew they had to run it."

He looked downstream at Little Niagara, the first plunge. "Yeah, I knew that fellow who swam Cataract. He wanted to be a hero, but he ended up a zero."

The Cour d'Alene man could relate, at least to the drowning part. Turned out he had been on the Selway in '97 when the water rose from nothing to several feet in a day. A Class III and IV stream became Class V instantly. Or Class VI, if you asked the dentist. That was during preseason when the only people on the Selway were hardcore river rats, guides training, and cultists. When the water came up, people got stranded on rocks for days, whole platoons of raft guides got swamped and trashed, and the river was a highway of flotsam. It was all over the papers. Snowpack had been 150 percent of normal before the melt-off happened.

This guy got knocked off his raft just like everyone else and was then sucked underwater. Couldn't see, couldn't breathe. Every time he came up for air, a wave hit him in the face. Every time he got a breath and thought he could swim for an eddy, he dropped in a hole, feet hitting the bottom, somersaulting forward into white foam. Convinced he was going to drown, he gave up. Then he hit a tree underwater, and grabbed on. He clawed his way back into the world on a tree limb, a Darwinian move, not quite a fish crawling on shore, but a man grappling along a dead tree underwater back onto the earth. It was a Cour d'Alene creation myth.

My take was this: He had been so frightened by that experience that the thought of the big drops was petrifying. Out there alone, he wanted somebody to run the rapids with, especially a group like ours with two kayakers that could fish him out of the water. No trees here, and he knew you only get lucky once or twice on the river.

THAT NIGHT WE got hit with the equivalent of a Saharan sandstorm. We cooked steaks on the edge of the big fire, and they were peppered with sand. We ate them slowly and remembered the anthropology class with the story of the skulls found with molars ground flat from sandy food. Couldn't remember if that was the Anasazi, or Piltdown Man.

With Piltdown man or whoever he was, what was going on? Was it like the dentist, who, from his stories it seemed, kept getting scared, but kept coming back? Hand me another one of them sandy steaks: They're so good I'm just going to grind my teeth to dust. Or is that kind of thing insidious, like getting addicted to Vicodin? One day after two weeks of back pain you turn on the cof-feemaker and you've got the shakes if you don't have a pill; one day you wake up and your teeth are all ground down to nubs. Or you look in the mirror while flossing and you've got several kids, a beer gut, and you've lost your edge. Maybe that's when you grab your fins, your goggles, and wait for the high water.

THE RAFT GUIDES on the Grand Canyon say, "You're always above Lava." They mean you may have just knocked off the big one, but there's always another hazard ahead, something to dread—maybe even Lava Falls on the next trip. So you might as well deal.

But I think they got it wrong. I think you're always below it. Because being above Lava Falls is a rare and great thing: You have that bowel-loosening excitement in your life, an anticipation that keeps you going and makes you feel alive—like a MAN, *Maxim* might say—because you're going to face the purest of nature's challenges. You know that when you're hitting the V-wave on the right side and disappear in your raft, you really will break away; you really will find that purity that's so elusive. You'll have escaped, at least for a second, not just the commercial jingles and the kids and job and debt and the sagging waist, but also your own biases and failings, your idiot congressman.

When you're below it though, you're just done.

Editor's note: Neither the author nor the ranger who referred to the drowned swimmer as a "zero" knew that he actually was an experienced Grand Canyon river guide and a humble soul. In the words of friends, Stan Hollister was "brilliant, outrageous, a minimalist . . . always helping people, usually behind the scenes and without being asked." I leave it to the reader to decide who the real "zero heroes" are—those who die, or those who never try.

Though he has kayaked many western rivers, **Auden Schendler** is a desk jockey by trade. He works as environmental affairs director at Aspen Skiing Company, where he plans his next trips from an office without windows or ventilation. His essays on mountaineering, sustainable business, and life in the West have been published in the *L.A. Times, Salon.com, Harvard Business Review, The Denver Post, Rock and Ice, Canoe and Kayak, Mountain Gazette,* and *High Country News.* Auden and his wife, Ellen, live in Basalt, Colorado.

das marlboro abenteurer team

Mark Sundeen

I ALWAYS LIT a cigarette above the big rapids. I knew they would like it. Summer had come and I was running rafts for the Marlboro Abenteurer Team. They were German. They had won an action trip to Utah by filling out a form that came in the cigarette pack. If there were any qualifications or requirements, I never learned.

Having adventures was the one thing I was good at. I'd been on plenty of them before. Now I was getting paid for it. It was my job. This one had sponsors and uniforms and photographers. It made it seem more real.

The Abenteurers wore red. They wore red caps and shorts and jumpsuits with the Marlboro logo. They stuffed red Abenteurer sleeping bags into their red Abenteurer backpacks. Across the bow of the rafts, foot-tall letters said MARLBORO. We bobbed on the river like cigarette boxes. They gave me a hat and T-shirt so that in the photos I looked like part of the Team. When we paddled down Westwater Canyon on the Colorado we had a J-rig run ahead and wait below each rapid with the cameras.

Hit zee vaves in zee center, cried Fritz. Jürgen and Fritz were the organizers and had bushy walrus mustaches and my boss told me to do whatever they said. They liked the Team members to wear the uniform, perform cheers and calisthenics, and eat sausage sliced from heavy tubes. They had told my boss that I ruined a photo because in my straw hat I looked like a hillbilly fisherman. So after that I wore the Marlboro cap and smoked a lot.

I knew how to act. They liked me for it. When one day the photographer demanded to be tied into a harness on the bow of the boat, I wanted to warn him he would drown if we flipped. But when I saw his glare I just said okay.

And I didn't complain when a helicopter buzzed ten feet above my raft with a video camera and blasted my hat off and blew the whitecaps upriver. It was my job.

Fritz and Jürgen thought plain rafting wasn't exciting enough. They wanted the boats to flip. It was June and Westwater Canyon was peaking from the snowmelt. Upstream the campgrounds were underwater. All the rapids but Skull were washed out but the water was fast and scary as it boiled along the rock walls. It was like one big toilet getting flushed. Once you started you couldn't slow down or stop. At Little D Creek my stomach was in a knot. I didn't eat any lunch. Then we untied the boats and launched.

The Germans had told me to eddy out often to give the photographers time to set up below. I tried to pull into a cove above Funnel Falls. The boat hit the wall and folded and started to ride up the rock. Water rushed in from upstream and paddles and arms and legs flailed around. I got a shoe in the face when somebody went overboard. Now we were on an adventure. Finally we spun off the wall. I was still in the boat with water to my waist. The river was churning with paddles and bailbuckets and Abenteurers.

I pulled in two swimmers but a third was way downriver. He went under for a five count, popped up, spit, went under. I chucked my throwbag but missed him by a lot. Then one of the Germans either found another rope or coiled up mine and hit the guy on the ear from about forty feet. We pulled him in right above Skull. Since only two of us still had paddles I told them all to just hold on and highside. We drifted sideways into the hole. The cameras flashed and Fritz and Jürgen howled. We got pummeled. The boat was so swamped that it stayed upright.

It was a pretty good job. It paid eighty-five dollars a day plus tips and at the end of each adventure was a party at White's Ranch with steak, ribs, and chicken, plus a trough of Budweiser and an athletic German man mixing margaritas. Cowboys yodeled western songs. The Abenteurers danced with whatever women they could find and then with each other. Packs of Marlboros were arranged in neat stacks on all the tables. I filled my pockets.

In midsummer Beach Philips came back to river guiding. He still thought it was beneath him, but he needed the money. There was no backhoe work. It was this or toss pizzas. We were working for the Man.

Beach and I took the Abenteurers down Cataract Canyon. The river had dropped. They were bored. Not enough vitevasser, Fritz complained. Beach Philips had an idea to add some excitement. Instead of motoring off endless Lake Powell, we'd hike them up and out Dark Canyon to the Sundance Trail.

The Abenteurers packed their Abenteurer backpacks. Neither Fritz nor Jürgen wanted to make the hike but they sent the team doctor with us. He was about two hundred pounds. The weather was over 100. The Team was slow at scrambling and rock-hopping. It was hot. Beach and I ran up above the next waterfall and smoked and waited in the shade for them to catch up.

By the time we reached the mesa the Marlboro doctor was wheezing and sweating and had to drop his head between his knees. And Fritz was waiting there for us, leaning against his jeep touching his mustache, suntanned and very satisfied.

When the Abenteurer Team returned in August, Fritz and Jürgen had thought up a new adventure to beat all. The Team would be helicoptered to Hite Marina airstrip, shuttled to the Sundance Trailhead, hiked down Dark Canyon, whisked off the lake in motorboats.

My boss called me into the office and handed me the credit cards. Drive to Lake Powell, rent two boats, tow one up to the mouth of Dark Canyon and pick up the Marlboro boys.

He said there were two types of boats to rent. A sixteen-foot skiff with a 25-horsepower outboard and an eighteen-foot speedboat with a 125-horse. He wanted me to rent the smaller boat because it was fifty dollars a day. The water-ski boat cost $180. I would have to decide when I got there if the aluminum skiffs were big enough for all my Abenteurers.

The tricky part was insurance, he said. You couldn't get insurance to travel upstream past the Hite Bridge to Dark Canyon. There was current from the river and driftwood and debris. It was considered dangerous.

You've run motorboats, he said. I couldn't tell if he meant it as a question. It was peak season and all the qualified people were down the river. I had driven a rubber raft with a two-stroke outboard a few times.

All the time, I said. No problem.

Beach and I left Moab in two company vehicles. I had a jacked up four-wheel-drive Ford van and Beach was in a 1976 Land Cruiser. We drove out Indian Creek then up Elk Basin to the Marlboro camp on Cathedral Point. From the buttress pushing out over the Needles you could see hundreds of snaky cracks in the mesa, split by the gorge of the Colorado. It was too deep and twisted to see the river.

In camp was a bonfire and a mess line with beef and beer. Someone in a cowboy hat sang through his nose and plucked a guitar. Jürgen welcomed us and told us tomorrow's plan. We were to get up early.

It rained all night. In the morning, instead of taking the old clay prospecting roads between the Bear's Ears we backtracked to the highway then cut south. We stopped in Blanding for coffee but it tasted bad and I saw Beach dump it out the window on the highway. He pulled over at Fry Canyon Lodge and made me charge some eggs and bacon and hot coffee on the company card. He said the Germans could wait.

We were late to the Hite airstrip and the Abenteurers were already sweating and pink. The helicopter was gone and they were huddled beneath the tin sunshade. We are waiting here forty-five minutes, one of them said. Yeah, yeah, said Beach Philips, get in. They got in. We raced over the bridge and turned onto a dirt road.

Dark Canyon carved down from the Abajo Mountains across the mesa. Beach and I had meant to get there early and reconnoiter the trailhead but now we were late and didn't know which way to go. We couldn't find the map but we'd been to the trailhead before. It would be hard to miss

Beach was racing the Toyota. He sailed over the bumps and his passengers floated up toward the ceiling. My van with nine Abenteurers felt like a plane crash when it hit sandstone so I slowed down. Beach had to wait at the forks. I didn't know where he was leading us. Somehow he found a wide dirt turnaround, which turned out to be the trailhead.

The sun was already high and hot and there were no shadows. The mesa was a flat range of red clay and piñon in every direction. A few square buttes jutted up in the distance. Blue mountain peaks were far off and blurry through the heat. We unloaded the Team and I told them I'd see them at the lake. They hefted on packs and plodded single file down the trail.

Vee meet at half past tree, said Jürgen with his finger on his mustache. No later.

Beach's job was to hike the Germans down to the lake. It was a steep but easy walk so the Abenteurer Team brought along a rock-climbing guide to make it more of an adventure. They would find a chasm to set a Tyrolean traverse then rappel to the canyon floor and follow the stream to the lake. I'd be waiting there with two boats and we'd motor them back to Hite to their helicopter.

Down at the marina I looked at the rental boats on the docks. The skiff was like what my grandmother used to fish in. I hopped in and it rocked dangerously. There was a plaque riveted to the hull that said the Coast Guard only allowed six people in such a boat. I would have seven.

I moved over to the speedboat. It was deluxe. It had a steering wheel and a windshield, padded vinyl seats, and a convertible sun canopy. Whattaya say, said the dockhand. He could see I liked it.

I'll take two.

Next I had to learn to drive it. I signed some forms then putted out past the buoys. My vessel was called the *Funseeker*. The throttle lever was bound in leather and had the high-quality worn feel of a sit-inside video game. I pulled it.

The boat lurched and bucked and as it shot forward I gripped the steering wheel. The speedometer spun to 45. It was fine. I pressed a button and heard a satisfactory whirring noise. The motor cocked outward and the *Funseeker* floated up on plane. It was sunny and the water very smooth.

Back at the marina the dockhand eyed me when I said I needed to tow one of my two boats up to Dark Canyon, but gave me a coil of cotton rope anyway. Did I know that there was no insurance up there above the bridge?

It's okay, I said, I'm doing this for my job.

I tied up the boats and sputtered onto the lake. When I gunned it the rope stretched taut like a slingshot. The *Funseeker* didn't move, but then the rope recoiled and in the moment of slack we shot forward like I was driving a yo-yo. I passed under the highway bridge into a narrow canyon where the lake looked like a river with no current. My boat strained at the bit dragging the other one up the lake. I had a map but all the cliffs looked the same so I just kept going. The twelve miles up to Dark Canyon took three hours.

The lake was high and the canyon mouth was flooded. Willow and tamarisk stalks poked up from underwater. I steered between the reeds in a deep green channel until driftwood and scum blocked the way, then I tied to the cliff and killed the motor. The creek had flashed and it looked like chocolate.

My watch said it was three o'clock and I lay down and slept until the Abenteurers arrived in their Marlboro knapsacks. They sloshed through the muck with brown grime all up their legs.

That's your boat, I said to Beach, and showed him which buttons to push and he turned the key and roared away. He'd never driven one either but he just knew how to do things like this. My passengers loaded in and I took off after him.

At the canyon mouth we throttled up and made a wide turn onto the lake. We raced each other, and Beach Philips took the lead and I cut behind him and launched off his wake and splatted down cockeyed and felt the weight of the Abenteurers rock to one side. I straightened it out and we flew past water and cliffs and sun. The boats were fast and everything was going right.

When we delivered the crew to the airstrip where the helicopter was waiting, Jürgen told us to meet him seven sharp the next day to start over. Same adventure, different Abenteurers. The blades beat the air. The Team loaded up and the chopper sailed away.

Beach Philips and I drove back to the marina and walked out on the floating dock. Out past the houseboat colony, jet skis and water-skiers zipped back and forth in front of the desert cliffs. It was 94 degrees and there were two hours of sunlight left on Lake Powell and we had nothing to get done till the next day.

We gassed up the *Funseekers* with the credit cards and motored onto the lake. Without any passengers they soared up on plane and I pulled back the throttle as far as it would go. It was fast and smooth and with every turn a sheet of water fanned out behind me, and the hot wind gave me tears and spread them across my face. I could feel the molecules evaporate off my eyeballs and I felt a million drops of air jet up my nose and bounce around my skull and spill out my ears and I felt good. After a lap we stopped and dropped our clothes and dove into the clear water, then back on the boats we drove faster, the motor sang and my stomach fell and I bounced on the wind-waves and the walls of Glen Canyon blurred in the sun, houseboats were like tin cans in the distance and there was enough gasoline to go forever, and we carved circles and arcs and figure-eights naked, charged chicken and veered away, full speed up some canyon I don't know the name of and spun to a stop where the drowned willows poked up, and I breathed out and breathed in and gunned it out of there in the direction we came.

The lake was wide and flat and there was a lot of it to go.

Mark Sundeen was born in 1970 in Harbor City, California. He is the author of *The Making of Toro* and *Car Camping*, and was co-editor of *Great God Pan* magazine. His stories appear in *Outside* and *National Geographic Adventure*, and he has worked as a guide in Utah and Alaska for eleven years. Sundeen lives in Moab, Utah.

frozen ro-tundra

Katie Lee

THERE ARE SOME, I suppose, who don't mind having their derrieres exposed to the arctic winds of the frozen North. Those who live there have probably grown used to it. But being a desert dweller, I'd rather cuddle up to a catclaw bush than have my poopdeck exposed to elements that freeze the stuff as it drops.

This is not the kind of adventure Joey and I envisioned when we decided, one early August, to run the Noatak River in Alaska's Gates of the Arctic National Park, three hundred miles north of the Arctic Circle. Friends had run it before us, shown us photos of a whoop-dee-do wild and beautiful river abundant with fish; its banks decorated with a few grizzlies, arctic fox, elk, moose, and caribou; its acclivities with Dall sheep and bald eagles, to name but a few unusual sights for desert dwellers.

I should have paid more attention.

"Beginnings are a bore," says my friend Bruce Berger. Only now and then, beginnings send a message, usually unclear at the time, but if we had light-year vision we'd be able to see that red flag waving before a torn-out bridge. When a trip begins with the lilting flow of a gentle cataract, we can only hope it will increase in tempo—whatever little blips and stutters clog the serene—and tumble into more and more serendipitous delights as the days pass. But when it begins like a snake trying to swallow a hairbrush, shouldn't we heed the message? Alas, we rarely do. Our gears already shifted into *go!*

We are an hour and a half early for the flight from Phoenix to Fairbanks. Better early than late, we settle into seats, happy and smiling, ready for take-off. Wrong seats. Move to correct seats, other side. Can't see Mts. Hood, St. Helens, and Rainier as I'd planned, but oh my God, I can see the clear-cuts!

Mile after hundred miles of chessboards on the snow-covered mountains; cuts so steep that avalanches are prevalent, the tops of mountains completely bare; nowhere a whole range or even part of one left untouched. To my great relief the ground clouds over past Vancouver, blotting out the chess players' wreckage.

Arrive Fairbanks.

The baggage cart machine takes our money, keeps the cart. We phone the motel, get a busy signal, no coins return. Second try, no answer. It eats more quarters. Third try, got 'em! The motel sends a car for us. We settle into the room. Wrong room. Wait half an hour for the clerk to decide which room and then drag our gear from 114 to 107.

It is nearly five in the afternoon and we are jet-lagged enough for a snooze before dinner. No way. Planes rev, zoom, land, take off. Kids yell. Parrots screech. Wait a minute. What are parrots doing in the Arctic? My observation deck was kinda fogged over from the flight when we checked in. Then I remember there were seed hulls all over the floor by the registration desk and some things with feathers pooping in cages. Aha, they were his! How very thoughtful of an innkeeper to own wake-up birds. After an hour of toss and turn, we give up and ask for the courtesy car to take us to dinner. Here we sit outside on the deck to enjoy a couple of drinks, serenaded by the melodious snarl of Jet Skis racing up and down the Chena River.

If our instincts were sharper than our mental derailment of them, we would stop, look, listen, and reset the goal and our mental picture of the trip we're about to make, backpedal, flip a coin, do something else. God knows there is plenty to see, do, hear, discover, and become enchanted with in Alaska, a land we know relatively little of. I was here once before, but didn't have the opportunity to shave as much as a whisker off its fascinating face. And, as I was to discover, neither have half of those who live in Alaska's cities, where they stay, just as we do in ours down yonder. I even have friends we don't bother to look up, who would point us toward a dozen treks even better than the one we've set out for. But the red flag simply quits waving on the torn-out bridge to new adventure.

After our deafening dinner, we go back to the motel and actually sleep from

11 P.M.—despite the racket from heaven and earth—until we get "the bird" at 7 A.M. next morning.

OUR QUARTERS LOOK as if a bomb has struck. Clothes are strewn, flung, draped, balled up, or hanging from every protrusion in the room—a few from splinters in the rough wood—as we try to separate our gear for the river from what we will leave here for the remainder of our trip. (Little do I know that what we leave will find its way to a hidden place in the unknown. We won't even remember where we stashed it.)

Should we take this extra waterproof tarp? The outfitter is supposed to have that kind of thing. Hunch: Take it. What about the heavy liner for my sleeping bag? It's eighty degrees out there! We're going wa-y-y north of Fairbanks: Take it. Do we buy those knee-high rubber boots we couldn't get at home for the glacial prices we see here in the store? Absolutely!

For this Noatak run I have enlisted a friend who has rowed rivers from South America to the Arctic. He, in turn, is leasing services and supplies from a company here in Alaska that has outfitted every kind of trek from Arctic sledging to glacier skiing. There will be only one other couple joining us— experienced river runners who have spent many of their days canoeing the Boundary Waters on the U.S.-Canadian border. We'll be five souls, have three boats, and plenty of time to go at our own pace.

One P.M. We're to fly from Fairbanks to Bettles, about three hundred miles as ravens go, where we will lodge for the night, then bush-fly to the Noatak River tomorrow. F-f-frontier F-f-flight S-s-service. Very casual, these folks. We wait an hour for the plane. Our pilot doesn't like it—magnetos not doing their job, or whatever. Return from runway to hangar and take another plane. This gives us a moment's pause, but once in the air the view becomes so magical that the "moment" is left at the airport, forgotten.

Ahead are cumulus piled on cumulus, with cirrostratus bisecting their billows, a bolt of low sunlight flaming the southern end where some wisps have broken away to float down and join the land. On the ground are tangled, multilayered brush and trees of the absolute wild; a silver river winding through like a skein of witch's hair, braided, knotted, let loose to flow over a shoulder, down a back, over a rump. A slight shudder passes through me, looking down on that dark green pelt of wild earth, putting me in mind of a friend who left the frantic forty-eight in the late 1970s to come here and build herself a home.

How in Christ's name did she do it?

For starters, she strapped eighty pounds on her back, carried a twelve-gauge shotgun that wasn't exactly light, and walked, waded, stomped, and slithered some ten swampy miles from the nearest village, through the kind of impenetrable stuff I see below me, to find the site for her house, mark off and stake it, return, and file for ownership. Sort of like a mining claim, not a homestead. She knew where she wanted to be, but she needed the foot trail—actually a moose, wolf, deer, and bear trail—for the many times she would be hoofing it in winter when the grizzlies were snoozing. She chose a spot a quarter mile uphill from a river that would serve to transport material for building the house in the summer. Came winter, she hauled everything in on a little red sled behind snowshoes or skis. Joanna is one tough lady. As for the gun, she told me she never had to use it on a bear she didn't mean to kill (for food) for the fourteen years she lived there before moving back to semicivilization. Once only, when she wasn't there, a black bear broke into her house and entertained himself to the max.

From Fairbanks to Bettles takes about an hour and a half in this little four-passenger job; winging northwest; crossing and recrossing the Tanana and Yukon Rivers, the Tatalina and Chatanika, plus a hundred streams, creeks, and flushes that vein the landscape wherever you see them through the tangle. Bettles is a collection of gas and oil tanks, heavy trucks, husky kennels, cabins, trading post, and airstrip beside the Koyukuk River. Jim, our guide/boatman/cook/gopher/friend, has come to meet us. When we unload our gear, my film can is not in the pile! I swear I saw it go aboard. Before the pilot takes off for his turnaround to Fairbanks, Jim goes through the plane with a packer's practiced eye and finds it stuck behind a port-a-potty. So glad my can lid is down tight.

After we're assigned our cabin, have a snack, check out the trading post, read the sign—BETTLES—POPULATION 8—LOWEST TEMPERATURE –70°—HIGHEST +92°, take some photos, walk along the river, check out the moose

racks on the grounds, talk to the huskies, take some more photos, eat a leisurely dinner, and enjoy a bottle of wine and some river talk with the boatmen, I
instinctively glance up to check on the big clock in the sky. It's at much the
same angle as when we got here. Hmmm. I hate watches when I'm going to be
outside with the real elements, so I'd ditch it deep in my luggage for the dura-
tion.

Hesitantly I ask, "Jim, uh, what is the time here?"

"Eeee-leven Peee-emm," he says, eyebrows dancing as he smirks. "I didn't
say anything because that's how you learn about daylight saving itself all the
time up here. When I first came, I didn't go to bed for two days 'cause the sun
never went down."

One of the other boatmen cracks, "Makes it easier to see the bears. They
can't creep up on ya in the dark 'cause there ain't no dark."

THE NEXT MORNING, Mark, our bush pilot, tells us that if we agree
to it, Joey and I will fly to the put-in first with our gear, food, water, tents, and
wait there for the arrival of Jim and the other couple who have not yet shown.
(Seems someone forgot to change their reservations to F-f-frontier F-f-flight
S-s-service.)

Still blindsided by beauty and the imminence of a spectacular wilderness
river trip, I don't ask what happens if we don't agree, and after nodding our
assent, he hands each of us a can of bear repellent. Damn me if it doesn't say
that on the can! Click. In my talks with Doug Peacock, I seem to remember,
either this shit doesn't work or if it does, it has a reverse action. Then I figure,
what the hell? I'd rather be eaten by a bear than chewed up in a traffic accident.
Mark assures us we'll only be there two or three hours before Jim and the
other couple join us.

At this point I look up to see clouds rolling over the Brooks Range where
we're headed. Clouds of incredible variety: vicious, smoky, tumbled, and
streaked with sun; the whole range cut down to size by their immensity. In retrospect, I understand what happens to the human mind in places as grand and
glorious as this. Our instinct and intuition, along with our common sense, go
dormant beside all the grandeur and newness, allowing us to see, without ask-

ing what it all might mean.

Here the sun is brightly shining.

As we turn toward the airstrip, Mark shakes his head. "No, no. This way. Plane's out on the river."

"In the river!"

"*On* the river. We're using a floatplane. You know, pontoons instead of wheels. We land on water." He gives me the "stupid tourist" look and I return a sheepish smile; it's the same look I've given to others at least a million times.

We leave at noon.

The flight is surprisingly smooth in a wee four-seater stuffed with barrels, much gear, and us. Mark dodges most of the cloudy stuff, following a braided river up a valley heading west-northwest. We wing over glacial lakes and backwaters, crossing and recrossing the snaking Continental Divide. I wouldn't have had a clue if he hadn't told me; I thought all of Alaska was west of the divide. Dumb tourist. The plane seems to skid as we round a jagged rock uplift by a horseshoe bend in a river that is swallowing its banks. We sneak between this clouded mountain and that vibrant green, sunlit one, sometimes coming so close I can see the hair rise on the backs of Dall sheep. Yet Mark's skill, his knowledge of this range, and a photographic memory of peak-dodging through it allow us to relax and enjoy the flight.

In less than an hour, we're down alongside the right bank of the Noatak River, skiing on a little tarn, in these parts often called a slough. The earth is tundra now; nothing but knee- to waist-high scrub, mostly matted ground cover and some grasses around the edges of the tarn where we've landed. Up a three-foot bank to higher ground and maybe a hundred yards from the plane is a drop-off into the Noatak. In the distance, on this level span, I see one upside-down canoe, patched here and there with duct tape.

"Where are the boats?" I ask Mark. "Surely, that's not . . ."

"No, it isn't. I'll bring one on the next trip with Jim and his passengers and another one with the final load." Seeing my questioning frown, he continues, "We strap them to the pontoons. Do it all the time—works really well."

I don't understand why they aren't already here, but since there's no time to waste asking more tourist questions, we unload the plane and in less than fifteen minutes Mark has taxied, skied across the tarn, and is on his way to Bettles, to return, so he said, around four o'clock.

As soon as the plane is out of eye- and earshot, it begins to rain.

Joey and I wander over the tundra seeking the best place to put our tent, and find a spot for the kitchen. We can't do a whole lot in the strong wind, intermittent heavy to light rain, nasty low-hanging clouds, teasing blue sky, and occasional sun. Having been told at one of our briefings to walk only on existing trails, animal or otherwise, we try to comply, tundra being a delicate, easily destroyed surface that will not regenerate for years, similar to the sandy/silty microbiotic soil of the Colorado Plateau.

Two tents get put up and we manage to carry, roll, or drag most of the equipment to the highest spot around. Between spates of heavy rain, we wander over to the bank of the Noatak, looking down ten or twelve feet into its swirls and burbles, wishing we were out of this and on our way downstream where the sun is making a grand display against the northwest end of the Brooks Range. Turning around to retrace my way back to our tent, I halt in midstep and start laughing. Circling one branch of a head-high shrub is the familiar green, upraised fist of an Earth First! sticker: NO COMPROMISE IN DEFENSE OF MOTHER EARTH. Wonder if anyone we know put it there? Anyhow, it gives me the first smile of the forever afternoon.

Back in the tent, we wait . . . and read . . . and wait. I can't tell if the sun is going down, around, or under in this depressing weather. All I know is that it never gets really dark. Like the boatman said, easier to see the bears. We don't. Just as I'm about to have real doubts about life in the frozen North, about six thirty—yes, I've taken to my watch again, it's the only way I can even tell what day it is—Mark finally arrives with Jim and the other couple, but no canoe, because of too much gear.

Sincere rain greets their arrival.

After hurried introductions, we help unload so Mark can return for the last load of food, more Coleman fuel, Ann's vegetarian stash, camp gear, canoes and paddles, and more water. Water, water everywhere, which only animals can drink. Ann and Eric, well-seasoned outdoors folks in their sixties, watch the takeoff and disappearance of the plane with a lingering apprehension that prompts me to ask if their trip from Bettles was okay.

A mite disgruntled over the screwed-up reservations, to say nothing of the bracing weather, Eric tells us he saw very little between cloud-dodging and mountain-hopping. Ann agrees that she felt some interesting updrafts and downdrafts, but it rained a good part of the way.

"Yeah, same thing here, it looks like," observes Jim. "Let's get the kitchen set up and the other tents."

The men rig a cook tarp off Jim's tent onto the longest twigs found anywhere on the tundra so Jim can light the cookstove out of the wind and rain. Meanwhile, I rifle through the gear for a waterproof ground cloth to spread under our tent because it leaks. Is this outfitter really together? When the last load gets here this afternoon? evening? morning? tomorrow? it'll be light enough to fly the whole night. All I want is to get gone, down that river—if they don't forget the paddles. Having kayaked, paddle boated, and rowed, but never canoed, I still can't wait to split this sponge.

It is almost 10 P.M. when we eat. Maybe the sun went behind the mountain, maybe behind a denser cloud, maybe I'm in Russia. To me this looks like a five-day rain, one that's here to stay.

It is. And so are we.

I NEVER DO find out if I can assist paddling a canoe with Joey, Jim, Eric, or Ann. It continues to rain the whole night and most of the next day. We lie in the tent and read, sit under the kitchen tarp, drink coffee or tea, tell stories, and wait for the plane. The wind is relentless, and perhaps two or three times in twelve hours, a tease of sun appears. The plane does not.

We move the tents to higher? drier? ground.

Temperatures continue to go down, the river to come up. It was something like ten feet down the bank when we first viewed it. By the end of day two, it's more like two feet below our feet. Gradually, then with increasing velocity, the Noatak chokes on itself; with nowhere to go but into and out of the tarn, it surrounds us completely. We can no longer get to the mainland. We're on an island that is approximately nine hundred feet wide by twelve hundred feet long, with one duct-taped canoe that we've pronounced un-sea-water-ice-or-snow-worthy and *no paddles*. In a pinch, which seems more than likely, we can use the canoe for meager shelter.

We watch what we use and go easy on the drinking water. Who's thirsty? Just open your mouth. But seriously, there's not enough Coleman fuel to boil what we drink. Ann's special food is a dicey problem; it isn't here yet. I'm a bit less tense than I would be if it weren't for Jim, an expert on knowing how to keep it together, what to ration and what not. With all his experience he's the best person to have a-tundra. We talk a lot about having positive thoughts: Mark will return as soon as he can get through— this weather can only last a few days—there's food enough for a week if we're careful—we can collect rainwater for drinking—everything will turn out all right and we'll be downriver soon. Bless all the gods for these knee-high rubber boots.

We see two planes but they never come near us. Hmmm. (1) They've forgotten we're here. (2) Each pilot thinks the other has come for us. (3) One crashed. (4) Impossible to get here (wrong—another plane went and came back from Lake Matcharak). Jim says that doesn't always mean they can land here. So they don't. We have all been in tricky situations of one kind or another before this, and have found that panic takes energy needed for survival. Luckily we're not on some guided tour with a group of novices. By now, a number of them would be well on their way to severe nervous disorder.

Music helps. I sing after dinner, breakfast, lunch, whatever it is, though without my guitar, or great sandstone walls to reflect the voice, the sound gets soaked up in rain and squishy tundra. But it's different from talking, and lyrics take us to another world of hope and dreams, give us something else to ponder, invent, laugh, or wonder about.

If you've never spent 24, 48, 72, 96, 120 hours of daylight in a rising pond on a lily pad, in a wild, unfamiliar place, hoping you won't be left there to rot, you may not understand to what extremes the mind can wander. When you can't read another word, can't move from your tent, don't have a deck of cards, have exhausted all topics pro and con, can't sleep anymore, and are trying desperately to keep your gray matter on positive thought, nonsensical to utterly ludicrous visions will float up to save your sanity. My "wig bubbles"—a term my dear deceased husband used for "imaginative thought"—were energized when I had to leave our shelter to perform the simple task of dropping scat, and found it to be a big problem. There are no porta-potties out here, no places to hide. This island is flatter than an old maid's chest. Yet to sneak over the edge into a river drainage that is now about a foot from taking you with it, or to slog into the tarn that is now part of that river, is not an option. Certainly we shouldn't defecate on the precious tundra, since we can't even walk on it unless we follow a trail. So-o-o, lying here in our tent, I begin to have fantasies—even time to psychoanalyze them—and conclude that this particular fantasy is based on envy.

I have always wanted to witness a man piss an arc from some high place, as they are wont to do, and have it freeze. Would it hurt? Anyway, it would be colorful (if we had sun). Even under cloudy skies, it would be more colorful than a squat-dribble-type freeze with no lights to play on the rainbow, so to speak. However, there is no fantasy when it comes to the poopdeck. Here we have pure realism. Oh my! To let down thy drawers in falling sleet and a brisk wind at zero temperature is an experience few can appreciate. One must not let this stuff go into the river, though I don't know why. Hares do it, mares do it, even copulating bears do it. Let's do it. Never mind. We must do it on that "delicate" tundra, and unless we yank up a hunk of endangered moss to cover our scat tracks, there's no place to hide it on this sopping tundra sponge. A few inches beneath, the earth is frozen solid. We're in permafrost country.

And we pace—pace—pace, up, down, and across our island each time we get out of the tent, when it isn't raining. We'll grow mold if we just lie here and read. Anyhow, we've come perilously close to our last game of musical books. So we slosh around in our rubber boots, which have begun to feel more like rafts, at first trying to keep to existing rills, but after three or more days we give up. What a poor substitute sloshing is for paddling and learning about this fine, now very fat and fast, river and how it carves its way from here. We keep an eye out for bears over on the mainland. They can swim over here even if we can't swim over there, and though we have no way to hang our food, Jim knows how to keep it contained and what to do with any scraps that might attract them. Again we move the tents, squashing low shrubs, in the hope we can elevate them above the swamp.

One evening—I think it is the fourth day—we are treated to a live Wildlife Adventure program.

After dinner it stops drizzling and we all walk down to where our tarn flows back into the Noatak to see if the floodwaters have dropped at all.

Two ducks are floating on the slow-moving water fairly close to the opposite shore, quacking serenely. Then Joey's eagle eye picks up movement on the bank. After a moment we see two arctic foxes hiding in the grasses, creeping low, stalking the swimming ducks. For a few moments, Mr. and Ms. Fox sit down side by side, out of sight of the swimmers, just watching. Then—and you can almost hear this conversation—she says to him: "Plan A, dear. I'll walk along here where they can see me while you circle around in front of them." He glances at the ducks, licks his chops, sneaks through the brush and away. Acting as a decoy, she pussyfoots along the bank while the two ducks, certain of their advantage in the water at least ten feet from shore, wiggle their sassy asses and keeping a duck eye on her, move ahead slightly faster. The bank bends toward us, but they don't seem to notice. Intent they are, watching Ms. Fox, when *crash!* off the four-foot bank right in front of them sails Mr. Fox with mouth wide open. He hits the water inches from the lead duck, who does what?

Ducks, what else?

Mr. Fox disappears underwater for a few seconds, but has forgotten his snorkel and has to surface almost immediately. Ahh, no dinner tonight, at least not that one. The ducks have flown. So much for teamwork.

We stand on the bank, holding our sides laughing. The only real entertainment we've had for ninety-six hours. Our laughter continues far into whatever-time-it-is as we recount fox tactics, analyze strategies, wander into all sorts of animal behavior, and discuss the nature show from every angle, scientific to anthropomorphic. Heavy on the anthro side, an old folk song pings into my memory, one I learned from a Burl Ives recording back in the late 1940s. Others remember it too, and so we hum and sing parts of it into the wee small hours that finally drop us into dreamland.

Fox went out on a chilly night
Prayed for the moon to give him light
For he'd many a mile to go that night

Before he'd reach the town-o, town-o, town-o
He'd many a mile to go that night
Before he'd reach the town-o

WHEN I CRAWL from the tent on the fifth day to take my morning's morning, sometime about ten, my throat is sore, my nose snotty, and what I know will sabotage this adventure is in full bloom. A bronchial infection. Added to this, I see the surrounding hills topped with snow.

About the same time, everyone else is witness to the whiteness. We gather beneath the cook tent, stomping around and drinking coffee. It's not the same as other mornings. For one thing it isn't raining. And something besides atmosphere fills the foggy air. It's our attitude. We aren't taking this anymore. We have got to get the hell off this sinking lily pad *now, today.* All brains on deck.

Jim:"Lets go have a look at that canoe. If we stuff rags in the holes, it might give us a few trips to the mainland with some necessary items."

Eric:"No paddles."

Ann: "If the canoe will float us, even taking turns, we can't row with our hands in that icy water, they'll freeze off."

Joey:"We can make a paddle out of something: piece of plastic on a couple of sticks . . ."

Me:"I saw a native paddle in Bettles. They take a branch, little over an inch thick, split the end up about a foot, bind it with thong or string to keep it from splitting further, and at the bottom of the split lace a five-inch twig to keep it spread open. Next, they put three or four consecutively shorter twigs up to the wedge, then weave leafy saplings in and out of the twigs until they have a nearly solid surface."

Eric:"I think it would take a whole day to make one of those, even if we could find the fixings."

Ann: "Joey's idea about a piece of plastic would take care of the woven twigs."

Jim:"The canoe. Let's go look at it."

We turn it over and decide that it might actually float—with a bit of stuffing here and there—slide it across the precious tundra into a foot of water, and push down to see if the bottom, at least, is leakproof. So far, so good. It's about two hundred feet to the mainland, some of it bordered by grasses rising above the water, so we don't actually know if, or where, we might bottom out before getting to the bank.

We go back to the kitchen to mull this over while we eat a very light breakfast of bagels and cream cheese, orange juice, moldy toast and jam, and a little more coffee, because we're near the end of our drinking water and the Coleman fuel is almost gone. Mugs in hand, Jim and Joey search for pieces of plastic that might serve for rowing parts.

Then we hear it.

Between two low mountains capped with a layer of mist, a plane appears. With no formalities of circling—the pilot already knows the direction of wind or reads it from ripples on the water—the plane drops, beelines for the tarn, and skis in, looking heavier on one side where a canoe rides. I spot this instantly. One canoe, with paddles, not two.

It taxis to our lily pad.

There is a special urgency this time because the plane is over half filled with emergency rations for other drop-offs and pickups Mark has to make. This means only one of us can return with him. Ann and Eric have elected to tough it out, wait for the second canoe, and make the run. I'm the logical returnee with my hacking bronchitis, gear, and lighter weight; but I hope to hell Mark will be able to pick up Joey and get back to Bettles before more bad weather sets in. Fifteen minutes later, we're gone.

Halfway there, we see smoke rising from thick brush on the steep side of a mountain. Moving closer, we spot four people in obvious distress, gesticulating wildly, waving a yellow tarp. Mark circles, sights their position, wiggles the wings, and flies on. (I learn later that they burned one of their sleeping bags to attract attention.)

Midway to Bettles, Mark lands on a lake where more folks are stranded. He leaves some cargo, picks up one person who barely fits, and tells the others he'll be back in two or three hours—or someone else will. Since I've "been there, heard that" already, I can only pray I'll see Joey sometime before midnight . . . tonight.

Elsewhere, during the five days and nights we were awash, Mother Nature has really done a number on the land. With the kind of weather that fosters the saying "There are no old bush pilots in Alaska," the Koyukuk has flooded Bettles and taken several cars, plus other trash, along with it. Close to the middle of the river, what I thought was a runaway barge turns out to be a huge oil truck half submerged in the flow. It just squats there at the mercy of a pissed-off river that is slowly burying it.

While I wait apprehensively for Joey, I go to the office of the company that supplied Jim's equipment. There I learn the aim, the rationale, the excuse—whatever you want to call it—for the two canoes that were *not* at the put-in for our trip.

"The Park Service won't let us take the canoes and leave them out there before a trip because it damages the tundra, the ground cover."

"Excuse me? A couple of overturned canoes are going to damage the ground cover?"

I can't believe what I'm hearing. Then I recall the dozens of similar national park and monument, recreation, and Forest Service rules and regulations in my own state, and groan over the actual harm they cause because some deferential superintendent hasn't the balls (or boobs) to move against what is obviously stupid, if not dangerous.

"What in hell do they think five pairs of boots do to that precious tundra in almost a week, walking all over to keep from freezing, to say nothing of the poops, the tarps, the tents, the . . . ?"

"I know," she interrupts. "We've argued that point for over a year, and this isn't the first time we've lost money on the tours." The woman motions with her thumb. "Park's office is over there if you want to express your opinion."

I rave at the guy for an hour and hope his ears are still burning. I also hope that his boss, and the boss above that one, and the next find themselves up some creek in the frozen tundra, far above the Arctic Circle, without a paddle!

Mark arrives with Joey about ten thirty and we toast each other with a warm and potent bedtime beverage.

The clouds move in. Again.

The "Grand Old Dame" of Glen Canyon, **Katie Lee** has worked for over forty years to preserve and enrich the river tribe's traditions. Filmmaker and photographer, activist, singer, songwriter, storyteller, poet, and former Hollywood actress—she is probably best known for her reminiscences *All My Rivers Are Gone*. Katie knew The Place No One Knew intimately, better than most who visited it before the deluge. Her collection of cowboy lore *Ten Thousand Goddam Cattle* is a western classic, and her latest essay collection *Sandstone Seduction* delivers more of the bawdy and irreverent humor for which she is known.

games

Jeff Wallach

KILLER GOAT BEACH, on the Lower Salmon, may well comprise the best baseball stadium on the entire river. It was known for many years as Packers Creek Camp; the BLM first officially printed the more evocative name on its 1995 river maps. I was riding in the crew cab with Joel on the way to the put-in one day when somebody mentioned the change on the new map. I never saw Joel light up like that before or since. Killer Goat Beach was named after an incident in which he was the undisputed co-star, along with a feral goat.

You really have to hear Joel tell the story, hear him describe various people "coming unglued" to appreciate it, but here, at least, are the details: When one of Joel's trips was camping on this beach a few years ago, a feral goat stood on some rocks above camp, watching them. One of the guests on this trip was "a fitness nut," and after pitching his tent in the sand high up the beach, he began doing stretching exercises, which inexplicably upset the goat. Joel, who was working in the kitchen, noticed the goat's agitation and asked the man to stop, but he refused. After a few more minutes the man began jogging laps around his tent, which really irritated the goat, and though several other guides suggested he quit it, the man still refused. Shortly after that the goat charged, and as it chased the man in a circle Joel yelled at him, "Stay away from the kitchen! Stay away from the kitchen!" So the man headed directly for the kitchen, with the goat in hot pursuit.

Joel stood beside one of the prep tables as the man ran past him, but the goat just stopped and lowered his head and he and Joel had a long face-off. After a minute or two of staring at Joel, the goat finally charged again. Joel picked up a piece of wood lying on a nearby table, swung it like a baseball bat, and smacked the goat right between the eyes. Nobody can replicate Joel's lanky imitation of the stunned goat staggering and falling to its knees before retreating drunkenly back up the beach.

Following this incident, several different outfitters reported to the BLM that while camping at Packers Creek their groups were attacked by a crazy killer goat. The goat earned such a fabulous reputation that when a couple of BLM bigshots from Washington were visiting the Salmon River a few years ago, local rangers motored them to the beach in the hope that the lunatic goat might make an appearance. While they were standing on the bow of their government jet boat, the goat not only showed himself: He charged the rangers like an angered plains buffalo. One of them pulled out a gun and—supposedly in self-defense—put an end to the terror of Killer Goat Beach.

It's a pleasure to hear Joel—who is not a showman like some guides—tell this story without self-consciousness and describe his own role in modern Salmon River history. None of which has anything to do with the fact that Killer Goat Beach—long, wide, and flat—constitutes the best baseball venue along the entire river. A few days before we ran The Slide Rapid on this Lower Salmon trip, we made camp at Killer Goat Beach during the hottest part of a blistering afternoon. Before we'd even begun unloading the boats, Leon began talking about having a baseball game.

Despite the heat, we cajoled about half a dozen guests—men, women, and children—into playing under the glaring sun in the burning sand. We began a bit lethargically, but as we got into it I noticed that even the adults—especially the adults, and even more especially the adult males—were starting to take things a little more seriously. For one thing, everybody seemed to be keeping score.

Two of the players were Tom, a large, slightly menacing physician from Tacoma, Washington, and Stew, a distinguished-looking prep school teacher from Pennsylvania who sported a brand-new, dapper, white beard. Late in the game, with the score tied, Stew roped a line drive up the middle that got him to second base. Although the next batter struck out, the hitter after him knocked a lame-duck Texas-leaguer just over Tom's head where he was playing first. Stew took off for third base as Tom struggled in the sand to go after the ball. He picked it up just as Stew arrived at third.

The two men considered each other across the white-hot sand of the infield in much the same way that Joel and the killer goat probably took measure of one another in that earlier, ill-fated confrontation. They weighed their options, each waiting for the other to make a move. Stew took a tentative step off third base, and Tom edged a little closer toward home. When something snapped in Stew's brain and shouted at him to *just go!* Tom reacted instantly, too, and both men ran as fast as they could in the heavy sand toward the plate—a race that progressed in slow, exaggerated motion. When it appeared that they were destined to collide in a perfect tie, and that one or the other of them must back off, Stew thought he saw his chance and *dove* toward home plate, leaping headfirst through the air in a manner that would have made Pete Rose proud. Not to be outdone, Tom saw that he'd have to dive, as well, and without a second thought he launched himself toward home. The two men crashed head-on in midair, fell to the ground, rolled around in a heap, and came up coughing, laughing, and spitting sand.

Although boatmen present virtually unlimited examples of arrested development, it's always entertaining to watch otherwise normal adults acting so much like children. This baseball game stands out as one of my favorite moments from the summer because you could actually see each of these men as little kids. In the backcountry, we often fail to consider how things look or what other folks might say; we don't measure our actions against what's appropriate behavior for a lawyer or a doctor or a CEO. Instead, we turn virtually every activity into some kind of a game. It is part of the unlimited freedom provided by our kindly host, the wilderness.

A hundred examples of this occur every day. At lunch, once we've set up the peanut butter bar and the water pump and lugged a few of the heavier items up on shore, we guides return to our boats to pull lunch food out of coolers and rocket boxes, at which point it's requisite to throw these items—blocks of cheese, stalks of celery, tomatoes, fruit, boxes of cookies—from the boats up to the lunch table one at a time, preferably just fast enough to make them difficult to catch. There's no real objective; it's just that we so rarely have an opportunity to really chuck a tomato or wing a carrot back home, so we take advantage of these circumstances. Contrary to what my mother might say, I've never seen anybody lose an eye to a bag of Fig Newtons.

Or consider the breakfast item/ritual known as "drop zone eggs." Once the griddle has really heated up, a guide—preferably a tall one, or one standing on a bucket, or a light one sitting on the shoulders of another guide—holds an egg as high above the griddle as possible, and then cracks it so that the egg wobbles down through space and then splatters on the hot surface, cooking instantly. In the advanced version of this game, two participants put on hot-gloves and protective kayaking helmets and hold the griddle up between them like a strike zone while someone else runs down the beach and then pitches fastball eggs at the sizzling target.

Only actual children like to play in the kitchen more than boatmen do. Among the most entertaining kitchen-related games are the amazing pyrotechnics produced, for example, by stuffing a bunch of steel wool into a metal can poked full of holes, attaching a long string to the can, rowing the whole thing out on a dory into a big eddy at night, then lighting it on fire and swinging it around on the string. On a dark evening these poor-man's fire-works release dazzling wheels of white sparks against the pitch-black horizon.

Many guides also aspire to create the largest grease bomb ever ignited on the river—which involves saving up sausage and bacon grease and drippings from grilled steaks in an empty tin can over the course of an entire trip. On the final night, just after we give out awards to all our guests—Most Likely to Become a Boatman, for example, or The Mark Spitz Award (usually given to someone who fell out of a boat in a rapid and survived a harrowing swim that we can now joke about)—one guide slips down to the river and dons a wet-suit for maximum protection against splattering grease and flames, and using a long pole lowers the can of grease by means of a wire handle into the mid-dle of a roaring fire.

When the grease has begun boiling and smoking, the guide takes another can full of cold river water and, using the pole again, pours the water into the burning grease—something we seriously advise against trying at home. A good grease bomb looks a lot like those films you've seen of nuclear testing, if on a slightly smaller scale. Of course, since grease bombs are dangerous as well as illegal along the Salmon River, I've only heard about them, and have never actually seen one in person. I've certainly never seen a guide, who for the sake of anonymity I'll call "Robert," ignite a series of amazing grease and margarine bombs right by the river's edge at the bottom of French Creek Camp on the night of the Fourth of July.

Many old-time boatmen also revere a game that involves seeing how fast a rookie can set up the roll-top table, a kind of clumsy gear puzzle that many trainees try to avoid dealing with altogether. This year, when Trista was unable to put the table together on land in under one minute, Leon encouraged her to try it while standing in the river so the water could help her balance the tabletop while she tried to attach it to the legs. Chris Quinn claims to hold the record for assembling the table in under seven seconds, but the most amazing part of his feat was that he'd remembered to bring the table at all.

On trips where we've brought along a paddle raft, we sometimes flip the empty boat upside down in camp and set it on a piece of beach that slopes precipitously toward a deep spot in an eddy. A boatman stands on each side of the raft with a bucket and tosses river water onto the bottom to slick down the surface, creating a sixteen-foot "Slip-n-Slide." There's nothing quite like the spectacle of a retired lawyer from Seattle running down the beach in her frumpy bathing suit, leaping headlong across the bottom of the raft, and disappearing into the river in such a way that for a moment only her feet are visible before they, too, disappear over the edge of the boat; or the sight of a portly, gravel-voiced businessman from Chicago showing off for his daughter by performing a giant belly-flop on the Slip-n-Slide and bouncing into the river.

Guides also possess a limitless repertoire of verbal games for passing long afternoons rowing against the wind on flat water, or for playing around the fire in the evening. Minute mysteries provide a foolproof way of spending a slow hour or two on the boats, and are perfect for quieting down unruly kids. For example: A naked woman is lying dead at the bottom of a mountain with a matchstick in her hand. You can ask me "yes" or "no" questions to determine what happened.

Some of our evening games also provide a great way for trip participants to get to know each other and begin bonding. Leon often leads a game called "Two Truths and a Lie" on the first night of a trip. The game requires players to offer three brief statements or stories about themselves to the rest of the group; as you may have already guessed, two are true, one is a lie. The stated object is for the storyteller to try to fool everybody else, but the real purpose is to give each group member a moment in the spotlight, and provide them with a means of introducing themselves in some entertaining way. My own stories often included the following:

—that I received a speeding ticket while taking my first driver's test;
—that in college I was a nationally ranked croquet player;
—that I once had an out-of-body experience.

AFTER THE SEASON was over, I spoke to Sandra Gaskill about the trip we worked on together that included guests (and baseball legends) Tom and Stew, as well as guides Joel, Leon, and Brannon. We both agreed that this was one of the best groups we'd encountered all summer, and I asked her why she thought this had been so.

"It had a lot to do with that first night, when we sat around and played Two Truths and a Lie," Sandra said. "That really set a tone and people felt they were in an environment that was comfortable, and they pushed themselves, and grew."

Strange and magical things occur when two dozen folks sit around a fire on a sparkling clear evening and sip drinks and tell stories and play games such as Smurf and Aardvark; Elves, Wizards, and Dwarves; or In the Manner of the Word. But it's hard to explain. You'll just have to come out there with us and experience it for yourself.

Is there a point to all of this? Is play somehow a metaphor for how our primordial instinct to have fun emerges fresh and wild when we step away from all the serious and mundane rules of society? Is there a deeper, hidden meaning—an undercurrent or subtext or inner frontier—to these games? And would Frederick Jackson Turner have taken his turn on the Slip-n-Slide?

In answer, all I can say is that if you thought I was going to reveal how the naked dead woman ended up at the bottom of the mountain with a match in her hand, you've got another think coming.

Jeff Wallach is the author of five books of nonfiction including *What the River Says*—a literary account of guiding on Idaho's Salmon River, and also about the idea of The Frontier in the American West. He has written for *Outside, Men's Journal, Sports Illustrated, Men's Health, Sierra,* and dozens of other national publications and recently completed an as-yet-unpublished boatman novel, *Pool and Drop.* Wallach has guided on rivers throughout the West since 1985. When not burning the peach cobbler he can be identified by the puffing sounds he makes in preparing to row even Class II rapids. He lives and writes in Portland, Oregon.

tempting the river gods

Alan Kesselheim

OUTINGS WITH KRIS had a way of gravitating to the unpredictable extremes, either life-threatening, like the time we ran out of water hiking in the Grand Canyon, or outrageous and bizarre, as with the canoe trip that ended with me standing on a boulder in the middle of the Rio Grande wearing nothing but a visor and a pair of weathered tennis shoes . . .

THE SETTING IS idyllic. Fall in northern New Mexico—desert-toned landscape under a dome of seamless blue; cottonwood trees rustling with yellow leaves; warmth that rekindles memories of summer but without the searing heat. A reminder that we've already slipped into accepting the inevitable coming of winter, a subtle slide toward attitudinal hibernation. A day to be out in.

It is one of the rare weekends that Kris and I get to share time. The curse of working as outdoors instructors in the same program is that we are often saddled with alternating rotations. Even though we live together, some months we see each other only on a handful of days.

Kris suggests a jaunt down the Rio Grande in the dented Grumman lake canoe I have borrowed from my parents while they are out of the country. Any other waterway within striking distance of Santa Fe is too low by October to be much fun. By autumn the rivers are ebbing toward their quiet winter pace; the Rio Grande is rippling through the canyons it charges down during the melt season, relaxed as a Sunday drive.

We pack up a lunch, and an hour later we have launched the canoe. Mostly we float along. A few families have responded to the fall day by driving down to the river to fish or picnic. We exchange greetings. Only minor fast water punctuates the steady tug of current; we proceed at a sedate pace into the deepening canyon. Basalt cliffs begin to rise higher above the river, constricting our view. Fewer roads penetrate as we approach the boundary of Bandelier National Monument. We are alone.

Once in a while we practice an eddy turn or another maneuver, but it feels good just to cruise, to watch the landscape. Ravens croak overhead, their outstretched shadows diving across the brown cliffs. A few rapids challenge us, but at this water level we handle them easily.

We pull over above the one formidable bit of whitewater along the run in order to scout it from shore. At higher water the constriction rapid is a fast, big-volume chute with huge waves. Even at this moderate level I feel the familiar tightening knot of anxiety and excitement. The canoe is by no means designed for whitewater, and I am still in the early part of the paddling learning curve. As a team our canoeing skills are only adequate. Across the river I can barely make out the aluminum glint of a submerged canoe pinned under a rock by the full brunt of current, a shiny warning against complacency.

We discuss strategy, focusing on the loud water before us, and forget the spell of the day in the tension. Then, with life vests on, we are back in the boat, setting up, kneeling for stability. The river sucks us along more and more irresistibly. The waves are big enough to give us a rollicking ride. The canoe twists and plunges, taking some water over the bow. I feel an inch of cold river sloshing around my knees, but we are right where we want to be, our strokes solid and tight. I glimpse the battered underwater casualty again as we sweep past on the back of the river, and we're through.

It seems a good time to have lunch. A sunny sandbar offers itself. Content in the knowledge that we've passed the tricky part of the river, we soak up warmth and readjust ourselves to the desert surroundings. It gets hot, so Kris and I strip down for a dip in the cold, silty water and then let our skin dry under the friendly sun. When we get back in the canoe, we don't bother to put our clothes on but just toss them loosely into the bottom. It's that kind of day.

At the mouth of Frijoles Canyon, inside Bandelier National Monument, a final boulder-strewn riffle precedes the lengthy flatwater paddle that a downstream dam has inflicted on canoeists. The water level is much different from what it was the only other time I've run the rapid, a year earlier. That time I was with a group in a raft, but I remember the spot well.

"You think we should scout?" Kris calls back from the bow. I stand up, looking for the route I remember, and identify what appears to be a clean line. I resist going to shore again so soon.

"I think we're okay," I say. "Let's head for that top V.'"

But as we approach, I see things I couldn't from upstream. What I thought was a clean shot is littered with hidden obstacles. Instead of taking us through, the V actually feeds right into a rocky barrier. We should have scouted. By the time I see our error, it's too late to get to shore.

"Let's ferry left!" I shout, knowing it's not going to work.

The ferry angle goes wrong. We're more broadside than we should be. The whitewater has us; the boulders loom close and large. Kris yells something that I don't hear. The boat is almost fully broadside and our paddling harmony is gone.

Then, the shock of cold, green water. I hear myself sputtering. The boat is in front of me, gaping into the current, filling with river. Kris has disappeared. I flail toward the near end of the canoe, but as I reach it, I hear the dull *thunk* of hull against rock. The boat shudders to a stop, pinned across two boulders, a sickening crease in its hull. As the current adapts to the new obstacle in its path, the canoe fills and settles.

I scramble to the top of a rounded volcanic rock and look anxiously downstream for Kris. She is only ten feet away, clinging to a tree root wedged down by the current. Her face has the universal expression worn by victims of natural calamity—astonishment, shock, personal affront.

"You okay?" I ask.

She nods. "I got sucked right under the boat." She begins hauling herself against the current toward her own midriver island of basalt.

My attention turns to the foundered boat. Damage has been done. I can tell that some of the rivets have popped out. An oblique crease dents the boat toward the stern, but by being pinned across two rocks the canoe has avoided being folded in two.

I am still berating myself for being too lazy and confident to stop and look at the run. The rapid is embarrassingly minor. With a brief scout we could have shot through and been a mile downstream by now. Gingerly I work my way back into the river next to our craft and find that I can actually stand upstream of it to get leverage on the hull.

Initially it doesn't even occur to me that I might not be able to free the boat. But as I test different angles, even get my whole body underwater and heave up mightily, I begin to appreciate the power of the river. The canoe is immovable; it doesn't even wiggle.

Kris has made her way to the other rock the boat is lodged against. For twenty minutes or more we struggle against the current. Then, each standing on our tiny island, we appraise each other. Kris is wearing running shoes and a cap, nothing else. I sport tennis shoes and a visor. The rest is sunburned flesh. We chuckle at each other and then laugh out loud for a bit.

The humor doesn't last long because now we're going to have to walk two miles on a well-used trail to the park headquarters and then hitchhike to our car. I can tell that Kris is pondering the same conclusion. We laugh a little more, but now it's nervous laughter. I kneel over the boat and search through the roiling water for bits of clothing. Nothing.

I imagine various all-too-possible vignettes—meeting young families along the trail; arriving at the busy parking lot; explaining to a receptionist at the visitor center why I need a towel; standing on the highway, offering our thumbs, and everything else, to passing recreational vehicles.

"Hey!" Kris interrupts my morose thoughts. "What about that stuff sack with my running clothes? Didn't we tie that to the seat?"

She's leaning out over the boat as she talks, feeling back to the stern seat. The current is strongest there, but she finds the string and the bag, bouncing and tugging in the river.

"Careful! Don't lose that stuff!" I walk across on the hull of the canoe to help. It takes a full ten minutes to unhitch the knot, but then we hold the precious bag of garments, scanty as it is.

Kris peers inside and then pulls out the wet contents—one pair women's size medium running shorts and one women's size medium stretch leotard. I ponder momentarily how to wear the stuff sack, but the applications elude me.

Kris looks at me and then looks back at the clothes. "I guess I get the leotard, you get the shorts." We laugh again, briefly.

I'm not a small man. Running shorts are diaphanous things, made to economize on weight and wind drag. Even though I'm quite motivated, it's a struggle to wiggle into Kris's shorts. The coverage about equals that of a small bandanna, and I am uncomfortably reminded of junior-high locker room pranks we called wedgies. Kris, in her skintight, sleeveless leotard, looks oddly attired for hiking, but not nearly so outlandish as me. I decide to carry one of our paddles along as sort of an explanatory prop for the hikers we might meet.

We hop to shore across a string of rocks and start off, shoes squelching water, my gait visibly affected by the constricting garb. Now and again I hear Kris giggling softly behind me. I make menacing gestures with the paddle, which only goad her into hysterical laughter, so I ignore her.

Within a quarter mile the shorts are uncomfortable enough that I'm thinking about splitting them apart at the seam. That may happen anyway. About then the first hikers come upon us, a couple with two young children. The adults choose feigned nonchalance and an inner-city aversion of eyes. The kids gape. I mutter something that is supposed to be construed as a greeting.

Soon we start encountering lots of people. We grow brazen and callous to our effect and stride past them, making no attempt to communicate; I use the paddle as a hiking staff. At least Kris isn't laughing anymore. Between groups of hikers I try to pluck the shorts out of my crotch.

Finally, we arrive at the busy parking lot. We shortcut to the exit road and start hitching. Kris is clearly the more presentable envoy, so she stands in front. I half hide behind her and extend my bare arm toward the roadway, wearing a benign expression, as if hitchhiking in a loincloth were normal weekend fare. A great many vehicles pass by, seeming to accelerate as they do. They are mostly station wagons, campers, and motor homes. Children turn around in their seats to gawk. Adults pretend we're invisible.

It's remarkable that anyone would stop and more remarkable still that the car that eventually does is a Mercedes-Benz driven by an older couple. They politely refrain from inquiry as we settle into the plush rear seat. Thinking the canoe paddle a little scruffy for the interior, I leave the window rolled down and hold it outside as we drive through Los Alamos toward our vehicle.

It is a quiet ride. In less than half an hour we're back to the car. We retrieve the keys we hid under the bumper and are on our way home. It isn't until we're halfway to Santa Fe that we discuss strategy.

"You know," Kris begins, "I don't think anyone knew we went paddling today."

Another mile slips by. "Maybe we could get some rope and carabiners and go back tomorrow. We could have the canoe sitting in the yard before anyone knows the difference."

These days **Alan Kesselheim** takes along a designated clothes bag for those impulsive moments on the river. He is farther along the paddling learning curve too. Alan and his partner, Marypat, have paddled across Canada, spending several winters in the wilds along the way. They live in Montana with their three children who are all avid wilderness paddlers and mostly keep their clothes on. Alan is a contributor to magazines, including *Canoe & Kayak*, *Backpacker*, *Big Sky Journal*, and *Sports Afield*, as well as author of *Threading the Currents*, *Water and Sky*, *Silhouette on a Wide Land*, and *Going Inside*.

catch and release

Bradley Davis

THE FLY AND ten inches of leader flicked across the neck of the bird and back into a lasso. It was 1966, in September, on an unnamed bar ten miles upriver from Agness on the Rogue River. Boyden made the cast. He has said for thirty-eight years that it was a slight shift of wind that drifted the fly upriver of the rock. Wind, a lie, the truth we will never know, but I was with Jane, his beautiful bride of a year and a half, when it happened. We had all been guiding on the Middle Fork of the Salmon for two months—away from our families—and on the way home with boats and all gear decided that if we called from Boise, our wives and families would have time to meet us in Grants Pass. We could all have a great reunion in a five-day trip on the Rogue River. For two months Boyden and I had spoken about our lives and wives and how it was so difficult to teach those we loved to become partners to fish. Boyden was very frustrated about it. He had made a fly rod for his wife as a wedding present, and she had broken it in the car door on its maiden voyage to the Firehole, prior to use: a disaster scene. Boyden told me that he had not been a gentleman about it.

The year before, Boyden had taken Jane to the Blackwater River, west of Quesnel in British Columbia, which was so thick with fish that it was impossible not to catch them. But essentially the only fish Jane caught were the ones she hooked when the line slapped into the water behind her. Boyden said she just wouldn't listen. He said he had spent endless hours attempting to teach her how to cast. He was in a fit entirely. I should say that thirty-eight years later Jane is probably the finest female permit fisherman in the world, a steady hand, and, with a Winston five-piece ten-weight rod, can lay out ninety feet of line.

But here we were in 1966 and half-pounders were all over the lower Rogue.

A beautiful late lunch on a small gravel bar and submerged gravel bed behind an exposed boulder a hundred feet from shore at the beginning of the tailout of the hole. Boyden was a really great fisherman. At twenty-four, he had fly fished for twenty years and was well trained in biology and aquatic entomology. He just understood what was going on in the water—and all around him for that matter. He was the finest fly caster I have ever seen—before or since—and so, even after thirty-eight years, I am inclined to believe that Boyden did not tell the truth about how it happened.

Under the soft cloud cover, Boyden had caught fish after fish off the submerged gravel, hooking them, then handing the rod to Jane so she could land them. They were really in love and it was beautiful to watch. At the head of the tailout, where the boulder tip lay exposed, a large seagull landed. Boyden made another cast and it was the sort of thing he would do but not admit to: He lassoed the bird around the neck, tightened up the line a bit to get the gull flying. Then he turned and handed his beautiful wife the rod. Already most of the backing was gone and the bird almost a hundred yards out. We were all laughing and cheering, while Boyden was giving copious advice, particularly about not getting the seagull caught in a big tree. As time and luck would have it, Jane landed the bird. She was very happy to have this done with. Jane is a very gentle, loving person and her face showed concern for the bird, which was flapping about, appearing to be tremendously frightened—and also pissed off. Boyden took off his shirt, grabbed the bird, and hooded it. It became instantly calm, so Boyden undid the lasso and handed Jane the wrapped-up bird, which she cradled as if to nurse.

Everyone had gathered and some cameras were ready. Boyden was directing the scene. The program called for the removal of the shirt and a spate of photographs and the joyous release of the poor animal. Jane held the gull as Boyden attempted to remove the shirt. The head of the seagull popped out of an armhole and it looked up and grabbed hold of poor Jane's nose. Its sharp beak just locked around her septum, piercing it. There was a lot of blood and Jane let go, while the bird, completely enclosed, but thrashing about in the T-shirt, was hanging from her elegant nose. It just hung there with blood squirting all over its head. Then it let go, falling crazily in the shirt to the gravel bar.

The most unfortunate situation then occurred, one that Boyden has never been allowed to forget. Instead of helping his wife, he spent the next minute or so helping the bird. More unforgivable was the fact that he doubled over in a fit of laughter so consuming that he could hardly extract the gull and release it. It took years of redemption before the story could be recounted, and it happened so fast that—unlike the fishing journals documenting the results of Jane's more recent fishing exploits—no photos exist of the incident.

Editor's note: During a telephone conversation, Jane revealed that she bore a scab from her encounter on the Rogue for about six months afterward. She became quite good at telling *her* version of the story to inquisitive friends and acquaintances.

Bradley Davis fishes full time from September to November every year. Here is a short list of rivers he has fished in North America: Utukok, Linik, Nestling, Naha, Alexander Creek, Smoke, Thelon, Kaskattama, Liscomb, Grey, Manatee, Niobrara, Dismal, White, Surley Run, Nestucca, Shell Creek, Bruneau, Sturgeon, Point Creek, Sprague, Chetco, Rattlesnake Creek, Tongue, Blitzen, Little Owyhee, Little Red Deer, Owl Creek, and Rio Hondo. When he can find time in February and March, he fishes in secret locations in Mexico's Yucatán. When he can arrange artist workshops to support his activity, he fishes in Scandinavia and Mongolia.

the nechako

Tim Cooper

IT WAS VINCE who made me promise to follow through for once. "You've got to write it down before it fades to nothing," he'd said. "Promise me that you'll do it." I promised. It was long ago already, and the central event took perhaps only five minutes to play out. Still, it was one of those occurrences around which the personal histories of the witness and participants are dated. This is particularly true in my own case, though I'd begun as a player of a very minor part. Vince thought I should call it "The Price of Friendship," but I thought a better title might be "My Biggest Wreck."

IT ALL STARTED when our trip leader RD was out reassuring himself of the location of the "goalpost" run in Unkar Rapid, all by himself. He slipped on a rock, fell down, and busted his thumb. He couldn't hold a fork, never mind an oar, and we had to pull Vince off the trainee raft to replace him. That left Lori in the raft, our one rubber boat, all by herself.

It was thought that Vince should probably row the only aluminum dory we had. In a metal boat you can be a little off course and tap a rock without sinking the thing. Vince had never been down the whole Grand Canyon before. It's not rocket science, but it takes a little practice.

The only drawback was that the aluminum boat was the *Nechako*, a vessel of unprecedented girth and a reputation for being unwieldy. Her lines had been sketched on the back of a cocktail napkin and lofted to full scale by dumpster fabricator that same evening—or so the story went. You sat at the rowing station and couldn't see anything but boat for fifteen degrees either side of the bow and stern posts because she was shaped like a section of cantaloupe and your butt was down where the seeds and stringy stuff would be.

The gunwales swept down from the lofty ends, in an arc that came perilously close to the water's surface. In the middle of the boat, the *Nechako* had the free-board of a log raft. She was so beamy that during a night of revelry we once got eleven people in the front cross hatch alone.

The location of the laden waterline had been severely misjudged and the oar-locks had therefore been raised six inches by a wooden frame made from pieces of an oar shaft bolted to the sides. The oars had to be two feet longer than usual just to reach the water, which put them at an angle where the average-sized person was more hanging from the handles than pulling on them. The exaggerated flare of her sides and a continuous fore-and-aft curve of her bottom made her set deep, but still bob and pitch about wildly in rough water.

She was a tough boat to love and since O'Connor had left the company, nobody had. The deck seals were shot, latches were missing, and the oarlocks knocked in their stanchions like a '53 Hudson with two bad rod bearings. Still, she was stable on the water, in the same sense a driftwood log is, and stout as a fireplug, both qualities we deemed useful in a rookie boat. While it was more likely that you were going to end up going somewhere besides where you'd hoped, the consequences were less dire. It could take all day to put a wood boat back together. The *Nechako* could sustain a canyon-ringing hit and you would-n't be late for lunch. Her wobbly heft and bone-deep sluggishness would be like wearing ankle weights. Everything seems much easier once you take them off.

Vince put on a pair of rowing gloves, which none of us neighborhood types had ever seen, and took over the *Nechako* like a good soldier. The gloves seemed a little unboatman-like, I thought, but hey, different strokes . . . Tuck, the company manager, got in RD's boat, the *Makaha*.

Tuck had come on the trip to prove to the skeptical staff that it was really no big deal to put five people, instead of the usual four, in a dory and row them down the Grand Canyon. An accountant had pointed out that the company would never make any money with a four-to-one client: staff ratio. A fifth pay-ing passenger was the difference between profitability and extinction. The arithmetic had to be made to work. Boats the size of the *Nechako* were part of the answer. In this case, as it somehow came to happen, it meant the rookie was pulling an overloaded boxcar down a river he'd never seen before. He took it really well. Unkar is arguably the first of the Grand Canyon's really large rapids, and Vince's first strokes aboard his new commission were to set up for the entry. Events weren't cutting him a lot of slack, but he made it to the bottom of that one, and all the rest of the big ones that day.

Over the course of the next few days, Vince proved equal to the task at hand. There are some moments when extreme exertion is called for—and worthwhile. Below the bigger drops I would find him leaning on his oars, spent and shaking his head, staring into the bilge. Then he'd look up and grin. If you got within earshot he'd start the narrative right there. He paid attention as if his life depended on it, which it actually did. He never complained, and you had to give him credit for that. We quickly became friends.

Vince had rowed most of the big stuff and most of the doldrums too, where the current seems to simply spin in circles and the wind often blows like a bastard. The Nechako's square waterline made her particularly unruly in the swirlies, and her towering stem and stern could send her skittering into the eddy like a water strider in the mildest gale. Vince's hands were raw through the gloves. We'd gone two hundred miles and were heading for the top of Lake Mead that afternoon. On the last day of moving water, we decided he deserved a break. A couple of us offered to trade boats with him now and then, over the course of the day, so he could try out the other dories.

But there are still some significant rapids in the lower gorge.

I had already taken my turn in the Nechako, and when we got down to Travertine Grotto I was ready to switch again. The boat I had been rowing since I started with Grand Canyon Dories was a 1976 Briggs dory, the sweetest watercraft to ever displace her weight of Colorado River water. She was made of Doug Fir marine ply and Port Orford cedar in a wizard's workshop in Grants Pass, Oregon, and I rather wanted her back.

You can develop a relationship with a rowboat much more readily than you can with most inanimate objects. Sure, people love their cars, but it would certainly be a different matter if they had to pull them to work. You might start to appreciate how easily that old VW rolled or cuss the brand-new Ford Exhibition till the paint all blistered off. The Roaring Springs and I were a team. It had taken her about three years to teach me to row. I just wasn't that adept.

Persistence can often win out over ineptitude, though, and I had developed a few good moves.

The *Springs's* designer and builder, Jerry Briggs, had grown up building boats and put everything he knew about them into one design during a rare conjunction of the planets one winter solstice night. The dogs stopped barking and all the sheep lay down at once. Briggs boats have a straight section of waterline, about eight feet, which we all thought was responsible for their ability to track like a freight train. The hull speed seemed to be about two miles an hour, a pretty good clip for one person pushing three quarters of a ton of stuff through still water. You could get them going that fast with half a dozen solid push strokes and keep it up all day without breaking a sweat.

If you stop rowing a raft for a moment, it is anchored in the surface tension like a lily pad. A Briggs boat will skate over the eddy lines, bounce off the crosscurrents, and hold her momentum like your maiden Aunt Bertha. It's uncanny, and a person can get spoiled. There's something about the way the bow rises out of the water that gives the stem a clean entry into the biggest waves and still shortens the waterline to where you can turn on a dime. You don't want to examine it too closely. Just row the damn boat and smile. You're getting paid.

The *Roaring Springs* was equipped with a set of oars I had picked out of a fresh shipment of a hundred one spring, before anyone else had gotten to the warehouse. They were ten feet of flawless, laser-straight American ash that would flex through the middle of the stroke and whip at the finish like a fish's tail. The blades were long and narrow so they didn't try to twist in your hand, though they had as much flat surface as you could pull through the water. They could be feathered in an instant and cocked for another stroke with the boat heeled over in a North Sea chop and the blade still under two feet of green water. (Try that with your three-hundred-dollar, axially wound, carbon fiber sinkers and your silly blade locators.) These sticks were very nearly perfectly balanced at the oarlock when the blades were in the water, because wood floats. You could let go of them and grab another beer from the side hatch before they crabbed under the boat. Usually. I don't care what you say, plastic will never come close.

The thing I liked about them most, though, was the way you could angle the blades into the water, matching their entry to the speed of the boat and have the surface of the river heal up behind the blade with a gentle *pock* like a raindrop hitting the water. You could move fifteen hundred pounds around in absolute silence except for that sound. If you could get everyone to shut up for a minute.

But I digress. When we got down to Travertine nobody wanted to finish out the last few rapids in the *Nechako*. So I reenlisted. In an hour we'd be tying all the boats together and it wouldn't matter which one you were on. We'd mount an outboard engine on the transom of each of the two back dories and motor across Lake Mead for a couple of days.

The water was sort of low, around 10,000 cubic feet per second. At this level 231 Mile Rapid turns into a set of short steep drops instead of the roller coaster it is at 18,000 cfs. It was heads-up boating.

The next rapid, 232 Mile, deserves its nasty reputation. The honeymooning Hyde party is thought to have drowned here in 1928, and wrecks occur frequently. Debris fans from tributary canyons on either side constrict a river already narrowed by the vertical black walls of the inner gorge. The rapid scrapes down the right wall in a series of substantial standing waves with breaking crests. Toward the bottom are The Fangs, a group of bedrock granite pinnacles smack in the middle of the current and sharp as scimitars. They are either exposed, or just below the surface, depending on river level. More towers of polished stone stand just off the right wall. We scouted 232 to see if The Fangs were out or not. The consensus was that The Fangs were covered.

All the boats gathered at the scant beach on the right. I left the sandy spot to the wooden dories and tethered the *Nechako* among the rocks. The hard metamorphic and igneous strata along this stretch of shore have been carved into a gallery of oddly sensuous forms. The passengers wandered around rubbing the rocks and taking pictures.

We were running the rapid in two groups. Half the people could take pictures of the run from the top, the others from the bottom. The boatmen had stood in a knot and talked through the run. There's a sharp hole on the top left that keeps you from getting into an optimal entry position. You have to stay out in the glassy water of the tongue, picking up speed as the river pours over the pile of rocky outwash from two lateral canyons.

I had a strategy that had worked so well on previous trips I actually looked forward to doing it. I never considered anything else.

I'd start pushing the oars well above the tongue just enough to get some steerage, then lean on 'em like a madman when I could see the bottom corner of the hole. Where the stream tilts and accelerates, I'd slide down the slick incline, irresistibly pulled by the river. Squeezing as close to the hole as I'd dare, I would then try to blast the crest of the left lateral into shimmering mist with my bowpost. By adding all the hickory wind I could muster, I might get most of my Briggs boat airborne if that wave was big enough. Once I was surfing down its backside, still headed left, I could just straighten out and watch the deadly dentition of 232 sail by two boatlengths to my right. It would be a beautiful run.

We watched the first group grease it. Dimock, a pioneer of the new school, pushed bow first, as I favored. Others pulled, their backs to the rapid. It all worked. I gathered up all five of my passengers. The youngest was around seventy. I piled them into the boat and took up all twenty-four feet of the *Nechako's* oars.

They were plastic-wrapped aluminum flagpoles with blades shaped like a speed-limit sign. A metal tube stiffened the blade and when you dipped them in the water they sounded like someone had slung a poodle off the rim. Urging the wards to hold on in earnest, we splashed into 232 like a sternwheeler, pushing toward river left to beat hell.

The top lateral stopped us dead. The *Nechako* rocked back on her stern and rode the crest to the center with her nose in the air. The next one stopped us again and we came out with momentum—toward the wall. I was still pushing left, but it obviously wasn't working. I was going to have to crank her around and pull, which maneuver I initiated by taking a couple of prodigious strokes on the right oar.

I had gotten her all the way around broadside in the current and was just starting my first stroke to pull away from the wall when we hit the uppermost Fang a foot forward of the oarlock. There was a terrific deafening crash, like a car accident. Everyone was thrown into a jumble on the left rail and I almost went overboard. My head was out over the side, which gave me a good look at the paramount Fang, inches away and undamaged. It had been lurking just under the surface, but the eddy caused by our boat now left a hand span of its tip visible. I scrambled back to the seat and hauled on the right oar to spin us off because we weren't moving at all, which is a little disconcerting in the middle of a large rapid. The boat came peeled off easily but we were careening down the wall, and totally out of control.

The current pushed the stern into a tight little eddy among the rocks, and the dory whirled into the wall in an instant. The right oar blade clattered up the vertical rock and jammed in a crack, snapping in half. The jagged fragment of plastic flew right at my head but the oar handle had already hit me in the sternum and flattened me to the deck, pinning me there like a bug. My feet were up in the air, kicking wildly, so I'm told. Struggling to keep my head up, I was looking right down what remained of the oar, which was bent into a parabola by pressure against the canyon wall and my chest. I still had a hand on it but could no longer breathe.

Somehow, I wedged my other hand under the handle and pushed up for all I was worth. I remember shaking with the effort as I slowly forced the shaft off me and let it crack down onto the deck. The handle broke off with the force of the impact and sailed into the front footwell: the only oar I've ever broken into three pieces. "I'll have to do something about that pretty quick," I thought, but at that moment noticed a more immediate problem.

Free now of the oar snag, the boat was slowly drifting into a passageway between a tower of stone and the wall. A quick visual comparison between the width of the passage and the beam of the *Nechako* indicated a bad match. We'd stick like a driven nail. I had but one oar. The only water available for it was part of the rapid, and flowing in the wrong direction at fifteen miles per hour. Leaping to the starboard side, I grabbed two handfuls of fluted granite and willed the boat to stop. Then I began to claw my way back up the eddy, dragging the *Nechako* along the wall, leaving a trail of blood and fingernails, with the boat repeatedly surging into the cliff and ringing like a Chinese gong. At the upstream end of the eddy towered another rock. The water right behind it wasn't going anywhere. There was a tiny lot where I could park the boat without straining to hold it. Maybe I could regroup, get in a spare oar, save our lives, and so on. But I had yet another problem.

The initial impact had been right on a seam in the plate aluminum, splitting the *Nechako* from gunwale to chine. It had also blown out an internal bulkhead, so the tremendous gash in her hull was leaking water into the cavernous front cross hatch *and* the left side. We were sinking. The *Nechako* didn't have much freeboard to begin with, but I noticed the water was already sloshing in with each surge. It was probably only the fact that the front cross hatch was jammed with lightweight gear in waterproof bags that was keeping us afloat. Then I noticed all the latches, save one, were missing on the twisted hatch cover. Buoyant black neoprene sacks were bulging from underneath it like monstrous entrails. If that single latch were to blow, we'd loose our flotation and go to the bottom like a marble.

Two tiny #6 screws and a $1.89 sash latch were postponing our demise for now. Quick action was called for.

I loosed a spare oar from the keeper and made to insert it in the vacant right oarlock. Unaccountably, I was unable to do this. Every time I'd get the throat of the oar close to the lock it would seem to jump out of my hand. The damn thing was so long that I had to lean way over the opposite side to keep it balanced, attempting to drop it into a two-inch space eight feet away, while wallowing in the swell. I tried hard, but it wasn't working. The oar seemed to be twitching around as if alive. After several tries I happened to look behind me where Martha was seated, eyes wide with terror, waiting for me to try to bludgeon her with the oar once again. She'd been fending it off with both hands whenever it got within reach. "Martha," I cried, "stop that." These were the first words anyone had spoken since we entered the rapid. I slipped in the oar. We were only going to get one try at this.

We sat dead in the water, sinking slowly, with the right gunwale scraping against the wall and a sizable rapid immediately to our left. I was going to have to get enough of the *Nechako*'s bulk into the main current to ensure that she would continue downstream and not wrap on the rock pinnacle immediately below. This from a standing start. Never nimble, a *Nechako* burdened with a thousand pounds of river water seemed a poor choice for this maneuver.

Options were limited. Our predicament was rapidly worsening.

"Be ready to highside," I suggested to the crew. When we hit the current it was going to suck the upstream gunwale down, raising the left side like the bow of the *Titanic* going under. By throwing themselves on the high side my passengers might keep the boat from being rolled right over by the force of the incoming water. Remaining upright would probably be best. We were going to hit some more rocks. That was certain, and I didn't care. If we didn't get out of the eddy, the molars of 232 were going to be flossed with elderly people. We just needed to get out of the rapid.

I stood up and hiked over to the right side where I put both hands on the polished stone. "Get ready," I told them. Giving my best heave, I shoved the boat away from the rock and leaped to the oars. There still wasn't enough room to use the right oar, so—praying this one wouldn't break also—I jammed the blade in the rock, pushed us off a little more, and levered the boat toward the current.

About three hundred tons of Colorado River pounded the *Nechako's* aft starboard quarter, whipping her stern downstream. "Highside," I suggested rather loudly. Everyone waded to the left rail. I only got one real stroke. The blade was still in the eddy, and all I had to do was prevent the force of the current from folding the oar against the boat. I was looking right down the length of the miserable thing, at the looming black obelisk. I had both hands on the left oar, which was bent like a soda straw, but the *Nechako* was still coming around fast. There wasn't time to do anything else. So I grabbed another stroke and held on till we went broadside into the tower, dead amidship.

I remember the echo it made. Flushed with adrenaline, I'd missed the reverberation of the first clash, which must have been terrific. But this one seemed to return from miles away. I'd been thrown out of my seat by the impact and was trying to get resituated when I heard the echo. "That must have been really loud," I had time to think. Then the right oar was in my hand somehow and I was trying to get a stroke in the rocketing current to spin us off the rock. We were very near the point of a perfect "postage stamp" pin, which would wrap the *Nechako's* aluminum hull around the rock protuberance like the foil on a baked potato. With the forces involved, I wasn't likely to be doing much, but I did it with everything I had.

Like a glacier making up its mind, the *Nechako* rolled off into the current and wallowed into the tail waves, gulping great slugs of river. My passengers sat uncomplaining in navel-deep, frigid water. Bless their hearts. The slightest wavelet slopped onboard. "We're sinking," I explained. They didn't seem to have any problem with that. Tuck rowed up and asked if we could make it to camp. "We might not make it to shore," I said.

We managed to get over to the right side, where we beached her on a flat rock and bailed her out. Duct tape and contact cement would serve to get the *Nechako* to the welders. The ten miles I rowed the *Nechako* that morning were the first and last time I would ever lay hand to her oars. And these days, I seldom volunteer for anything.

Editor's Note: To honor the wild rivers that sustain us and as a reminder of our desecration of them, Martin Litton—founder of Grand Canyon Dories—named each boat in his fleet after an environmental atrocity. The Nechako River is a tributary of the Fraser in British Columbia, which was impounded by Kenny Dam to form an enormous reservoir. In an ironic twist on Tim Cooper's metal-hulled protagonist, this dam was constructed primarily to supply power to aluminum refining plants.

Tim Cooper spent thirteen years as a professional boatman in Grand Canyon, where he met and married fellow guide Lori. Together they are raising a couple of promising boaters, one of each gender, near Dolores, Colorado. They spend as much time as possible on the rivers of the West. Cooper writes when he can but was spoiled by thirteen years of regular meals. His stories have appeared in *The Hibernacle News, Mountain Gazette,* and the Grand Canyon anthology *There's This River.*

taz

Jeri Ledbetter

TAZ IS AN OLD TRUCK like one my grandfather, Elwood Ledbetter, used to drive in the 1970s. It was a great vehicle in its day, but this is no longer its day. We climb into the bulbous white cab and slam both of the heavy doors two or three times before they remain closed.

This truck will start—or might not—in any gear. But it's hard to tell which gear it's in, as the indicator arrow is out of alignment. This makes it extremely important to double-check that it's in "park," as well as to stand mightily on the brake pedal as I turn the key. The starter whines inauspiciously at first, then reluctantly gains speed. I pump the gas pedal a few times, and just as I'm considering giving up the engine roars to a start.

I sit there for a while, suspiciously eyeing the cab. Last week when I started it, tendrils of smoke poured from a mysterious wire that emerged from the engine compartment between the seats. Not thinking, I reached for it, searing my fingers. I shut off the truck and pulled off the cowling to investigate. The thin wire was tied into the engine so it picked up a charge. Curious. Seeing no reason for its existence, I untied and removed it.

Reassured that, at least for the moment, the vehicle isn't going to burst into flame, I put the lap belt on as tight as it will go and back cautiously down the tree-lined driveway. I point the truck down the steep gravel road that leads toward the town of Crouch, Idaho. The brakes squeal and complain against the momentum of the massive vehicle, built in a day when steel was cheaper and gasoline seemed an infinite resource.

"Did we put brake fluid in today?"

"We topped it off yesterday," my sister Jacque reminds me. "So it should be okay."

I struggle with the gearshift, finally managing to clunk it into second, although the arrow now points at "neutral." The truck slows. I hold on to the lever, knowing that as soon as I let go it will pop back into "drive." I'm careening down a steep hill on loose gravel, approaching a sharp turn. I can't wrestle the wheel around with one hand, so I let go of the gearshift lever to grab the wheel. We speed up, again in "drive."

I claw at the lever, frantic to get back into low gear. I desperately want to stand on the brake pedal, knowing that would be disastrous. We lurch around the corner. I've seen Jacque make this drive in total confidence, with a beer in one hand. She sits in calm amusement in the passenger seat, and I contemplate uncharitable thoughts about her for a while.

Our kayaks, paddles, life jackets, helmets, and a cooler full of beer bounce around in the cavernous red box behind the cab. That's this truck's job these days—shuttling gear for day trips down the various forks of the Payette River in Idaho. Perhaps at one time it delivered fresh linen, or maybe Dolly Madison doughnuts. It would be well suited to such work.

Painted on a roll-up door on the back of the truck is a huge Tazmanian Devil, the cartoon character, pushing a striping machine. The previous owners used the truck in their business of marking parking lot spaces. We are confident that Taz is much happier shuttling boaters and gear.

After ten minutes of maneuvering down the steep, winding road, my palms sweating, we reach the asphalt that leads into town. I point the indicator at "neutral," as now we want to be in drive. We open all the windows, trying to blast air into the cab as the engine, eight inches off my right knee, heats up. I slowly gain speed, but not too much. The speedometer needle hasn't ventured above zero in years. After a few minutes my right foot, pressing the accelerator, burns from the heat. My little toe, naked in flip-flops and closest to the hot engine, can finally take no more. I move my foot away, but the accelerator pedal is stuck down so we don't slow. Slightly panicked, I move to the brake pedal as the engine continues to rev. Jacque, unruffled, says, "Oh, the pedal has been sticking. I tied a wire to it so you can pull it back up."

The wire eludes search. We're not exactly speeding down the road, but I am uncomfortable with the quality of vehicular control. Finally I reach down, grab the accelerator pedal, and pull it up. Then I remember the smoking wire that I removed last week. It had been attached to the engine, not the pedal, but that must have been Jacque's "emergency brake." With two mysteries solved and control regained, we continue toward the curious rural town of Crouch.

The entire town and its population of 154 is concentrated on less than half a square mile of land near the confluence of the Middle Fork and the South Fork of the Payette. The most prominent and heavily frequented establishment in the main square is the Longhorn Saloon. Other buildings are scattered about like afterthoughts—a hardware store, lumberyard, Laundromat, grocery store, and a library not much larger than an outhouse. The proximity to rivers, plus the town's layout, with all true necessities of life located within fifty yards of the saloon, is Nirvana to my sister. This is why she chose to settle here.

Crouch and nearby Garden Valley are populated mostly by rednecks. Over the past two decades, however, boaters discovered the Payette River and greater numbers began swarming into the community each summer. During the 1980s the disparate mix was volatile with mutual disdain—it was like living in a popcorn popper. Unattended kayaks were sometimes used for target practice; boaters referred to the area as "the Garden of Hate."

But kayakers and rafters kept coming. And although the locals couldn't fathom the draw—particularly since several boaters drown each summer— most grudgingly recognized that they were selling more food, beer, and gasoline. The owner of the saloon developed a fondness for thirsty kayakers, and an uneasy truce settled upon the valley.

Taz rattles through town, across the Middle Fork bridge, and out onto the highway that follows the South Fork upstream. The beauty of our put-in vehicle, I realize, is that neither the other boaters nor the rednecks know how to categorize us. We are Ledbetters, after all, granddaughters of Elwood from War Eagle, Arkansas. He owned a "movin' bidness" in Oklahoma, and talked out of the corner of his mouth like Johnny Cash. So we know the language. My sister works on oil rigs, can swear like a sailor, and frequently joins the locals for football night at the saloon. Yes, we kayak down the river, but neither the other boaters nor the locals know quite what to think of us. We therefore have earned tacit acceptance from both.

We careen into the parking area where we will launch our boats. I put the beast into "park" and thankfully turn the key. The engine grumbles, sputters, and stops. I grab the door handle, eager to escape, then remember it doesn't work—hasn't in years. I reach through the window and feel for the button on the outside handle, desperate to flee from the heat. Finally I wrestle the door open, my right foot still firmly on the brake pedal. I fumble behind the seat for the "Idaho emergency brake," a split pine log. I step out of the truck, chock the tire, and hear a sputtering sound. I follow the noise to the front of the truck and see a luminous green fluid spattering on the ground. Taz, like an out-of-shape distance runner, vomits radiator bile onto the pavement.

A group of young boaters stop pulling their kayaks from a Yakima roof rack atop their shiny red SUV to stare blankly at our ancient shuttle vehicle. A young man blinks at the widening green puddle and eyes me curiously. This truck likely ticked off its first hundred thousand miles before he stopped soiling his underpants. When we begin to unload our kayaks from the back of the truck, he understands, and goes about his business.

From the back of our beloved Taz, I retrieve a jug of antifreeze and put it on the seat to remind me to replace his precious fluids at the end of the day. He will need it for the drive back up the hill. The vomiting slows, and finally ceases.

We remove our kayaks and paddles from the van, ease them into the swirling river, and paddle downstream.

Jeri Ledbetter spent the early 1980s building mini-warehouses in Indianapolis, capitalizing on Americans' insatiable attachment to stuff. Those who knew her—with manicured nails, power suits, and spiky heels that matched her leather briefcase—would hardly recognize her today. She fled Indianapolis, landing in a community of folks who ran boats through Grand Canyon—misfits, geniuses, and lunatics, drunk on adrenaline and crazed with attention deficit disorder. She spent two years careening down the river in ponderous baggage boats, and the next twelve rowing wooden dories. As former director of the Glen Canyon Institute, she has followed the path of many: from river rat to activist. These days, as she eases into retirement from commercial guiding, she enjoys messing about in boats even more.

confessions of a cat lover

Eddy Fence

THE STRUCTURE PUT-PUTTING down the Colorado River below Moab resembles a Klingon mother ship. Or perhaps the microscopic view of some weird protein: Six H-shaped molecules are grouped around an elliptical one. The molecules are lashed to a motor-powered support raft. Bold letters on the tubes proudly announce the name of this traveling circus: OUTWARD BOUND.

This is, however, a private trip, an "invitational," solely consisting of Utah instructors who work for this well-respected outdoors education program. These people were *not* sent by their parents. They are here because they are fearless women and men. Almost all of them have as many river miles under their bow as wrinkles on their faces. But there are a few rookies along, as well as logistics staff who keep the Moab program base stocked with boxes of hard-tack (the infamous "plate armor"), dehydrated onion soup, summer sausage, two different kinds of flavorless cheese, and bottles of Pepto-Bismol.

Most of the figures on board recline to the stuttering of gangsta music punctuated by coughs from a four-stroke with a mind of its own. Only one man—the program director—stands proud and alert at the helm. Occasionally, he tilts the motor and lifts the propeller to avoid plowing sand-banks or gravel bars, which in a low-water year seem to make up the bulk of the river. The raft's repair kit holds a spare propeller, just in case.

They are on a three day-trip through Cataract Canyon, in November, after a long and rewarding summer season. A three-day trip through "Cat"—as river rats call it affectionately—is an unforgivable sin. But this is all the time they have, before they move on to more gainful unemployment, on the ski slopes of Colorado.

Their run through Cat is a first, a piece of history in the making. They are test pilots all, about to take on formidable whitewater, on crafts with a reputation for being "capricious." The boaters call them "paddle cats," or sometimes less flattering, "pieces of feces."

What exactly does a paddle cat look like? Imagine a medieval apparatus of torture, strapped to a set of inflatable tubes. Two seats resembling the rock-hard benches of workout machines ride atop twin pontoons. They are integrated with aluminum foot guards and front bars, under which the pilot may wedge his or her knees for leverage and balance. Between the tubes sags a drop hatch of very limited storage capacity. In it, watermelons, signal flares, Band-Aids, instructor manuals, driftwood for campfires, a drybag with costumes, or other essentials may be carried. Seated, paddlers are easily mistaken for Easy Riders of the waves, or for monkeys straddling oversized Hypalon bananas.

The frame of this Procrustes chair has been specifically designed for our program. No expenses were spared. Rumor has it that a miniaturized prototype was tested in the program director's bathtub, with a blow dryer operated by his girlfriend simulating strong headwinds. The laudable idea behind the design was that student pairs would have to communicate and cooperate to maneuver this . . . boat.

That is the theory. But it does not matter much yet, on this overcast late-autumn day. Right now, bags of peanut-butter-filled pretzels are ripped open, and the crew contentedly chews their cud.

Soon enough, we beach our unwieldy landing craft near a camp known as Tamarisk Hell. The scene that unfolds is reminiscent of the Omaha sector in Normandy on June 6, 1944. Instructors leap into the shallows. (At this time of year they make it to shore without being strafed by mosquitoes.) They unload the boom box, crates of food, stoves, pails, sleeping bags, gas cartouches, camp chairs, Therm-A-Rests, jerry cans of drinking water, a grill, and a fire pan; they clip life jackets, uncoil ropes, wrestle with tents or tarps. Someone in a rush finds a room with a view for the Thunderjug—a portable toilet required by Park Service regulations. One also may hear the troops refer to it more soberly as "The Unit." This device evolved from a primitive ancestor. Its prototype was the Groover, an army-issue steel box for grenade launchers, bearing a stenciled warning: CAUTION—EXPLOSIVES! Before the era of cushioned seats, lengthy sessions on this rocket box caused additional indentations in bare backsides—hence the name.

The evening is spent pleasantly enough, over tall tales and burritos, washed down with liberal amounts of mood-enhancing beverages.

NEXT MORNING, THE time has come to face harsh realities. The mother ship is broken up, and instructor pairs launch their cats. My copilot is Heather. Heather is half my age, twice as graceful, and works three times as hard at the Moab base. Her doe-brown eyes brim with an unspoken question. "You know what you're doing, right?" While I ready the boat, I try hard to avoid her gaze.

Our rig immediately displays typical cat behavior: It turns as if on a swivel, but the tracking sucks. I try my best to keep its nose pointed downstream. Unlike an oar-powered cataraft with a single boatman (ideally) in control, it is much harder to synchronize the paddle strokes of two people—especially when nobody wants to be captain. As a result, we zigzag down the placid river like a drunken water strider.

Despite that, my mind finds time to wander to Outward Bound courses I've worked with these craft. A favorite pastime of students on calm stretches is "flatwater polo." Two mobs of kayakers attempt to toss a water bottle between the tubes of a paddle cat, while "goalies" are defending that space viciously with their paddles. (We always make them wear helmets for this.) It's a free-for-all, without rules whatsoever. Tackling, biting, splashing, ramming, flipping, and dunking opponents, slinging mud or holding them back by their stern loops—anything goes.

Some cynics maintain that this is the only use for a P-Cat.

One time on the San Juan, after fierce upstream winds kicked the river into frenzy and formed an invisible wall, everybody had to de-board. With throw-bag ropes clipped to the frames, we waded the river, dragging cats downstream and to camp. Except when we stepped into holes in the river bottom, momentarily disappearing. A few kayakers even harnessed their boats in front of the deadweights, pulling them like building blocks for Egyptian pyramids.

Another low-water year, that one.

BEFORE I EVEN get to feel the onset of Quasimodo Syndrome, the rumbling of Brown Betty, our first rapid, jolts me from fond memories. The river is flushing with sediment from recent rainfalls upstream, and right now its eponymous convulsion resembles a Bloody Mary more than anything else. Those old backpacker knees hurt like hell, so I don't bother folding my six-foot frame into the contraption. I am sure I can ride this baby like a rocking chair.

Due to slight communication problems, we enter the rapid sideways. Next thing, I look up at the raft, catching Heather's expression, the age-old "Why are you leaving me at a time like this?" Her face could use some rouge, right now. "What do I do?" she yells over the din. "Try to keep the damned thing . . ." I swallow the rest of my answer with a pint-sized gulp of sediment-laden Colorado. At this point, I seriously consider finishing this trip in the water, safe and snug in my life jacket. But solidarity gets the better of me, and—with the help of my maiden in brilliant neoprene—I remount. No need to mention that I did not dress for a swim. I begin to shiver instantly, and my teeth are clacking castanet-style.

On a previous trip, I was lucky to retrieve a half-full pint bottle of Jim Beam doing rounds in an eddy. It probably washed out of a boat flipped by one of the munching holes for which this canyon is known. In my present state, some of that antifreeze would certainly come in handy.

Perhaps it would even improve my aim. Sober, I miss the fun of the standing monster wave at Rapid 10 by overcompensating for the current pushing outward at the bend. The half-moon shape of our camp directly below promises heaven. Everybody else who lands looks as dry and unconcerned as the surrounding desert.

Tonight's entertainment consists of various party tricks, including pouring blue flames from a bottle, and walking around with bottle caps in your eye sockets and belly button, without dropping them. The starred attraction is a grease bomb, which leaves everybody in awe and the performer with singed eyebrows. A proposal to run an obstacle course with quarters pinched between butt cheeks, to be dropped at the finish into a bucket, finds only limited resonance with the crowd. Most of us retire early, satisfied by an honest day's work and a steep learning curve.

ON OUR LAST day, a challenging trio of big drops awaits us, bellowing downstream. The lump in my stomach may not entirely be the result of over-dosing on syrup-drenched pancakes, eggs and Cowboy Coffee for breakfast.

Rapid 15 is merely a warm-up. Early river runners on a mining expedition christened this roller coaster in 1891. Their version of Kilroy-Was-Here—scratched on a boulder on shore—cheerfully reads: CAMP # 7, HELL TO PAY, NO. 1 SUNK & DOWN. "Number One" was half of their miserable fleet of wooden tubs. A purported ledge of pure silver in Grand Canyon they were chasing turned out to be nothing but mica and schist: fools' dreams glittering in the sun.

Four notorious marker rocks spiking this stretch of river are aligned like a baseball diamond. Perhaps the fact that I grew up playing soccer affects the nature of our run. While we are scraping first base the old Abbot and Costello routine flashes through my head. I don't know who or what is on first, but without the cat's foot guard, my toes and kneecap would be. This feels more like pinball than baseball.

"Left turn." "Not so much . . . I mean, *right* turn!" "STOP!" "Back . . . PADDLE!"

We barely miss the pitcher's mound, and a merciful current carries us clear of second base. Not exactly a home run, but we are alive.

While my brain soaks in a marinade of adrenalin, memories of a past near-disaster rear their ugly heads. Only a few weeks before, one of the rafts on a course had smashed sideways into first base. As a result, the metal pin of one oarlock broke, and the oar itself bent like putty.

But improvisation is a leitmotif in every river runners' life, a talent equally well applied in finance, dressing, cooking, car maintenance and courtship. With a dexterity acquired over decades in the Great Outdoors and somebody else's penknife, I sawed a length from bleached bones of driftwood that littered our beach. I whittled it down to the diameter of the fractured pin. Thrilled by my own cunning, I rammed it into the oarlock, then inserted our spare oar.

We pushed off into the current. After a few strokes my homemade splint shattered under the strain. Climbing back onto my seat from the bottom of the raft, I felt consoled that, at least, they don't chain us to the benches anymore. Not easily defied by the river's verdict, we replaced the useless joint with three buff paddlers on starboard. Under the scrutiny of other outfits our lopsided act negotiated the rest of the rapids with the grace of a crippled crab. The guides of the competition hooted and catcalled from recliners on shore, toasting our effort with cans of cold beer. Beneath life jackets adorned with graffiti and the company logo, chests inflated with pride. Not only had we saved face as individual boatmen once more, but also upheld the reputation of our fine outdoors program.

AT BIG DROP One, our only job is to keep her straight and not get bucked off. If I wore a hat, this is the part where I would slap my thighs with it, whooping and hollering. I feel like a centaur—half man, half . . . rubber duck.

Our run through Big Drop Two is so-so, but at least uneventful. Idyllic Little Niagara rushes by, too fast to allow us to make a mistake. The cat in front of us is less fortunate: It sits on a rock, tubes sticking half out of the water. The pilots shift their weight, frantically trying to wiggle her off—in vain. Eventually the captain steps out, onto the boulder. She puts some muscle to it, straining until I'm afraid her head might burst. When there is sudden movement, she almost misses the boat.

Then comes the *big one* of the Big Ones. Naturally, I/we miss the boulder-flanked entrance slot, running a pour-over this side of Mossy Rock instead. We stick both tubes almost vertically into the accompanying hole, leaning back in our seats like choreographed bull riders. In an out-of-body experience, I observe the peculiar response of the cat as it bobs back out with a corklike move. Before I have a chance to thumb my nose at Satan's Gut, we have been flushed out at the bottom of the rapid.

By now, my copilot has even stopped cursing me under her breath.

The worst lies behind us, or so we think. A rambunctious wind starts to blow, crimping the water's surface. It pushes the cats into a wide eddy, where they sit like decoy ducks. When I look to shore, the scenery still floats by—in the wrong direction. The oar-driven baggage boat manned by our junior instructor Mikey seems to fare slightly better.

Eternities of paddle strokes and teeth gnashing later the mouth of Gypsum Canyon cleaves sandstone parapets on river left. The four-day hike to the highway should feel like a Club Med vacation. I am glad I announced my intention to leave our party here, *before* the trip. Let nobody blame my Momma for raising a quitter.

I soon stand on shore, trying to straighten from my Neanderthal posture. Looking at boiling clouds the color of lead, I wonder what further boating adventures I shall miss. With a sigh of relief and a strange popping from my knee, I hoist my eighty-pound pack and wave the disappearing flotilla good-bye.

After stints as a wrangler, cop-in-training, potter, counselor of juvenile delinquents, river guide, Civil War reenactor, and conscientious objector, **Eddie Fence** is now considering a career as a haiku poet and hermit. Among his humble, temporary abodes, he has counted an Irish monastery; an oven-hot storage locker; an unheated sauna near the Arctic Circle; a houseboat parked on a ranch in British Columbia; and a blue hut—shaped like a Tootsie Roll— on the banks of the Rio Grande. Eddy has not driven a car since 1982, when the army forced him to. He currently lives out of his backpack, trying to keep things simple.

much ado with almost nothing

Abigail Polsby

(Dedicated to the wonderful people of Arctic Village, for lending a hand and making this fateful trip possible.)

SMOKE PLUMES FROM the handheld ground-to-air radio as I drop it, adding another burn hole to the already filthy bedspread. This is the same hotel where last year—after a month and a half spent north of the Arctic Circle—I walked into my room, exhausted, only to find puke on the bathroom wall and trash in the can.

So why return once more to this fine establishment, you may ask? First of all, this is the cheapest hotel in Fairbanks. Second, it is close to "Freddy's." And if you have ever been to Fairbanks, you know Fred Meyers is the only place you really need to visit if you are outfitting yourself and nine others for a twelve-day trip up north. Finally, the Gold Rush Motel is where my boss provides a room for his guides—probably related to reason number one. In my experience, it isn't half bad, better than most of the warehouses I have been put up in. To the Gold Rush's credit, it does boast its own liquor store, across the street from a bar with the same name. The bar harbors a dark and dingy restaurant that looks a lot like the rooms, but serves the best prime rib sandwich in town. What else could you possibly need?

My three-night stay here is about over, and I feel ready for adventure. I have checked the gear lists at least a dozen times. I have compared the "list-of-what-we-take-on-our-flight" to the "list-of-what-has-already-been-shipped-to-Arctic Village," our halfway point to the river we are about to float.

DAY ONE, 5 A.M. I am awakened by the sound of a jackhammer. Each time I try slipping back into sleep the jackhammer starts up and wrenches me out of it. I decide to get up and take advantage of the extra hour. After I ditch the melted radio in a trash can, I walk to Freddy's for some coffee; they have a Starbucks inside, of course. (Fairbanks is practically a suburb of Seattle.) I buy some motion sickness pills for the bush plane rides ahead. Then I head to the university district to stop by my company's storage shed. I pick up an extra tarp for shelter, and two tents that are marked for another trip. Call it a guide's intuition; I still don't know what impelled me to drive out there and take these things.

I rush back to the motel to meet the clients. They, too, look like the jackhammer roused them early, but at least appear ready to go. My assistant guide Nicholas resembles Santa Claus—or rather his corrupted twin, complete with ratty clothes, big silver beard, and a belly to match. On top of his looks, this morning he smells as though he indulged in some of the finer libations the Gold Rush has to offer. We all pile into some cabs and get a lift to the corner of the airport where bush planes land.

We load our gear onto a rolling cart and proceed to the scales. All clients have to step on the scale, and then weigh their personal belongings for the next few weeks. Each passenger has an allowance of forty pounds. I have been instructed to abide by this limit and charge clients the same as the flight company: $1.50 per pound over the limit, round trip. I was reprimanded last year for disregarding this rule. "Excuse me, I know you just paid close to four grand for this journey, but it seems as if you packed too many pairs of underwear, and I need to ask you for three more dollars." That just wasn't going to come out of *my* mouth this morning.

Soon we are droning in our twin-prop plane across the Arctic Circle, toward Arctic Village, the much-anticipated Athabaskan Indian village of about 150 Gwich'in. The Gwich'in still live a subsistence lifestyle largely dependent on the Porcupine Caribou herd and are therefore very much opposed to drilling for oil in the National Petroleum Reserve. They are generally accepting of travelers, understanding that the more people visit the neighboring Arctic National Wildlife Refuge, the more supporters are likely to enlist for their cause.

Nicholas and I find our pile of boxes and begin inventorying gear. "Boxes number 10 to 14 aren't here," he whispers. He is wise to keep his voice low. The clients are already anxious. He hands me a list of things that came in the boxes and another of those that didn't. The inventory of missing items is almost as long as my forearm. No group gear has arrived: The entire kitchen and all tents, bug shelters, tarps, repair and first-aid kits, library, water filters, extra paddles, and life jackets got lost in transit.

All we have at this point are the fresh groceries bought in Fairbanks and the extra gear I grabbed out of the shed this morning. There is also the stuff that *was* shipped, including camp fuel, dehydrated food, and—most important—our boats. Mind you, these are different boats than the ones I was told were shipped. We have one eighteen-foot Avon Pro raft sans thwarts and rigging (much too large a boat for the Kongakut, the river we are about to run), one twelve-foot Riken (much too small for the amount of gear we intend to tote downstream), a single inflatable kayak, ten life jackets, ten paddles, and one puny blow/suck pump. I try to remember what I brought as my own gear and how it might replace some of the missing group items. A quick tally shows that all of this is still insufficient to run a trip. But I am determined to make it work.

With two hours to spare before our shuttle flight to the put-in, I decide to walk to the post office, which huddles north of the airstrip. I approach an elderly gentleman and ask for a ride to "town." With a big toothless grin he waves me onto his four-wheeler. I swing a leg over as he pulls my arms tight around him and hits the gas. In the trail of dust we leave behind I notice a white puppy following as fast as his tiny legs carry him. I learn that "Ear" is my chauffeur's dog. We find Betty the postmistress, and inquire about packages labeled "10 of 14" through "14 of 14." I hand her my written confirmation of their arrival at Arctic Village.

She is on her lunch break right now, but tells me to jump into her truck. We drive to a shed at her house, where she keeps overflow and on-hold packages. Near desperation, I rummage through a mix of garbage, packages, and belongings, but only find packages for the next trip—all eight. I tear into them to discover nothing but dehydrated food.

Running out of time, I go into scrounging mode. I look around the shed and locate a cooler, a bag of plastic cutlery, as well as some paper plates. I ask Betty for these treasures, promising to return the cooler in ten days and to send her some new picnic ware from Fairbanks. "Of course you may borrow the cooler." She asks me what else I need and volunteers to introduce me to her neighbors, for some more loaners.

One of them takes us out back into *his* shed and donates a rusty Coleman two-burner camp stove complete with last season's fish skins caked to the top grill. It's perfect! I thank him profusely, take down his name, and draw a crude map, to remember where to return what to whom. The next neighbor lends a ladle and steps in as my escort, since it is time for Betty to return to work. My new guide is just that, as it would be inappropriate for me to go door to door by myself, without a tribal member. As we walk down the dirt road I am amazed by the fences surrounding bare yards: Rows of caribou racks from years past line streets and separate houses, strung out like the white picket fences of my New England youth. Inside one of these enclosures skinny chickens scratch the dirt around two large, silver feed bowls. I ask to borrow a bowl for three weeks, indicating I'd gladly settle for one of those in the yard. The man who answered the door disappears inside and returns with his wife. After a quick exchange, she hands me one crusty—yet also slimy—feed bowl. Of all the possessions I rounded up this is my prize. Oh, the salads I will serve in this bowl!

We move on down the street until it is time for me to abandon my mission and head back to the tarmac. The scavenger hunt has yielded a good load and my loot at this point almost makes the trip look possible.

Proud of my wares, I hitch a ride back to the airstrip. The pilot has already left on his first shuttle run, with Nick, some gear, and a few clients. The rest are calmly basking in the sun, reading next to piles of gear. I pace the airstrip one more time, scanning it for anything useful. I dig an old mug without lid from a trash pile, together with some aluminum foil and a pie tin. Scores of other items I unearth would be useful if they hadn't already been used for target practice.

I bump into Lady Luck again, in the guise of two hikers who just finished a two-week trek, and mooch a large plastic spoon and two Tupperware bowls. A group of birders also flew in, headed for the Canning River. Without self-restraint, I beg, and score two extra cups, a couple of spoons, a small pot, and *four* water bottles. I take their addresses, promise to return the goods, and return to our growing pile of utensils.

Next, I decide to write a letter to my friend and fellow guide Julie, who is still on the Kongakut but will take out in six days. She and I will be guiding the next trip together, and I hope she might dream up some sort of assistance. My letter is sprinkled with a fair amount of venting and invective, mostly aimed at our boss. I attach a wish list for things missing and one of supplies I pilfered from the next trip.

About an hour later Kirk—the pilot scheduled to pick up Julie—stops by. I hand him my letter, explaining the situation. Chuckling, he forks over the spoon his mother packed for his lunch. "It's all I have," he insists, and I refrain from patting him down.

As soon as the plane returns, we transfer clients and my motley collection of gear into its fuselage and take off. We touch down near the put-in late in the afternoon. Before our pilot takes off, he hands me his spare radio. It's a welcome replacement for the contraption that burned up in my Fairbanks hotel room. For good measure, he throws in his pot and emergency stove. He warns me that it is filled with some kind of airplane fuel, which tends to make the stove fussier than normal. "Better keep an eye on it," are his parting words.

Since another party is camped nearby, we decide to inflate boats, throw in the gear, and float downstream for a mile or two. While Saint Nick gives the river speech to the clients, I chat up our neighbors for yet another small pot.

Finally—having collected a semblance of kitchen—we are off.

We make it downstream for about two boat lengths before our flotilla grinds to an abrupt stop in the middle of the river. Grounded! The water is very low for this time of year, barely knee-deep in most spots. Everyone de-boards and we drag the boats. After hauling rafts loaded for a major expedition through an evening that seems endless, we arrive at a perfectly flat beach backed by a beautiful mountain. It has been hours, and we are only a half a mile from the put-in. "This is going to be a long trip," Nick mutters, mindful of the clients nearby.

Before we even unload, we circle up to discuss how camp will be organized. We already talked about bears and reiterate not to spread camp out too far. On this trip it's not much of an issue, because we only have three tents, for eight clients. We managed to bring enough shelters for everybody, but it will be cramped. "Bill, meet Jake and Sam your new tent buddies." For most, it's a flashback to summer camp, but nobody complains. Perhaps it has something to do with ferocious wild animals and the fact that it's warmer to sleep in a "puppy pile."

Though our nerves are on edge after an already long day, Nick helps clients to set up their tents. Meanwhile, I assemble our miserable kitchen inside a Megamid nylon shelter and fire up the stove. I use our pilot's, because the Coleman is still filthy, and I'm too worn out to clean it just now. As recommended by Flyboy, I watch the pot a few minutes—but it cranks like a jet engine. I leave to tend to a fussy zipper on a couple's tent.

By the time I reach their domicile it has almost taken off, and the wind just ripped an eight-inch hole into the rain fly. While I try to locate our "repair kit" (a euphemism for some duct tape wrapped around my water bottle), Sam compliments me on the nice fire in the kitchen. "Could we perhaps bring it out into the open to stand around?" he inquires politely. Fire? Did he say *Fire?*

I see jets of flame erupting from Dirk's MSR International stove—illuminating the Megamid like a Japanese lantern. Nick and I notice the conflagration at the same time. We sprint to tackle the fabric surrounding our cooking area. What is left of it still works as a shelter, but our kitchen now has a take-out window, a two-by-two hole in the back wall. During the commotion the stove fell to the ground, which extinguished its flame. But it is now clogged so badly with sand that—even after several cleanings with an irritating tool smaller than a paper clip—it never works again.

So I scour Betty's neighbor's stove, cursing and praying it will work. Still rusty and fishy, it fires up right away and never fails me for twenty consecutive days.

A mere hour and a half later, dinner is ready, and I set it on top of our cooler. I carefully place ten paper plates, ten plastic cups, and the same number of forks at the head of the line, along with a Magic Marker. As people wash up I muster a serious face. In my best hostess voice I explain that these are our forks and cups for the entire trip and that the plate would be for the first five days and that they all would get a fresh one for the last leg of the trip. "Everyone is responsible for his or her own plate. Write your name on it and keep it in a safe place. I will be setting up a dish wash down by the river and you are welcome to wash your plate. But be careful scrubbing it or it won't last." I explain that we are "traveling light."

With full bellies we crawl into our cramped abodes, and for the first time since I awoke at the Gold Rush, I sigh with relief. We are here! I realize that all the trouble of this very long day is worth the moment: the intense quiet and beauty of the Arctic.

Breakfast doesn't go as smoothly as dinner. Brewing coffee takes more than an hour, as I only have three very small pots and one thermos. Without filters, we are preparing it "cowboy style." This works great in large quantities, but is slow and tedious when one pot only holds two cups, and each person wants at least one refill, including myself. This is where Saint Nicholas comes to the rescue. He is a born storyteller, and a damn good one. He already was an accomplished boater when I was still wetting diapers and has stories galore, from all around the world. He can yarn through an entire meal, almost making you forget what you eat. Today, Nick is truly a godsend, because we are taking our breakfast in shifts. With our small pots it's the only way to get all of us food and coffee. The hot beverage turns into personal trauma. After all the trouble, the coffee melts our precious cups and scalds people's hands when I serve it.

I hand out Band-Aids, then open all of our food cans. I whip up a large bean salad off which we will live for the next few days and issue everyone an empty can. "They work great as mugs but tend to get hot," Nick tells them. "So you people better put on a glove or clean sock before you grab 'em."

When they do, it is quite a sight.

What started out as a logistical nightmare is still turning into a great trip. So what if I spend seven hours a day cooking? So what if our group looks as if it's been outfitted by the Salvation Army? The weather is holding and Nick and I soon establish a workable routine. In order to cook, Santa has to lie belly-down on the ground. Head propped on one elbow, beard dangling dangerously close to the flame, he stirs the pot with his other arm. His old boatman's back cannot handle hunching over the miniature stove, and it looks as if the cook regularly falls asleep on the job. I usually feel bad and end up doing most of the cooking myself.

Every day of paddling, we have to wake people up earlier, due to incessant and increasingly fierce afternoon winds. They blow from noon until midnight, and always upstream. By day four we are getting up around three to be on the river by six and make it to camp before Arctic midsummer light grazes the tundra horizon.

Whitewater day. Rearing to go, Nick and I wake the clients at two. We are afloat by three-thirty. The rapids are fun: Nobody falls asleep, and we have only one wrap in Big Mama. Sam, our largest client, climbs out of the boat to help pushing, but slips and plunges into the icy river. He drifts by my raft, and—with a bit of huffing and puffing—I succeed in pulling him in. It seems the biggest man is always the one going overboard. Murphy's Law, I guess. One of the rapids on the Kongakut is Eddy Out, named after a 350-pound boater who swam it involuntarily a few years ago. We tell Sam we'd consider renaming Big Mama in *his* honor.

Next morning we decide to sleep in, to give the galley slaves a well-deserved break. While we pack up camp, a plane passes us rather low. A figure hangs out of the cockpit, laughing and yelling. It turns out to be Clint, a friend and fellow guide. He drops two big red stuff sacks, and we only catch one word through the din: "Enjoy!" The plane is gone as quickly as it came. I pick up the first bag, and it starts leaking on me. Instantaneously, I feel engulfed by the perfume of cheap whiskey. Both care packages contain leftover goodies from Julie and Clint's trip, which just ended this very same morning. Chocolate, Tang, coffee, Macs-and-cheese, jam, tuna and booze all exploded on impact, creating a colorful mess. We root through the ooze, to see if anything has survived the delivery. The only items intact are the ones most important. I pull eight multicolored plastic plates out and hand them to Sam to rinse off in the river.

"Plates!" I beam. "Real plates!" By now, everyone's have begun to resemble paper towels held together with duct tape. The bag holds one more surprise— a large pot. I have never laid eyes on an object more beautiful than this dented and blackened vessel.

IT WAS ALL smooth sailing from there.

I NEVER DISCLOSED to anybody all the items missing on this trip. No professional guide would have. No refunds had to be given to clients who had spent half a fortune for a fully catered adventure. Trained to improvise, adapt, overcome, it was just another exciting challenge for us. One, however, I never wanted to experience again. The following season I started my own river company offering trips into the refuge. And I vowed to always bring a complete mess kit and shelter for everyone.

My second trip of the season went smoother, as Julie brought additional gear with the next group of clients to the put-in. I *did* return all of the items I had borrowed and gave Betty our leftover food and coffee to spread around town. She wanted her old plates back rather than accept new ones. I tried to convince her that they had no longer been usable and that what was left of them had been burned and their ashes sprinkled into the waters of the Kongakut River.

A NOLS semester in Wyoming was all it took for **Abigail Polsby** to ignore her East Coast roots and Skidmore College education to migrate west for good. After graduating from Evergreen State College instead, she joined the ranks of struggling outfitters by running backpacking and ski trips in Olympic National Park and the Cascades. As fate would have it, she discovered the lure of rivers. Passionate about water ever since, she has turned into a successful river rescue and wilderness first-aid instructor through her company Sierra Rescue. After realizing that trips cause fewer headaches when she organizes and leads them herself, Abigail became a partner in an Alaskan outfitter company—Arctic River Journeys.

rafting? schmafting! i want my river back!

John Nichols

THE LAST THING I promised my dying mother I never would do was go down the Wild River Section of the Rio Grande Gorge in Taos County in a raft. Why? Because I am a fly-fishing enthusiast, and there is about as much good blood between denizens of this specialized trade and river rats as there used to be love in the Old West between cattlemen and sheepherders.

And besides, *my* gorge is a deserted, nearly inaccessible, and luminous canyon devoid of all humans except me, the solitary angler. In the autumn I descend a dozen secret *bajadas* to fish for trout in an ambience that is shimmering and prehistoric. I stop often, holding my breath, awed as I absorb the beautiful loneliness. And I always know I am the first human intruder in that spot for centuries.

Nevertheless, life is convoluted and full of contradictions. In my case, love made me do it, pure and simple. I hate to admit it, but a trusted friend lured me onto the wild river in a large rubber raft.

Her name? . . . Betty Read. Her métier?—beagle, mouthpiece, law books . . . specializing in domestic relations. Her disarmingly simple come-on? "Wouldn't it be fun to take a raft trip down the Rio Grande?" Lightly she touched my shoulder, causing my heart to flip-flop.

"Isn't it dangerous?" I waffled.

"It's exciting," she replied.

"You're not scared?"

"I'm scared, but it'll be *exciting*," she insisted.

Not long afterward I spied a guy named Seaver Jones seated at a smoky bar in Taos. The Ragtime Kid was playing a song, so nobody occupied the neighboring stool. I flopped down like a fool beside this large and boisterous man, downing some potent amber concoction in swift neat gulps. "Seaver," I whispered, "I know you are a river runner. Tell me all about floating the gorge from Arroyo Hondo to Pilar . . ."

For an hour that born-again evangelical water sprite calmed my fears and pricked my interest indeed. He spoke of Canada geese and their delicate goslings, of once domestic goats running wild among the boulders, of bald eagles cruising overhead, and of the thrill to be had in Powerline Rapids. When at last I skulked stealthily from that murky bucket of blood, I was a believer. Posthaste I telephoned some fellow travelers in Denver, and, after I painted a glowing picture, Rod and Mari and Wayne and Debbie agreed to join Betty and me for this once-in-a-lifetime escapade.

And at 8 A.M. on Memorial Day, 1983, with our hearts in our throats, our cameras in hand, and a serene early-morning sun pulsing warmly overhead, the six of us found ourselves gathered in the Tennis Ranch parking lot north of Taos, nervously awaiting our destiny in the shape of a big old ramshackle yellow school bus.

FAR FLUNG ADVENTURES had a reputation for being one of the best companies on the river in Taos. I had chosen it for that reason, and also because they advertised an early launch time. I wanted to float in morning purity, long before other rafters had polluted the Rio's precious bodily fluids. "Go early," Seaver Jones had intoned, "and you will see the Canada geese and their goslings. You might spy the wild goats among the rocks. And perhaps you'll even catch a glimpse of a bald eagle."

Right on time, here came the lumbering bus (full of jabbering recreators) loaded on top with four rafts and rowing frames and plenty more erudite paraphernalia.

"Howdy," the head honcho, Steve Harris, said.

Jovially masking our queasiness, we hopped on board. It was good to feel safe in the hands of an expert like Steve, a lanky and leathery man, brown all over, and right friendly to boot. He had an aura of being in control:

professional, good-humored, no nonsense.

Brimming with overconfidence, then, our conveyance rumbled off from the Tennis Ranch parking lot.

Three miles south of Arroyo Hondo a howitzer shell clobbered us. The bus shuddered, rattled, and swerved. A rubber raft spun off the top and bounced in the roadway. Another raft flip-flopped upside down, slamming into the western windows, and dangled there. A steel rowing rack clattered to the pavement as we skidded onto the shoulder. Somebody connected to Far Flung Adventures muttered with alarm: "Holy cow, *this* never happened before."

Our guides worked feverishly to change the blown-out tire and clear detritus off the highway. They clambered over the bus, jockeying clumsy rafts back into position, lashing them down tightly. Meanwhile dozens of buses, trailers, RVs, pickups, and assorted four-wheelers chugged by us full of jeering tourists and hooting oarsmen from other outfits.

But quickly we hit the road again. And as we descended the winding dirt path toward the John Dunn bridge west of Arroyo Hondo, I clasped Betty's hand tightly, worried about the danger involved. What about the terrible Ski Jump Rapid and the hellacious Powerline maelstrom? Maybe our venture was foolhardy, doomed, snakebit. Perhaps we should cancel at the last minute and—

Betty squeezed my sweaty fingers. "Don't worry, John Nichols; all is well."

On that cue, we turned a corner onto the bridge and entered a scene that I can only compare to the sacred Ganges at Varanasi in India at ritual burial time.

AS OUR BUS inched slowly backward down a side road west of the bridge toward the launching beach, I stared in horror at a riot of buses, RVs, trailers, motorcycles, and children. My god, *look at all those big adults, fat adults, half-dressed adults, apprehensive adults!* Twenty rubber rafts of various dimensions and colors were lined toe to toe along the shore. Swarms of tanned, healthy river rats in shorts, sandals, and yellow rubber boots were trying to act good-natured in this traffic jam, bumping into each other and jostling for room, obviously desperate to get on the water. Boys from the Bureau of Land Management, jaunty in government shirts and ironed shorts, scurried hither and yon, fretfully checking people in, casting aspersions, issuing veiled threats, and wondering how in hell things had come to such an impasse.

The guides hustled rafts off the tops of buses and began to pump them up, loading gear, tying down ammunition boxes for cameras, heaving in coolers of beer and sandwiches for lunch. Gas generators wheezed and coughed. Skinny and fat and perplexed and pink people were lined up twenty deep, waiting to use portable outhouses supplied by our friendly government agency in charge of the fiasco. Transistor radios played heavy metal music, country-and-western ballads, good old rock and roll. Everybody was choking to death on the dust. One hyperactive little kid kept firing a toy machine gun.

Steve Harris wrestled a rowing frame onto our raft, secured it expertly, and slipped in the oars. In the background animated human beings wearing tank suits, Bermuda shorts, purple sweat suits, yellow diving suits, tattered blue jeans, cowboy hats and baseball hats and magenta bandannas took thousands of pictures of each other taking pictures of each other applying suntan lotion to each other. Offshore, a bunch of kayakers, sleek seals compared to us ungainly whales, slithered on the wide, passive river, warming up, doing rolls, spinning around, floating sideways, checking their gear, their muscles, their egos.

Rod and Wayne and Mari and Debbie went for a climb in the rocks to see if they could, just before departing, inadvertently step on a prickly pear cactus or brush their palms against a nasty cholla.

The plethora of kids carelessly prancing through the turbulent scene caused me to remark to myself: "You know, maybe this isn't as all-fire dangerous as I thought."

Betty wandered off a ways, lit up a Kent, then coolly surveyed the zany carnival scene. Finally, by way of comment, she said, "Huh."

SUDDENLY STEVE HARRIS called, "Okay, let's go." In seconds we tumbled into the raft, pushed off, and were riverborne. My heart began racing again. I grabbed the hand straps and tensed to hold firm and weather the whitewater, screaming in excited frenzy as we plummeted through billows of angry waves just inches from certain death among jagged boulders.

Instead we began to float south with almost somnolent stateliness, a sensation about as exciting as snoozing on a waterbed.

The river was high and muddy. In the bland blue sky the sun shone brightly. It was eighty degrees. And rafts similar to ours stretched bumper to bumper fore and aft as far as the eye could see, like a train of barges toting a corpulent and noisy cargo of Texas beef toward New Orleans.

"This is nothing," Steve said. "One Labor Day, I eddied out and there were so many boats on the river, I couldn't get back into line for an hour."

Rod, Mari, Wayne, Debbie, and Betty glared at me, The Organizer. I shrugged, pointing ashore: "Look at the geese." Sure enough, there they were, those fabled Canadian honkers and a couple of goslings, resting peacefully near the old Manby Hot Springs. They stared as we floated by.

"Throw 'em some peanuts," I heard a voice say. "Anybody got any peanuts?"

Apparently not. But the party that swirled laconically up on our starboard side had bags full of Cheez-It crackers, fried pork rinds, barbecue chips, and Doritos, which they were washing down with lite beer. The handsome guide at the oars called with cheerful sarcasm, "Hey, gang, aren't we having fun?"

We responded, "You bet . . . yessir . . . *wow!*"

My pulse really slowed down; my heart quit fibrillating. Betty Read, master of the subtle remark, observed, "I should have brought my bathing suit." Wayne hollered, "*Pass me back one of them brewskis, cowboy!*"

We opened the cans and drank a toast to Rod, who perched nervously on the gunwale of our Avon Pro. He was outfitted in a cute green rubber suit intended to protect him from the splashing water.

We drifted for five monumentally uneventful miles and then tragically ran out of beer. Our oarsman advised, "Keep your eyes open for beer cans. Sometimes they fall overboard. They look sort of like bubbles. If they're low in the water, grab 'em, because that means they're full of booze."

Steve Harris is an amiable guy. He talked about his life on rafts in the Big Bend of Texas; he outlined plans for an Alaska float later this year. Betty bummed cigarettes from Steve, and Wayne regaled us with tales of his truck-driving days for the Teamsters. Mari and I took pictures of other rafts and rafters taking pictures of us. Rod began to feel pretty stupid in his green rubber suit that was absorbing sunshine and drenching him in sweat.

I yawned. In fact, I could not stop yawning. An hour passed . . . and then another.

We scanned the shore for other rare fauna, but all that came into view were rafters eddied out, noshing cookies, drinking beer, burping, slopping on the suntan lotion, climbing rocks, masticating pensively, staring back at us.

"You know," I said, "this doesn't exactly feel like a wilderness experience to me."

As yet one more raft filled with tubby jovials consuming baloney and cheese and Schlitz malt liquor twirled lazily by us, Steve pointed upward: "Are those eagles?" We squinted and agreed that yup, those two minuscule blips soaring eight thousand feet above our heads were probably golden eagles.

Then *that* thrill was over and the day settled back on top of us like a bottle of liquid Valium.

"I bet there's a coyote around the bend," I joked. "Preening on the bank, checking out its coiffure in a mirror, begging for little cans of bean dip, slices of white bread, and Hershey bars."

We decided the rafting companies had chipped in to rent the wild geese we'd seen earlier. Pretty soon a couple of trained beavers in Lycra miniskirts would be doing a cancan dance on the beach while five dozen tourists filmed them. After that, a pet deer with scurvy might appear munching on Bunny bread wrappers. And a mangy raccoon, at the end of a tether, would pluck salami from our greasy fingertips, then gleefully smoke a cigarette.

Some clown started yodeling, "*Oh, bury me not on the lone prairie . . .*"

ABRUPTLY STEVE WARNED, "We're approaching a rapid. Keep your eye on the right, and around that rock outcropping you'll see a nesting water ouzel."

Biff, bam, bumpety-bump, the raft squizzled into some whitewater. We woke up and searched for the "water ouzel nest" but found nothing. The rapids lasted two and a half seconds.

"That's *it?* That's a *rapid?*" Suddenly I yelled, "*I want my money back!*"

"Oh, there are better ones up ahead," Steve drawled. "You'll like Ski Jump."

But as we approached Ski Jump, I griped, "This isn't Ski Jump. This is the Big Trout Riffles south of Caballo Trail. Right here in low water there's a beautiful island of white stones in the middle of the river. I usually wade over to the island in water up to my thighs and fish the riffles on both sides. They're full of brown trout. Then south of the island there's a wonderful rock garden of fast-riffle water. I always hook a big one."

Today there was no island, no rock garden, no distinguishing features at all. Just the high muddy river boiling along carrying four dozen floating cocktail parties composed of obnoxious cultural imperialists wearing orange life jackets, Bermuda shorts, and yellow John Deere caps. Our raft heaved up, slewed sideways, bounced left, spun crazily, lunged and bucked twice, then skidded into smooth water again. We had just started to shout, "Eyeow!" when it was over.

Mari cried, "That's it? That's Ski Jump *Rapid?*"

Steve explained that there are different classes of rapids, numbered I through VI. What we had just come through was a Class III rapid. We immediately demanded some Class IV, V, and VI rapids; we wanted some *action*. Steve said, "Well, there's Powerline still. But right now we're gonna dock the raft and eat."

WE NOSED IN among a flotilla of lolling boats and toddled ashore like good children. They fed us baloney and cheese and salami sandwiches with imported mustard and mayonnaise, lettuce and tomatoes and sliced ham, apples and oranges and various juices and more beer. Then we lounged on the rocks with eighty other Joe Blows from Peoria ordering kayakers, "Do a roll, do a roll!" Usually they obliged, tipping over, then flipping upright again. They grinned as we clapped and cheered.

"Reminds me of the Colorado," Steve said. "Sometimes it gets real crowded. Often when we ran out of beer, we'd send the kayakers over to the big rafting camps and have them do rolls in the river for beers. The campers would cheer and toss in the cans, and they'd bring 'em back to us."

To Betty, I murmured, "This scene is so goofy and bizarre, it's downright campy." Betty glanced sideways, letting smoke trickle provocatively from her mouth, and, with just the hint of a sardonic smile, she whispered, "That's right,

John Nichols."

A teensy cloud appeared in the bright blue sky. We munched on apples as Steve recounted a dream that a fellow guide, Del DuBois, had once had. Del was rowing a raftload of people downriver. The gorge was quiet. All of a sudden he peeked into the water and blinked—what was *that*? For a ways he tracked a floating object and finally realized it was a Butterball turkey. Puzzled, he let it pass by and disappear downstream.

He had not progressed much farther, however, when—what was this? Another one? And sure enough, a big plump Butterball turkey twirled lazily past the tips of his dripping oars. Next a whole drove of the plucked birds bobbed into view and disappeared downstream. With that, Del realized the gobblers were prizes, released by the government as rewards to the rafting companies that deigned to tackle this sleepy river. Trouble was, when he plucked them out of the water they were always a tad rotten.

At which point he woke up.

Another diminutive cloud shyly appeared and a faint breeze riffled the water as we clumped lethargically back into our raft. "What's this bailing bucket for?" I joshed. "In case somebody vomits from boredom?"

And off we sailed on the lazy currents, accompanied by dozens of other jocular rowdies who by now had a thorough buzz on. Violet-green swallows darted gracefully over the water. I grumbled dourly, "If I had a cane pole and some chicken gizzards, I'd start jigging for catfish."

PRETTY SOON WE noticed some rafts had stopped along both shores and people were changing clothes, donning wetsuits and other rain gear.

"What's that all about, Steve?"

"Oh, they're just preparing for Powerline."

The sky went black: *Boom!* A stiff wind leaped upriver against us. The temperature dropped thirty degrees in five minutes. *Ouch.*

But we still felt pretty wiseapple. During our next scoot through mild whitewater, I stood up, snapping pictures. Wayne rode the back hump of the raft like a bull rider, grabbing a loose rope with one hand, his other appendage swinging free, while we screeched, "*Don't touch the bull with your left hand!*"

Then Powerline arrived. I had just begun to rise for another candid snapshot when we did a nosedive into an eight-foot-deep gulch. Betty lurched two feet into the air; I pitched across the bow as Rod toppled toward me, and we collided; I clobbered him on the head with my camera, knocking off his glasses, and we both swallowed a gallon of water and fell to our knees as the raft pitched riotously, slithered and bounced over a dozen mammoth boulders, and Wayne—none too soon—grabbed his loose rope with both hands, both knees, and, no doubt, both buttocks.

"Man overboard!" came the cry from a trailing raft.

"We got a swimmer," Steve Harris observed. "Let's haul him in quick. And bail your asses off, please."

Expertly, in the churning water, he waffled us sideways and reached the swimmer; Wayne and Debbie hauled him over the side. The guy was exhilarated. Steve barked, "Come on, bail harder—I can hardly control the boat."

So I bailed, then Betty bailed while Rod fumbled in the water for his glasses. Nobody wisecracked about using the bucket for boredom vomit. The swimmer, a complete idiot, chortled, "*Whee!*" at every lunge and buckle. Wayne pitched forward, then lurched backward, then jerked sideways: "Yikes!"

Powerline endured only a moment, then we had to eddy out again. A teenage girl in another boat had broken her collarbone. She'd lost her grip in a whirlpool and slammed into an ammunition box full of cameras. Steve and Debbie (a doctor) leaped out . . . and they sat her arm in a sling while I scrambled up and down the boulders, trying to get warm. The suddenly dark day had turned bitterly cold. I was drenched, rain was falling, icy wind whipped against me. I had goose bumps the size of nipples on every inch of skin. My fingers had lost their feeling up to the *elbows*.

Looking mildly concerned, Steve returned to our raft. "That's the first I ever had a swimmer *and* an injury at the same time," he said. "Come on. Hop in. Chop-chop."

BACK ON THE river our journey became excruciatingly painful. We bounded, flopped, and twirled, taking wave after wave in our faces. Most of us wore only T-shirts, shorts, and sneakers. Everybody turned blue. Tossing and twisting and bailing frantically, we hung on for dear life. I gave up trying to snap photographs. Every time we chucked out the water we'd hit another pocket, spin, splash, and sputter like spastics, take on more river, gulp traumatically, and commence bailing again.

"*More!*" we cried deliriously. "Come on, Steverino, give us something better and *bigger!* We want some *Class V* water, man. Isn't there any *Class VI* hereabouts?"

Waves smashed into our teeth, driving water like splinters down our throats, into our crotches, against our ankles . . . and hypothermia became a serious consideration.

I noticed—in the middle of all this—that Steve Harris was working hard at those oars, trying to keep us under control. And I realized—*duh!*—that maneuvering a boatload of half-snockered smart alecks safely through all that angry water was not easy. It took strength and know-how and plenty of moxie, too.

One rapid followed another, now, fast and hectic. We bounced high, bounced hard, held on; Betty almost got thrown overboard. We would have enjoyed it a whole lot more if we hadn't been so stinking *cold*. Rod's weenie rain suit didn't seem all that stupid anymore. My very *bones* shuddered. How come nobody had instructed us beforehand to dress up like rubber penguins?

The last rapid (*Finally. Thank Christ!*) occurred where the Pueblo River joined the Rio Grande. A hundred spectators populated the shore, taking photographs: I shot them a birdie. One last chilly thrill elicited a final shriek—then we arrived at the takeout point a few yards beyond the Route 96 bridge north of Pilar. By then we were so soggy and frozen our tongues had turned *white*.

Another amazing zoo awaited us. Boats lolled everywhere. Bewildered, frozen, drenched-and-catching-pneumonia tourists stumbled dazedly from rafts. Bedraggled, completely disorganized, the ensemble onshore could have been a decimated Normandy landing, or perhaps a comical retreat from Dunkirk filmed by Mel Brooks. Rain pelted down unmercifully. My chattering teeth sounded like frantic tap dancers.

With numb fingers our palsied crew grappled for drenched gear and ruined cameras as we floundered clumsily from the raft. "Bye," Steve chortled. "Thanks for choosing Far Flung Adventures." We staggered through the miserable crowd, searching for our bus. But when we got there we couldn't leave right away, because it took ages to maneuver the broken-collarbone girl on board. Then a hobbling kayaker appeared, his thigh all bandaged, probably hiding a broken femur. He collapsed on the seat in front of me. "Where did it happen," I asked, "at Powerline?"

"Naw, I negotiated that fine. Then I was just standing on the bank, watching the others go through, when some klutz kicked loose a rock and it bounced off my leg."

We made the return trip in a blinding deluge. The windshield fogged up and our driver could scarcely see. We remained seated, stunned, dripping on the slimy floor. Rain harsh as hail clattered against the tin roof. The exhausted passengers stared vacantly ahead like concentration camp zombies.

Mari and Debbie rasped hoarsely, "We're staying at the Sagebrush and they have a hot tub. We are gonna get off there and just lie in the warm bubbling water for hours and hours and *hours*."

The bus halted to set them free. They invited Betty and me, but we declined; I had to pick up my truck at the Tennis Ranch. Our fellow travelers wobbled bowleggedly toward the hotel like football players after losing the Super Bowl. Betty Read remarked coquettishly, "They're thanking you for this experience, Johnny."

We next stopped at Holy Cross Hospital. Helped by a pretty Far Flung Adventurer, the wounded limped inside. When she returned, the blond aide murmured, "Jeez, there's all *kinds* of victims in there. One lady busted her nose rafting; her face is a royal mess."

Finally, totally burned and drained, we reached the Tennis Ranch. Betty and I crawled painfully inside my truck, turned on the whirring heater, and headed home, feeling keelhauled, bruised from guggle to zatch, achingly cold and defeated.

"Well," I chattered triumphantly, "did you like *that*, Betty Read?"

She glanced at me, sticking her svelte tongue pensively between her teeth. Then her eyes sparkled with a mischievous gleam and her lips turned upward in a sweet, mocking smile: "Sure Johnny. I had a ball."

At home, I called Rod and Mari and Wayne and Debbie at the Sagebrush Inn. "Boy," I told Mari enviously, "I bet you all really enjoyed that wonderful hot tub."

"No, we did not," she whimpered. "The damn thing is broken."

I SUPPOSE THE River Gods had tried to teach me a lesson—and perhaps they succeeded. In a pinch—yes—I could understand the lure of whitewater. Nevertheless, I had lost something precious on that trip down the Rio Grande: a sense of place, inviolate, majestic, solitary. In just a few hours the "wild" and "inaccessible" gorge had been made smaller and more mundane for me. Too many people with nonchalant attitudes had used the river for thrills that had nothing to do with the awe and respect I had built up for it since arriving in Taos years ago.

But folks like myself are an anachronism. No doubt beauty ought to be shared, even if the sharing destroys the mystery that made it lovely in the first place.

And anyway, human perturbation is transitory. Nature always heals herself. To prove it, last night I had a dream.

It was autumn again, the river low and clean and clear. All rafters were gone, silence reigned, and the trout had begun to rise. Alone, I descended a steep *bajada*, rigged up my rod and reel, and, dwarfed by the magnificent high walls of the deserted canyon, I cast once more into the tumbling breakers. In no time, of course, I hooked a big one and played it for long minutes, scrambling spiritedly over boulders as it dragged me downstream—

Until finally, triumphantly, I swung my mammoth and noble adversary into a shallow alcove. Then I reached down and grasped gently and lovingly by the gills . . . *one of those friggin' Butterball turkeys!*

A deeply rooted Taoseño, **John Nichols** has celebrated the Land of Enchantment and its ethnic mix in image and word—for over thirty years. In addition to his best-known work, *The Milagro Beanfield War*, he has authored numerous novels and books of nonfiction, including *The Last Beautiful Days of Autumn* and *On the Mesa*. This trout enthusiast, naturalist, and political activist has managed to maintain his integrity and sense of humor despite a tangle with Hollywood and the increasing commercialization of his home pueblo.

beer and dinner

Chad Niehaus

THE SEASON HAD grown into an extension of my body. This reflection of me had become paramount to my existence. I wanted everyone to know that this was how I lived, that these things were what I considered important. I wanted a common passerby to see the sparkle of the river in my quick glance and instill in them a desire to experience a place like I do. My hands had roughened, my skin had grown dark, and the confidence that resided deep within me surfaced each morning before I opened my eyes and stayed with me until I laid my head down again. I had developed friendships with people who shared stories to make you weep, guffaw, and admire. I had learned from these characters that above all you must possess a deep sense of respect for special places and everything that depends upon them.

A plan made prior to accepting the job of Westwater river ranger was now · taking shape. Summer was coming to an end and the steady traffic of class registration, health insurance, and other mailings connected to graduate school reminded me that I was obligated to another place, another life. I suddenly questioned this shift in lifestyle vehemently. It felt reassuring to have such a complete plan when I was making it, but now that I was in the middle of its execution, I was seriously considering a bailout. My current job and residence created a smile that hadn't been there for a long time. I was earning money, I was working, I was doing good things, and I *was really enjoying myself.* If it was contentment I was chasing after, well, I had found it. I knew this job would change my perspective of "work" forever. The next time I considered employment that would be a "good career move," my hopes would race back to the time when I was earning enough to live and living enough to be fully satisfied. This experience was going to make it painfully difficult to enter Cubicle Land, a dreadful place that seemed to be eagerly awaiting my inevitable arrival.

My fate was essentially sealed. I had gone through the steps to make all of this happen, and would presumably give myself a black eye if I pulled out now. But the pain of detachment started to pulsate as I wrapped my mind around the idea of taping the box shut that contained my beaten river shorts, my sun-bleached cowboy hat, bug-stained and water-warped paperbacks, and a voluminous collection of memories created on and off the river. I couldn't do it, not yet anyway. I extracted the shorts and hat from their place of safety. One more run through the canyon was in order to feel right about this. I needed to say farewell and absorb another dose of the place's mystical elements that would monopolize my thoughts while I was away. It would give me a chance to say thanks.

I donned my sweat-stained and faded polyester button-up ranger shirt for a final patrol of Westwater Canyon. I was still not entirely comfortable with the concept and statement of a collared short-sleeved shirt tucked into shorts, but this was the image the Bureau of Land Management was aiming for. This was the look that conveyed bureaucratic competence and demanded public respect and adherence. Besides, who was I to question the fashion sense of the United States Government? My irrepressible quest for personal expression was pushing it as it was, with shorts depicting an aquarium scene and flip-flops conspicuously revealing my big toenail painted a low-key cosmic blue.

Routine duties had consumed the bulk of yet another beautiful day in the desert. I had spent it dusting, mopping, and polishing the trailer that had been home for the past six months, preparing it for the next damned lucky resident. It also took time to put the last touches of paint on a personalized oar blade that would be added to the ranger station alumni wall. Since the shadows were growing long I loaded dinner, breakfast, and my ammo can full of river life's necessities into the ranger raft. I shouted a word of appreciation to Alvin, a longtime ranger station resident, for giving me a hand with the shuttle and sympathizing with my likely-futile-but-worth-it-anyway attempt at closure. I kicked the river's edge and floated into a heavy world of reflection, determined to come to grips with my situation along the way.

The current was strong enough to let me stay off the oars, so I sat cross-legged, sipped a cup of milk tea, and slipped past what were now intimate features of the canyon. I watched cliff swallows depart their mud nests to graciously consume swarms of busy gnats along the river's glistening surface. I drifted past the spot where not too long ago four mule deer had ferried across the river a hundred yards in front of me. I took a head count at the great blue heron rookery. I marveled at the cottonwood and willow gallery highlighted by the soft, late-afternoon glow.

As the boat spun slowly around, I spotted a dot of a woman running frantically up and down the beach at the campsite known as "Fault." Upon seeing me, she waved her arms wildly and leaped into the air. The arm wave was close enough to textbook to signal that my presence was needed at camp. I pulled on the oars and headed in the direction of the distress signal. Words were cast my way, but the moan of the oarlocks and the distance between us made it impossible to understand any meaning. I shook my head, pointed to my ear, and yelled *"Louder!"* At this, the woman reared back and let out with everything she had. Two of my favorite words made their way to the ranger boat, words that always sound sweetest spoken in a female voice, *"Beer"* and *"Dinner."* What a treat, I thought, to be invited over for a warm meal and alcohol served by an enthusiastic and striking river goddess.

I moved the boat swiftly and surely, smiling at the luck of it all. I looked over my shoulder once more and noticed that the woman was still pacing back and forth, running from one collection of gear to the next. It pained me slightly to see that she was making such a fuss over little old me. I drove the boat high onto shore and performed a daring and graceful "tube bounce" exit, landing solidly on the beach with bare feet and a grin to make even the most ardent Ani DiFranco devotee go soft with yearning.

No words were offered to me, neither from the woman nor the family huddled by the commercial raft. But several trembling fingers of various sizes pointed toward the dinner table. Having nothing to refer to but my gut, I walked toward the roll-a-table in eager anticipation, rubbing my hands of any river dirt that might get in the way of enjoying a freshly cooked meal. Upon arrival at the dinner table, though, I was dismayed to find nothing but crumbs, not even enough for a light snack. Bowls were turned over, scraps of tortilla were strewn about, and I couldn't find a cold beer anywhere. I turned around and flashed a look of confusion at the raft guide. I watched her eyes grow large. She tilted her head to the side and motioned with her chin a little beyond me and just to the right. Must be more on the stove. I turned to prepare a plate and suddenly locked eyes with another dinner guest. He was roughly my size but seemed to be much more assertive and stronger. As he headed toward the table for another helping I reacted the only way I knew how: I stood way up high on the tips of my toes, puffed up my chest to its full capacity, waved my arms, and let out a booming blabber of gibberish.

As he continued his approach, absolutely unimpressed with my display of machismo, I had to smile. It was now quite clear that I had not in fact been invited over for beer and dinner. Instead, a bear was eating these poor people's *comida Mexicana*. I ballooned and shouted once more, this time louder and fiercer. I reached down and grabbed a skillet that had been licked clean of frijoles and pounded on it with a wooden spoon.

Behind me, an uncertain moan grew to a ferocious shrill howl. I looked back and saw the crazy-eyed guide gaining speed toward the bear and me, kicking up plumes of sand with each lunge. Impressed and intrigued, I joined her as she passed and contributed a wavering growl indicating, I hoped, power and immensity, not puberty. The bear looked at us, we looked at each other, and just like that the guide and I were digging our heels into the sand in true cartoon-braking fashion. We skidded to a stop within smelling distance of the beast, which hadn't even moved so much as one of his enormous muscles as a result of our storming. We stood our ground and profanely described all of the various places the bear could go besides right next to us.

Being a sensible bear, the seventh F-bomb was one too many. He huffily turned his shoulder to retreat to the few scraps of fajitas that remained in a tuft of tamarisk. We needed this bear to run away much farther, though, so he wouldn't develop a habit eventually leading to his demise. This was my cue. I brought back my shaking hand and held it high in the dusky air. Then I belted out a yodeling battle cry and delivered my big old hand squarely on the visitor's rump. It remained there long enough to feel his substantial body heat and coarse wiry hair. This bright idea triggered a unique amalgam of surprised gasps from the still-subdued and concerned family, a soft "whoah" from the guide, an "uhhhhh" from me, and a primeval grunt of disapproval from our hairy friend. The noise, however, was more impressive than the results. After three more ass-slaps and nothing to show for them but louder bear groans, it felt like time to switch tacks.

The guide suggested we remove the temptation of food and humans altogether and pack up camp. Hearing this, the family showed obvious relief and was suddenly more than happy to do anything that would speed up their departure from this different and definitely not-in-the-brochure experience. The kids hefted their little matching drybags back to the raft, the parents broke down the tent, and the guide disassembled the kitchen. I remained on bear duty, shadowing his movements and engaging him in a soft discussion about why he really needed to head back up to his home on the Uncompahgre Plateau to pick up where he left off. Once the raft was rigged and ready to go, I raised my hand one last time. Blackie had gotten the picture, though. I didn't need to follow through this time. As he sauntered away, I wished him good luck and returned to the ranger boat.

While we floated together toward their second attempt at camping in the wilds, the now fiercely brave kids chattered excitedly about the close call. The parents were still a little shaken. They wanted reassurance from their guide that the bear wasn't going to follow them down the canyon. "We won't see him again," she replied with confidence, "'cuz we'll be a mile downstream and on the other side of the river." I concurred with her wild-hair guess by nodding slowly with squinted eyes, my favorite and most convincing impression of someone who might actually know what he is talking about.

Once we arrived at Miner's Camp, and the family's anxieties had mellowed to a tolerable level, I thanked everyone for a memorable evening. I lingered after making my closing statement, assuming an engraved invitation to the "we survived the bear scare" dinner party was on its way. Once all backs were turned though and the group began speaking about me in the third person (and about my outfit in particular), I took the hint and headed downriver to warmed-over soup and a solitary perch.

I ROSE THE next morning, as the walls were glowing red with the coming sun. From the honeymoon suite high atop Hades Bar, I stared for a long time into the desert ether that always felt so pure, so right, so real. I gazed too long, though, and burned something bold into my brain. Closing my eyes and looking at what was there I found desert varnish, an impossibly blue sky, water reflected on black rock. I found contrasts of deep harmony. I saw a river home. This image—I knew—would be my memory of place, and I made a quiet pact with myself not to let it fade while I was away.

I realized the only thing crazy about our run-in with the bear was that it represented just another day in the canyon. I tucked the "beer and dinner" story onto the tightly packed Westwater shelf of memories, wondering how long I would be able to last in my new place between readings. As I walked down the path toward the boat, the commercial party drifted past. "You ready to go?" shouted the guide in an easily distinguishable voice. "Yeah," I replied, "I guess I am."

Chad Niehaus is happy as hell to be back in Moab, Utah, where he now serves as a river manager for the Bureau of Land Management. When he emerges from deep within the recesses of Cubicle Land, he steps into his other life as landscape artist, writer, and recreating dirt bag. More tales of "whoah" can be found in his book, *Living for the Epic*.

this river is out to get me

Bill Beer

Editor's note: In 1955 two young men were the first to swim the entire length of the Colorado River through Grand Canyon. Equipped with indefatigable spirit, swim fins, rubber shirts, and—theoretically—waterproof rubberized boxes for their gear, they negotiated 280 bone-wrenching miles between Lees Ferry and Pierce Ferry. About halfway through, they hiked up to the South Rim for supplies, where rangers of the National Park Service detained them, in an attempt to keep them from finishing their run. Incredibly, they talked their way out of it, and were allowed to continue. They captured their feat on celluloid, and Bill Beer later recounted it in *We Swam the Grand Canyon*.

WE AROSE THAT morning still elated by our visit to the rim, and at the absurd thought that while we were puttering around in our damp, grimy camp several million people were reading in their newspapers and hearing on their radios that the "intrepid swimmers" were continuing on their trip. Sore yes, cold yes, dirty yes, but intrepid . . . ?

Pity there was no one to watch the two "celebrities" as they stumbled down the sand to consign themselves to the raging waters of the Colorado.

And rage they did! What a day! We had nothing but rapids all day, with no time in between to take pictures. Salt Creek Rapid, Granite Falls, Hermit, Boucher, Crystal, Tuna Creek, Sapphire, and several smaller ones followed one after the other. These were some of the big rapids of the Granite Gorge we had heard so much about. As far as I was concerned, they deserved a reputation but not the one they had; I had wonderful fun bouncing down these rapids like a rubber ball down a flight of stairs. I yelled and laughed and the canyons shouted back until at times I sounded like a whole carload of people screaming on a roller coaster. It was a wonderful sport. I wanted to swim every rapid in the world! We no longer stopped to survey rapids; they seemed not to offer any real hazards to us.

Even though I was feeling no fear, there was still excitement and tension just before going down the brink of each rapid when I could hear the noise but all that was visible was the smooth edge where the river disappeared. Both John and I commented on that tense "before the game" feeling.

And, just as before a game, the tension was always accompanied by a need to empty our bladders. It didn't take us long, however, to learn to wait till *after* the rapid before doing that. With long johns on we found that the process infused a temporary warmth that would insulate part of us from the cold river for a few minutes—if we didn't move much. John grinned, "It's almost as good as a warm-up break."

In camp that night we calculated we had swum ten miles and had dropped 130 feet.

John said, "I feel like it."

Poor John hadn't shared in the fun today. All day long he had been bouncing off rocks, proving they weren't *that* far below the surface. He never hit too hard, just enough to give him a bruise or take off a little skin. His camera, lunch, and both his boxes had sprung leaks, so he had another night of laying out everything to dry. He had removed the splint, and his finger had opened up again; now it looked as if he'd wear the new splint till we were out of the river.

The next day, the river started out on him again. In the first rapid he dropped down a wall of water onto a rock that scraped his foot and dislodged his swim fin. Panicky, he reached down to rescue the fin and was somersaulted over the rock into the hole behind it. Still doubled over securing his swim fin, he was dumped onto another rock. And when he finally got the fin on and lifted his head for air, a wave squirted into his mouth and he inhaled a fair amount of muddy water. He coughed all the way to the next rapid.

The sun was shining brightly and there was, thankfully, no wind. It was far and away our most pleasant day so far. The water had warmed up to fifty-six degrees, not exactly warm, but we had finished the first hundred miles now and were a little tougher and tolerated it better.

Late that morning we stopped to look over an old cable car that spanned the gorge. We thought it might be fun to see if we could get the fifty-year-old device to operate well enough so we could run the car out to midstream and dive off, but it was rusted too solidly. We contented ourselves with a few photos and returned to swimming.

Around the next bend we saw Shinumo Creek, with its clear water coming into the river, and stopped again—this time to try taking some movies. Our damaged camera would no longer run by itself, but John figured out a way to jam a twig into the button so we were able to shoot a scene with both of us in it at once. Of course we didn't hear the spring wind down, so we carried on with our acting long after the camera was dead. Swimming down the Grand Canyon may not have been a silly thing to do, but how about two guys hamming it up in front of a dead camera?

Below Shinumo we raced through another series of rapids, dropping fifty feet in two and a half miles. Earlier that morning I had dropped into a big hole in one of the rapids and had come up bubbling that I had fallen into the "biggest one yet." But below Shinumo I seemed to find a hole in every rapid, each one bigger than the last. In Waltenberg Rapid, I believe it was, I was swallowed by a real whopper. After I came out of that one I was dizzy. I'd read estimates of the depth of these holes that ranged up to thirty-five feet. Even half that is an outrageous lie. A really big hole is perhaps only ten feet deep. But it still takes plenty of power for a river to suck a hole in its surface ten feet deep, and there's a lot of violence all around the holes. They often overturn a large boat in a trice, but the poor swimmer doesn't get overturned—he gets rotated.

After that last ride in the Colorado's cement mixer I was ready to take a break. So when we saw the granite wonderland the cliffs had become, we swam ashore. The water that was again in John's boxes caused us to stay. It seemed a perfect place to do some serious filming, too.

We worked till nearly dark staging a "typical" camp sequence for the camera, then quit for the real thing. Our little wonderland made a fine campsite, complete with a carved stone fireplace, which had its own hearth, mantel, and flue. After we had draped our dirty wet clothes all over it I wondered if perhaps we weren't taking too many liberties with Mother Nature.

She must have thought so, too. It was obvious the next morning that she was angry with us. We awoke to a cloudy, blustery, threatening day. It had been raining somewhere. Overnight the river had risen two feet and then dropped back one. With no banks to overflow, the Colorado just keeps rising in flood. We had passed clusters of driftwood deposited seventy-five feet up on the cliffs and knew the river had once reached that height. We could only guess how high and how fast it might rise overnight and hope we camped high enough above the water.

We were slow to finish our camping sequence the next morning. Considerable discussion—sometimes vigorous—over every single shot delayed us. It wasn't that we were angry, just cheap. Neither of us was willing to waste a single inch of expensive 16mm color film on superfluity. As we worked, argued, and planned that morning, and as the camera was unloaded and reloaded several times, I couldn't help remembering the repair job I had done on the camera in Marble Canyon and wished devoutly that I could find out whether or not we were making blank film or movies.

By the time we got in the water it was raining; soon it began to rain hard. The rain was freezing, and I couldn't understand why it wasn't snow or hail. Almost immediately we agreed to warm up at "the first pile of driftwood after the first rapid."

But there were no rapids. For miles. It became a contest to see who would give up first—which I lost. I gave up many times while John hung on, grimly refusing to quit. Since I couldn't leave him alone, I had to drift helplessly along with him.

Finally, six miles below camp, we heard a rapid. The rapid was insignificant, but the acre of driftwood below it was a gift from heaven. It was soon ablaze. We kept backing farther from the fire until we were about 150 yards away, each on his own boulder slowly turning, one side baked by thirty tons of blazing wood, the other freezing in the pelting rain.

No sooner were we afloat again than we began to plan the next warm-up break. We swam a few jolly little rapids and three or four miles downstream saw another huge pile of wood. By this time the wood was rather rain-soaked, so our fire sent up a huge column of smoke. As we stood well back and watched the column rise into the vastness of the canyon, we realized how insignificant it was. The chances of anyone seeing the smoke were about zero, and we gave up the idea of using a fire, however large, as a distress signal. Better save the effort.

A glimmer of sun tantalized us back into the river, but no sooner were we swimming than the clouds returned from their hiding places behind the walls and poured rain down on us again. It felt like standing in a cold shower while someone threw buckets of ice water on us.

Back in the river we encountered a few smallish rapids, which helped distract us from the cold for a while. Forster Rapid had a mansion-sized rock in the middle, which sent John swimming vigorously toward the side of the river. Two miles farther along we came to S-shaped Fossil Rapid. Neither of us negotiated it well, and we found ourselves grounded about halfway through. Just after Fossil the granite reappeared. While we knew we'd be able to find campsites in the granite, we also knew there would be no shelter from the rain. On top of the rising granite, however, were strata of sandstones and shales, which were deeply undercut, leaving wide caves that promised perfect covered campsites. These strata were riding up on the granite, however, and would soon be out of reach. By the time we had agreed on a place, the lowest sheltered ledge was a hundred feet off the water.

That was the night John was cleaning his pistol and dropped a vital little pin in the silt. He knew within inches where it had fallen, but before he was through he had raked our campsite with his fingers and his fork, had panned the area like a gold miner, and finally, after dark, had cascaded cupful after cupful of silt through his flashlight beam hoping to spot the pin. The process consumed a few drams of whiskey—maybe more than a few because the last thing I heard as I went to sleep was, "Pin's hiding . . . doesn't want me to find it . . . doesn't *want* me to have a pistol. It keeps moving, right now it's under this big pile of sand. Can't sit here and look for it, pile's too big. Go to sleep poor John. Go to bed. Poor-old-John-without-a-pistol-Daggett."

Our maps showed us we were thirty miles from Havasu Creek and the long climb to Havasu Village. From the first time we had heard of it, we had planned to stop at Havasu and visit the smallest Indian tribe in the U.S., Grand Canyon dwellers from prehistoric times. At one time we had considered resupplying completely there. Even after abandoning that idea as impractical, we still wanted to climb to the tiny, protected village just to see it. Now it was again becoming apparent that our huge consumption of food made supplementing our supplies there a wise idea. Also we could mail exposed film out.

The sun was up in the morning and the day promised to be another good one of shooting through the "granite." We tumbled through half a dozen rapids and between them drifted down some of the narrowest passages in the river. In these narrows there were no accommodating silt banks, no friendly piles of driftwood; this was the most remote part of the canyon with no trails on the plateau above, no early signs of man nearby.

The sun was bright and hot and reflected off the polished rock so intensely that we kept our eyes slitted. It was so hot we had to keep dashing water on the black rubber of our boxes to keep them from burning our bare forearms. The temperature in the airless side canyons must have risen to 130 degrees—the whole area had a dead, hell-like feeling. And yet the water of the river was as cold as ever. It was strange to be broiled on top and frozen below. At times we wished we could swim along upside down. At our one warm-up break that morning we couldn't stay out of the water long because we became intolerably hot in our black rubber shirts.

Shortly after the break we came to Bedrock Rapids. Even as we approached we could see this wasn't going to be easy. First the river bent left around the boulder fan of Bedrock Creek, then it shot directly at Bedrock itself, a great rock island, which split the flowing water as a whirling saw slices a log. Half the river was diverted sharply to the right, completing an S-bend, while the other half disappeared into unknown hazards behind Bedrock.

John, still fearful of all large rocks, hung back while I swam ahead. As I poured down the tongue, sizing up the problem as fast as I could, I saw no way to avoid hitting the rock island. The whole force of the river was dashing against it like surf pounding a cliff. Every few seconds the water rushed up the rock face then came back down again in a big curling wave, which formed and broke and re-formed again.

I was swimming furiously to the right side of the river, driving hard to try to keep away from the rock, when I saw that if I could catch that wave just right I might use it to push me off the rock. It was body surfing, pure and simple, but the timing had to be very good.

At what I thought was just the right moment I paused, going with the flow, and let the river hurl me at that rock with frightening force. I had guessed right—just as I was about to hit, the thousands of gallons of water that had gotten there first rushed back, carrying me with them. I came so close I could have kissed that big jagged red monster.

As I slid along its side, the river now carrying me parallel to the island, I saw a nasty little fishhook of a rock at its downstream end. With a few extra strokes I was able to slip past it and turn to watch John.

John was playing it safe. He was much farther to the right than I had been. I lost him for a moment in the spray—then he reappeared right up against Bedrock. He was fending off the rock with his hands. I started for shore, swimming backward so I could watch John. He was swept swiftly along the edge of the island. Then he got turned around backward.

Suddenly he stopped. He had been going so fast and was stopped so abruptly that I could see, almost feel, the shudder that shook his body. The water poured over him and submerged him. He was rolled backward for a few yards. I could see a swim fin or his head project crazily out of the water and then disappear in the brown.

Just past Bedrock he came up and stayed. By this time I was on a little patch of silt and stood up to see better. John was in a little whirlpool not moving. President Harding Rapid all over again? But this time there seemed to be no blood, and when he got out of the whirlpool and began to swim slowly toward me it was obvious he was furious.

As he got closer I heard him ranting and raving and saying bad things. When I could understand what he was saying I discovered that high on his list of targets was *me*.

As I helped him climb out on our little silt bank he moved very slowly, very painfully. Between groans he continued his expostulations.

"Damn you, Beer! You're the luckiest guy in the world. I was way to the right of you. When I saw you get by with no problem, I was sure I was safe. Then that goddamn wave disappeared! It was there for you, but when I came along, no siree. No way is the Colorado going to make it easy for old John. All of a sudden the way was nice and clear and all downhill into that rock. No wave for old hit-the-rocks John. I was pushing and shoving all along that rock. Right next to the son of a bitch!"

"Why did you turn around?"

"You don't think I wanted to, do you? I had just spotted that little hook when the river jerked me around backward and slammed me into it. Hard."

"Boy, I'll say. I could feel it from here."

"My back feels broken."

It looked that way from the way John was acting. He couldn't sit or stand erect. Every time he moved, he groaned a little. He had hit right on the base of his spine, driven by the full force of the river. Worse than the pain was his anger and frustration.

"I did all the intelligent planning. I watched you, Bill, and then figured I'd play it even safer. I did everything right but I was cheated! Robbed! It's like that damn rock reached out and grabbed me. You know, I think this river is out to get me. I mean it!"

"Hey, you could have broken a leg, or been killed."

That sobering thought seemed to mollify John somewhat, though he did carry on a bit on the theme that the rapids seemed to be getting worse and bigger and more dangerous the farther we went. It wasn't that he wanted to quit. John felt the Colorado River had hurled a personal challenge at him and he was determined to win.

In fact, he insisted on going on even though getting into the water was a slow agonizing operation for him. The water, however, gave him some support and the cold numbed the pain, so perhaps he was better off swimming than not. After a couple of fair-sized rapids—Deubendorff and Tapeats—we stopped for lunch at 135 Mile Rapid.

After lunch John took a few still photos of me swimming 135 Mile Rapid and then followed behind. He caught up in a section called Granite Narrows where the rocks close in on the river tightly; in places the river is less than forty feet wide. It is a gloomy place. Just downstream from the narrows we came upon Deer Creek Falls, one of the Colorado River's more beautiful sights.

Seeing this lovely waterfall dropping out of a dark slit in the cliff to plunge more than a hundred feet through the sunlight, we had to stop. I doubt if any canyon traveler, past or future, ever passes up Deer Creek Falls.

It was at Deer Creek that I wasted five dollars of film taking movies of a bird swimming underwater. I thought it was a freak of evolution, which had appeared in one of the Grand Canyon's micro-environments. Of course it wasn't—just an ordinary water ouzel. John thought I ought to pay him his half of the film cost when he found out.

We departed, regretting it was too early to camp, and swam downstream looking for the perfect rapid to photograph. We needed movies of one of us going through a typical rapid to illustrate what we did a dozen times a day. We wanted a rapid with a curve, a high, sloping bank for camera positions and a convenient eddy at the bottom to help the swimmer get out of the current. We planned to take multiple runs of one rapid.

We found our ideal rapid at Fishtail. It was really too early to stop, but a look at the map consoled us. Even with our late start and early finish we had logged fourteen miles, and though this wasn't our best mileage to date, we had fallen farther, 135 feet, than on any other day's run. At 139½ miles we were halfway to my car at Pierce Ferry. I commented, "Halfway, John old pal, it's all downhill from here on."

John, gently exploring the lump on his tailbone, groused, "Yeah, like Hell is downhill from here."

Our campsite was only a few feet off the water, but we did have a spring trickling out of the cliff nearby and both enjoyed clear water showers; it was nice to get all the silt out of our hair, beards, and underwear. We were camped by the talus slopes and John found the only level spot on the sand a foot off the water; I chose to dig a ledge out of the talus slope for my sleeping bag. John got clever and, before he went to bed, marched a line of little sticks standing up in the sand from his bed to the water. By counting them, he could tell if the river were rising. We were sure it was, as we had an unusual amount of driftwood floating with us today.

That night the never quiet Colorado with its rapids and whirlpools and bubbling boils was noisier than ever with the *schluurp, schlump* of sandbanks giving way to the rising water. John's stick system worked well. Every hour or so I was awakened by the beam of his flashlight as he counted stakes. There were always one or two fewer. At last count I saw only two.

But we were both too tired to keep it up. At dawn I was awakened by John grumbling below me. I looked down to see almost all our campsite underwater and John's sleeping bag half in the river. "Now I *know* the river is out to get me," he announced. "Well, I've had my warnings and I'm going to be *really* careful from now on."

That morning we cooked on a boulder. The river had risen by this date to about 15,000 cubic feet per second, and there was no sand left.

After breakfast I unloaded my boxes and repacked them with lighter driftwood, and we climbed to the head of the rapids. After some surveying and discussing, we thought we could get the film footage we needed in four runs. Because of John's painful back, the original plan to split chores had to change. I got to do all the swimming while he sat on a rock and took pictures.

After each swim through the rapid I had to get ashore, put on sneakers, put my boxes on my back, and hike along the cliffs for half a mile. After each trip in the hot sun wearing a rubber shirt, sweatshirt, and woolen underwear, the cold Colorado was a delight. I made the four runs while John sat dozing on a rock, trying to make it look like a great effort when he moved to a new camera site. It was well after noon when we started downriver again.

We took only one warm-up break that afternoon, but when we came to Upset Rapid it looked so ideal for movies that we again stopped to film. This time, back or no back, it was Daggett's turn to swim. I set up and waited interminably for him, sure the sun would set before he arrived. And when he did come around the bend into the rapids, I thought he was struggling unnecessarily much just for the camera. *Ham* was the word that stuck in my mind.

He disappeared into the shadows and I set about making camp. He was a long time returning. About two hours in fact, and well after dark. He explained that he had discovered he was going through the rapids with an overly friendly railroad tie and that by the time he got free of this dangerous companion he had missed all the good whirlpools and had landed about a mile downstream. There was no way back along shore so he had to do some swimming and some rock climbing. It was my turn to have the hot soup ready.

We were both feeling pain that night. John still couldn't sit or lie on his back—it was either stand or lie facedown—and his finger was still useless. My usual collection of nicks and bruises seemed to have concentrated in my feet, which were so swollen and sore that I walked with a hobble. The climb to Havasu the next day began to look like an ordeal.

In the morning we were again faced with getting into Upset Rapid from too close to the brink. I made it narrowly, but John lost his boxes and got sorely smacked while chasing them through the rapid. Even so, it was a great rapid and an exhilarating way to start the day! We were in the water, through the heaving, turbulent rapids, and around the bend before we caught our breath.

We were less than an hour swimming to the mouth of Havasu Canyon. It's a tricky entrance with little clue to tell you it's coming. The cliffs descend into the water so there was no chance to get out and survey the problem. I was slightly ahead of John and hugging the left side of the river so as not to miss the entrance. With no warning I went around a projection of rock and there it was! Bright blue water and hard swimming upstream against the current of Havasu Creek. I yelled back at John, "Wait till you see this!"

He hurried to join me but didn't hug the cliff as closely as I did. As he came around the corner I saw his astonished look as he saw the beautiful Havasu, then the even more astonished look as he was swept away toward Havasu Rapid. John is a powerful swimmer, but that morning he exceeded himself. It appeared he had an outboard motor he kicked his feet so hard. Pushing his boxes like a river tugboat he plowed his way up against both the Colorado and the Havasu and swam into the blue tunnel that is the mouth of this stream.

The creek joins the river through a thin cleft with overhanging walls. The walls and creek bottom are white with limestone deposits, and the water is a startling aquamarine. The bright sun shining into one end of this tunnel was caught and reflected a thousand times until even the air seemed colored blue. After the brown, harsh Colorado, we couldn't believe this. After a hundred feet or so of hard upstream swimming in strangely warm water we came to a place where we could climb out on the rock.

We made packs of our sleeping bags, enclosing exposed film and a little

food, and set off up Havasu Canyon, another of the delights of the Grand
Canyon.

It would be about twelve miles to the village, the first nine of which had no
trail. With no trail, the going was difficult. At times we inched along the cliffs,
sometimes waded upstream, sometimes stumbled through thickets, often
backtracking. Neither of us was walking very well; we both had acutely sore feet
and realized we had acquired more injuries in the river than we had thought.
Now that we were using our feet for walking—our bodies no longer both sup-
ported and anesthetized by cold water—the injuries showed up. We moved so
slowly that darkness caught us just as we reached Mooney Falls, less than seven
miles up the canyon from the Colorado. We made barely one mile per hour.

Facing us was a three-hundred-foot cliff extending across the canyon from
wall to wall—but not your ordinary cliff. It appeared to be made of fountains
of frozen stone, as if fan-shaped jets of liquid rock had shot out from a
hundred places on the face of the cliff and just as they curved down had
instantly congealed. Each of these curved fans seemed to drip scores of stone
icicles, which festooned the face of the cliff with a thousand vertical streamers.
In the center of these solid brown streamers fell the shimmering 230-foot
white ribbon of Mooney Falls, plunging into a marvelous half-acre blue pool.

We were speechless. The whole place was a fairy tale scene. The bats came
out in droves from the cliff. We thought better of trying to do any tricky rock
climbing in the dark. So we just camped there at the foot of Mooney.

The next morning we discovered a well-built trail cut up through the cliff
using tunnels here and there and offering viewing openings complete with
steel guardrails. And at the top of the falls the trail became well trampled.

A little way above the falls, hobbling worse than ever now, we came upon
campers having breakfast outside some old prospector's cabins. This group of
people was being shepherded by a professional guide who charged them for
this taste of outdoor living. John muttered, "Pretty good way to run a hotel. No
hotel, no beds, no food, and the guests do all the chores." And then with a
laugh we realized that these people, whom we regarded as civilization with
tents and cots and all the comforts, were themselves sure they were out in the
wilderness. We were a little startled when they almost immediately guessed

who we were and began with a flood of questions. I hustled us away, only to have John grouse that if we'd lingered we could have wrangled breakfast.

We passed the next two waterfalls in Havasu's series of three—both lovely, but neither as spectacular as Mooney—and arrived at the village. We would have walked right through it but for the church, a large stone-faced Quonset hut with a bell tower on one side. Under the roof was a big loudspeaker—to carry the word to any reluctant churchgoers who decided to sleep late on Sundays. This had to be the center of town.

Nearby was a flagpole with a U.S. flag. There were a couple of horses tied to the fence and some little boys swinging on the gate. Behind the flagpole was a nondescript building with several crude signs on it. HAVASUPAI SUB AGENCY —SUPAI, ARIZONA and HAVASU TOURIST ENTERPRISE OFFICE, REGISTER HERE were on one door; on the other we read, POST OFFICE—SUPAI, ARIZONA and BASKETS FOR SALE.

On the steps lounged a couple of Red Men. They began the pow wow.

"Hey, you guys them Frog Men?"

"Uh . . . yeah. Say, could you tell . . ."

"You guys didn't really swim down that river, did you?"

"Uh . . . yeah. Say, could you tell . . ."

"Who you guys kiddin'? Nobody's that crazy. Not even White Men."

"Uh . . . sure. Say, could you tell us where the Post Office is?"

At that moment a little white man with thinning hair came around the corner carrying a hoe. With the hoe he pointed to the sign in front of the door that read POST OFFICE—SUPAI, ARIZONA. We went in and at once faced the world's widest woman.

Her beam was not less than one yard. A perfect thirty-six inches across the shoulders and hips with proportionate face and feet. Havasupai are wide people, but this lady must have been mother-of-them-all. Her English was mostly mumbles and sibilants delivered with her hand covering her mouth, and only when the wife of The Indian Agent showed up were we able to understand how to get our mail entrusted to the care of the Federal Government. At that it took an hour. Starving by now, we asked about The Store. The Postmistress managed to communicate that it was next door. We went next door. Pretty soon The Postmistress lumbered over. She was The Storekeeper.

There were several holes in the floor, at least one of which we were told was caused when the floor gave way under The Storekeeper the year before. Goods were piled on the floor or in boxes scattered about. We spent every last cent we had on food. Once outside we wondered if we'd have to squat in Supai's main street to cook breakfast. Fortunately, we were directed to The Guest House, which had been The Hospital till The Medicine Man had it shut down.

Just as we finished our gargantuan breakfast the man with the hoe strolled in.

"Howdy," was our official greeting from The Indian Agent.

"Howdy, howdy," we replied, hoping to open things up a bit.

Silence.

"You fellows them Frog Men?"

We confessed.

"There's a few people been callin' you. Want you to call back. Don't know if the phone works today, though."

We strolled over to The Telephone, which was next door in The Indian Agent's living room. John attempted our calls with much shouting and repeating—the telephone worked only intermittently that day.

He informed the Park Service of our progress and timetable. He learned that our movies, mailed from Grand Canyon Village, had indeed been fine—were excellent in fact—and that excerpts, especially John swimming Soap Creek Rapid and me in Hance, had been shown on TV all over the country. Another spate of news stories had come out, including interviews with Park officials and others—even the honeymoon couple who had given me the lift. Now that we had reached Supai there would be a few more news stories. Publicity was of no concern to us—we felt so cut off from the world that it was as if the uproar were happening to someone else—but the news about the camera working was wonderful.

We should have left then to return to our river, but our feet were so sore and swollen and so cut up that we thought it wise to give them a rest. Besides, we were enjoying Supai and its people. We spent the day getting to know some of the residents and learning some of their fascinating history. We were treat-ed by the Havasupai as part supernatural, part crazy. They held the Colorado River in awe. They warned us of the dangers of Lava Falls, twenty-five miles downriver, though none of them had ever seen the rapid.

In the morning our feet were no better; my own dainty size thirteens looked like stuffed sausages with toes. Oh well, it was all downhill. About halfway down to the Colorado an old ankle injury of John's acted up and he limped badly. Both of us fell into the creek more than once—in my case scrambling a dozen fresh eggs in my sleeping bag. We arrived at dusk and camped at the mouth of Havasu Canyon, sure in the knowledge that swim-ming rapids and fighting whirlpools was easier than climbing up and down Havasu Canyon in tattered tennis shoes.

Bill Beer kept pursuing adventure throughout his life. He starred in a Disney film re-creating Powell's exploration of the Grand Canyon. In 1965 he quit a career as a news reporter and sailed with his wife and two-year-old daughter from Connecticut to the Virgin Islands, where he established a successful charter business. Bill was also an avid pilot. His last trip followed the Mississippi from St. Louis into Canada, then via Montana and the Dakotas to Arizona. He died of heart failure in his ultralight plane at the age of seventy-one. The sun was rising, and he had just completed another lifelong dream: flying Monument Valley.

hapless is as hapless does

Frederick Reimers

"HEY, WE MADE the Washington guidebook," Jeff told me over the phone from Seattle. "Check out page 321."

"For what?" I asked.

"Our first descent."

The Upper Upper Middle Fork of the Snoqualmie, he meant. Ah, here at last would be the recognition we deserved, and vindication for a somewhat misguided exploit.

Bill, Jeff, and I had plucked this first descent—the first we'd ever attempted—when the lumber company finally opened the gate on the riverside road that had been locked for ten-odd years. It was Bill's idea, and we went on a weekday as he worked weekends. This angered his roommate Shawn Wickstrum, who was equally hungry to have a first descent to his credit.

The river was low. Like forty-cubic-feet-per-second low. But rather than wait for more water and risk someone else swiping our glory, we proceeded down the creek. Furthermore, we were in a hurry, as Bill had to be at work by four o'clock the same afternoon.

The run was a series of precipitous slides and waterfalls. We ground our way down the early drops and over a fifteen-footer, snapping photos of each other. It was my first run of a waterfall and I was feeling pretty good. "Too bad Shawn isn't here," we all laughed, imagining him grousing along all day in his delivery truck knowing he was missing out.

A few pools below we found a monster. We all got out, stood on the ledge and measured the sheer drop with a throwbag. Seven arm spans: about forty feet. Pretty steep stuff, but looking over the lip, I had made higher cliff jumps. It would be easy—just nose in. I volunteered to go first.

However, in my youthful exuberance, and with my vision clouded by glimpses of immortality, I failed to take into account the little ski jump lip a third of the way down. Predictably, the boat flattened out, as occupied kayaks do when free-falling through the air, and I landed completely flat in the barely aerated water. I gasped in pain and pulled my skirt, afraid to further wrench my back by rolling. I floundered to shore and lay on the rocks.

"How was it?" Jeff yelled down.

"Not so good," I called up, barely able to breathe from the pain.

He came anyway, breaking a rib on the hull of his boat. As we both lay on shore groaning, Bill, not wanting to be late for work and figuring the portage would take too long, also came on down. Just like us, he winced in pain.

We portaged the following fifty-footer and groveled our way down the rest of the run. It was fun to make jokes at our own expense because every time Jeff laughed, he was shot through with pain from his broken rib. Fortunately, Bill was on time for work.

FIVE YEARS LATER, the episode all but forgotten, I located the new edition of *A Guide to the Whitewater Rivers of Washington* and turned to page 321. I had to search to find mention of us, but there it was, buried in the middle: "The next big landmark is a forty-foot waterfall just downstream. Although it has been run, the hapless kayakers that attempted it got beat up and hurt."

Yow. Sucker-punched by destiny. The fickle winds of fame. Who wrote this, anyway? I looked up to the contributor line. There it was, the last and loudest laugh echoing in my head, "contributed by Shawn Wickstrum."

Frederick "Rico" Reimers is the managing editor of *Paddler* and *Kayak* magazines. Rather than paddle Class V and take forty-day expeditions as in days of old, he instead spends his time sitting at his desk repairing and rejecting other people's accounts of those same experiences. He also recently won three games of computer solitaire in a row.

jug, not jig

Pete Fromm

THIS HAS NOTHING to do with hopping lead-headed blobs of feathers endlessly off some invisible bottom. That is sport—I suppose. Some people may really enjoy it. Either way, I don't mean to belittle the jiggers, and I don't put many of those fly fishermen ahead of them. I don't think any of them have tried jug fishing. If they had they'd know better.

As is, jug fishing wallows in obscurity, and perhaps that's for the best. There are no pay jug-fishing streams yet, at least that I've heard of. Here again though, more trendy anglers may have something on me. Maybe jugging is big in Argentina or Chile or Russia, or wherever they're going this year. I'm not the world's most well-traveled person, but I've seen a share of water, and only on one, the Rio Grande, have I seen a true addiction to the sport.

The Rio Grande, in Texas, is big, mostly slow, and always muddy—the archetypical jug river. I did my time on the Rio as a river ranger in Big Bend. At first it was hard for a northerner. My first appalled gasp of, "Holy mackerel, it's filthy," stung my boss, and I stuttered a little before I could get out, "Big runoff, huh?"

I looked around at the parched flats and the scorched black rock of the mountains. It was mid-February and I didn't think runoff was a very good guess. My boss said, "Northener," and that's still the only time I've heard that sound like a swear word. He said, succinctly, that the Rio was brown, not dirty, and I remembered to always remember that.

Even so, on my first few patrols I watched my brilliant yellow oar blades completely disappear upon crossing the waterline and I was vastly underwhelmed with what had to pass for a river down Texas way. There were some rapids in the canyons that made my heart go hard and fast before I could even hear the water begin to grumble, but mostly the brown water just oozed along, flanked by river cane and desert.

For wildlife I had to get along with the horses the Mexicans drove over for the better grazing on the Texas side. That and the ubiquitous heron, squawking and flying downstream only to have to repeat the process again and again and again. Sometimes I would try to sneak the boat across the river and come back in behind the heron, just to spook it upstream and give it a rest, but the heron always saw me in time to go a few hundred more yards downstream. I figured they must re-migrate at night. They had to, or after a float trip or two they'd all be clumped at the end of the river—a giant knot of great blues at Brownsville.

After checking out with the boss I started to float on my own. I was told to expect a crush of people during Spring Break and was assigned the Lower Canyons as my patrol float. The Lower Canyons section is an eight-day float through desert and canyon that is beautiful even to a northerner. I camped under peregrine aeries and at springs where I refurbished my water and I didn't see a soul until my boss picked me up at Dryden. After working summers on the Snake, it was not what I would have called a crush of people.

So with eight days to fill I picked up trash. There were old fire rings to clean up, a few bits of camp litter, and, on the canyon walls, there were the nails and strings from setlines. It wasn't exactly a legal way to fish, but on the Mexican side all we could do was pull the nails and reel in the lines. Usually they were old and empty, but occasionally they still held hooks and I reeled gingerly, not knowing what a rusty barb coming out of that water would do to me. There was never a fish on any of these hooks, and I wondered what kind of paddlefish-type beast they were after.

And there were the jugs. I picked up all kinds: bleach bottles, plastic liter pop bottles, plastic sixteen-ounce pop bottles, metal refrigerant cans, anything that would float and displace a fair amount of water. There were even some fragile, glass bottles—the juggers' equivalent of the bamboo rod.

My boss, I think to see if I could ever be anything but that sneered Northener, never clued me in to what the jugs were for. Most of them were simply flotsam I thought. Empty jugs discarded to pile up with the log and cane jams. But a lot of them had strings tied through the handles, or wrapped around the flare behind the bottleneck. I wondered about that, but before I could reach any conclusion I pulled up the first jug that was still armed.

Now, I know how big a #20 Adams is, and I guess some of the nymphs and Muddlers I've used go down to #6 hooks—I've never paid attention to the numbering at that end of the scale. What I found dangling from three feet of twine tied to this gallon bleach bottle was, at least, a double aught hook, and I only stop at #00 because I don't know if they go into the negatives. Treble naturally.

I fiddled that hook around in my hand and whistled. "Holy mackerel." I wondered what it could possibly be for. I looked into the flat, roily surface of the solidly opaque brown water. Fish? It didn't seem like a sucker could live in there. Probably not even a carp.

But I'm truly not that opaque myself, not all the time. I guessed catfish after a while, thinking if there were species of cats that would leave the water at night just to stroll around Florida, there must be species that could carve their way through this muck. Given the choice, I think I would have picked living in this silt over walking in Miami at night.

I didn't have any of my fly-tying stuff with me, let alone a rod. I mean, who would have suspected it, fish in here? I didn't have any idea of how to match the hatch anyway. I dug through my cooler, though, figuring in this water smell would be the key. I settled on a bit of salami the size of a good bluegill bobber. I sunk the hooks into the stiff chunk of sausage as best I could, then, not knowing exactly what to do next, I heaved the whole mess overboard. It's not a difficult technique and I mastered it in a considerably shorter amount of time than it had taken me to land a fly in front of me rather than behind.

I discovered more armed jugs, finding that refrigerant cans were the most common. This had to do with availability rather than performance. I'll take a bleach bottle any day of the week, especially for the truly grumpy lunkers.

I followed my drifting bleach bottle with what, in retrospect, was embarrassing attentiveness. Part of the joy of jug fishing is its sedate pace. Unlike dry-fly fishing, there is no such thing as missing the fish of your life while doing something as innocent as turning away from your fly long enough to sneeze, or, god forbid, actually talking to your fishing partner. You can even pull over and eat your lunch while your jug goes around the bend. After repacking you simply drift along until you find your jug. You check the hook of course, a bait check, and as often as not, you'll find a fish, safely stapled into those monstrous trebles. Relaxing yes, but exciting? Well, unsighted jugs are a bit more like nymph fishing, while trailing close in a jug's wake is the real thing, the dry-fly fishing of the jug world.

This first time I stayed just far enough back to keep from spooking whatever might be interested in a piece of soggy salami. That's kind of embarrassing too. Water transparent as a piece of oak, a bleach bottle for rod, reel, and bobber all in one, and a treble hook the size of your fist, tied to a piece of twine, and I'm worried about presentation and boat shadows. But I lurked along, ready for anything, backing when the bottle twisted into the eddies alongside the cliffs, drifting free when it had the main current. Sometimes, after four or five revolutions, I'd help it out of the eddies with my oar.

This went on for quite a while. The bottle crossed into another eddy, hesitating on the line so precisely that I was whispering, "That's it, that's it." The bottle was making a fine presentation and I was proud of it but then it was gone.

How much force, in pounds, does a gallon of air trapped in a bottle require to be submerged? I don't know, but try to sink an empty milk bottle in your bathtub. Even with two hands it's a job. Whatever had my bottle was doing it with its lips. And the bottle didn't come back up.

I backstroked some, a little surprised, looking at the eddy line to see if some swirl in the water could have sucked my fishing system under. The line was a gentle one, though, and I began to look around the water, feeling a little less comfortable about dragging my hands and feet in it as I had been.

My jug did not reappear for a full minute. Then it popped up like a submarine blowing all tanks, nearly in the same place it had disappeared. It drifted aimlessly and I suffered the same slowing heart and sweaty brow that afflicts me whenever I'm surprised by an extra-large trout stripping line away from me until it has so much dragging in the water the hook pulls out without letting me even see what had carried it. I rowed a little shakily to the jug and reached for it with my oar.

I mishandled the oar and banged the jug and the race was on. The jug left the eddy, half submerged and looking more like a submarine than ever. Its wake curled over it and broke and fell, only to be swept away by the next wave. Whatever had it was towing it downstream at a clip I couldn't hope to match in my heavily loaded raft.

I fought that jug for nearly half an hour, never touching it again, or even coming close to touching it. Anyone watching from the top of the canyon walls, where the jug would be too far away to see, could only have concluded that the oarsman in that boat was being attacked by yellow jackets. I veered wildly with the runs, backing when it charged upstream, pushing myself into a sweat when it went with the current.

Finally the jug disappeared again as the fish sounded in water where I couldn't even guess the depth. A minute later it was up again, in an eddy on the Mexican side, and I snuck over in my fourteen-foot boat, shipped the oars, hooked my ankles under the rowing frame, and stretched over the side, arms out, reaching for the jug. The jug moved slightly toward the canyon wall, and I've never seen a bleach bottle look so tired.

I wrapped my hands around it, barely touching, then I grabbed and pulled back with my entire body and that jug came out and the string went tight and fish just kept coming out of that impenetrable brown surface.

I saw a huge round side and thought I had found a new species, maybe a sludge salmon, when I was blasted square in the kisser by the tail and I dropped the jug more in surprise than hurt. But the whole mess landed in the boat, in the front section, where, thank god, the cross-tube stood hard and wide between that fish and me. I sat back on the frame and wiped at the water and slime on my face and wondered if it wouldn't be easier if I just slipped over the side. There was nearly three feet of slashing, sickly-gray/blue fish batting the hell out of a bleach bottle in the front of my raft.

I had my service revolver but, with the inflatable boat, that would be a definite last resort. I decided to wait it out, but even with the temperature over eighty by now, the fish showed nearly no sign of slowing down. Besides, watching a fish fight and gobble for breath at the same time isn't an easy thing for a catch-and-release person. I maneuvered the boat into a quiet stretch and undid my ten-foot-long wooden spare oar.

A club, well wielded can be a deadly weapon. A ten-foot oar, choked up half way, is less than deadly, but can inflict serious damage. With half of it pointed the wrong way, though, I wasn't sure whether I'd give or receive the brunt of the blows.

It was a messy battle and I gave myself a pretty good shot in the ribs before it was over. Not over really, but that catfish was pretty well slowed down. It was all a bit brutal, but there was no way I could picture to release this thing.

I circled around on the outside tube, with my knife out, trying to close for the deciding jab to the brain or the base of the spine. I steadied my knife over its head, the ugliest head I had ever seen in my life, and, not wanting to have the fish slide away while I cut open my raft floor, I lunged to pin him to the floor while I delivered the coup de grâce.

Catfish, as you may know, have spines incorporated in their pectoral fins. At the time I did not know that. For a moment I thought I had stabbed myself, but my Swiss army knife was stuck in the catfish, which, after that last outburst was very still. I felt somewhat Neanderthal, having completed a battle to the death, of which the outcome had been far from certain.

I pulled my knife out and the fish did not quiver. It was nearly quitting time anyway, and I pulled over and watched my wrist swell from the jab of the spine and taught myself the exhaustive art of catfish skinning. That night, and the night after, and once more the following night, because there was still ice in the cooler, I ate catfish until I thought I would die. There is little tastier, but when fifteen pounds has to be eaten before it spoils it becomes more of a stark challenge than an epicurean event.

As savage as my first venture into jug fishing was, I decided, over the next few days, that fish of that size had to be a fluke. With a little queasy spot in my stomach I threw another jug over the side, a refrigerant can this time, hoping that a smaller jug would nab a smaller fish. It went down almost immediately and the chase was on. I was even able to release this one.

My experience grew over the months, and I became as expert as anyone I knew. There was no use jugging if the temperature was over seventy-five or so, and I even took to moonlight jugging. The moon silvered the whole river then, but it was more ghostly than regular silver. The riffles held whole fields of pewter flashes, with the flatwater either black or an even shine, depending how the moon hit it. It was a different river altogether, silver, not brown, and jugging it was as beautiful as any recreation can get.

I advanced to some of the most complicated forms of the sport; double, then triple jugging, which can't be appreciated until two, or even three fish are independently towing jugs through a mud-colored river with a single boat in chase.

Over the months I never found better bait than that salami, not even different brands of salami. The makers, however, were not enthusiastic at the idea of a free plug—in a catfishing article. You'll have to experiment.

I moved back to Montana when the spring temperatures drove me out of a job, and haven't been back to the Rio Grande since. I gave up jugging a bit reluctantly. After all, in how many types of fishing do you hope not to catch a really big one? But I had no choice, I was back in clear, fast-water country and I took to fly fishing as if I hadn't been away.

However, I have recently made the discovery that the lower Missouri, out in the breaks area, flows wide and brown and slow. The catfish population is reputed to be booming. My fly shop doesn't carry #00 treble hooks, but I had one left and I tied my first salami pattern last night. And I'm saving bleach bottles.

Pete Fromm's latest novel, *As Cool As I Am*, earned him an unprecedented fourth Pacific Northwest Booksellers Literary Award. Earlier winners were his novel *How All This Started*, the story collection *Dry Rain*, and the memoir *Indian Creek Chronicles*. He has published four other story collections, as well as more than a hundred stories in magazines. He lives with his family in Great Falls, Montana.

hell and high water

Karen Jettmar

STANDING ALONE ON the edge of a gravel bar in the pouring rain, I stare at the maelstrom of copper-colored water racing by. Entire trees rush past, huge root balls pivoting in the swirling current. With three days of unabated rain, the river has come up five feet, surging bank to bank. In the last twenty-four hours, the rocky bench we're camped on has become an island as rising waters push a new path around the backside of bluff overlooking the river. Leaden skies hide the spectacular mountain scenery soaring above us. We're deep in the heart of Wrangell-St. Elias, Alaska's largest national park, on a remote wilderness river accessible only by airplane. How in the hell will I get seven edgy people, huddled in leaky tents and inadequate clothing, safely down the Nizina and Chitina Rivers by raft?

IN ONE OF the summers of my youth, I worked as a wilderness guide for a small Alaskan company that specialized in backpacking and paddle trips in Alaska's parks and refuges. My working arrangement was fairly casual. Chuck, the owner, left his house unlocked; the guides came and went freely. He left messages for us on the kitchen table.

In August, I returned from my last trip, only to find a note of instructions for one more. It was a five-day, one-raft voyage down the Nizina and Chitina Rivers, a benefit for a local conservation group. The note instructed me to drive 255 miles north of Anchorage to Chitina with a stove and the company's raft, frame, and oars. "All else will be taken care of by the McCarthy Lodge, which is doing the flying." Cool—no trip prep. I just had to wait for the raft, still six hundred miles distant on another river. Chuck's note said Steve, another guide, would return the raft to Anchorage the next day.

My part seemed simple enough. I packed my personal gear and waited for Steve and the raft to show up. Steve arrived, but without the raft. "I left it on a gravel bar beside the Noatak River," Steve said, "The weather was bad and the pilot told me, 'It's either the boat or the clients, but I can't take both.' He said he'd pick the boat up as soon as he could and ship it back to Anchorage."

"But that could be days from now," I said. "What am I supposed to do in the meantime? My trip leaves in two days."

"I don't know; it's not my problem. I have a dinner date." And with that, Steve walked out the door.

To bail or not to bail in this situation? I felt a sense of responsibility to carry out Chuck's orders, and made a list of everyone I knew that might have a raft to loan or rent. The following day, I started calling and found a fully outfitted raft to rent. That evening, one of the clients on the upcoming trip called from the East Coast. He said he and five friends would be arriving in Alaska the day after. I told him that I was only expecting four trip participants; I was operating on the premise that I only needed one boat. With six people, I'd need two boats and another guide.

"I'm sure you'll take care of all the details," he said. "See you tomorrow night in McCarthy." And with that, he hung up.

The odds stacked against the trip, but I was determined not to let anyone down.

I scrambled for an assistant. Through friends, I contacted a whitewater boater visiting Alaska from California. Catherine agreed to row the second raft.

I set out to find another boat. By the time Catherine arrived, and we'd driven to Chitina, we were a day late for our prearranged rendezvous with the pilot from McCarthy Lodge. Since there were no phones in McCarthy, the only way I could get a message to him was through the local broadcast message center, "Caribou Clatter," a community announcement service for bush residents with no telephones.

Will arrived in his Cessna 180. He had not heard our message, and he was not happy. "They're all waiting and anxious to go. I flew back and forth from McCarthy to Chitina several times yesterday and today looking for you. I'm flying you straight to the river."

"I don't feel too comfortable doing that," I said. "Have you checked out everyone's gear and clothing? I don't want people going out there unprepared. What about the food for the trip, and all the cooking, safety, and emergency gear? What kind of tents do they have? I'd like to take a look at what we're bringing along with us before we get all the way out there."

We struck a compromise. Catherine would fly in to the river with the rafts first, then Will would come back for me, and we'd stop in McCarthy to look at the gear. We packed up the plane and they took off, over the Copper River and up the Chitina River Valley to the Nizina River.

Some time later, Will returned for me. One of the participants accompanied him. "What about the food and gear check?" I asked.

He waved his hand. "Everything is covered."

I boarded the bush plane and we took off. Passing over the mouth of the Chitistone River, I shouted over the engine's drone, "Hey, where are we going? I thought we were doing the same trip I did earlier this summer on the Nizina. You're supposed to land on that gravel bar down there!"

"Tom, one of the clients, said he was told that the trip would start up at the headwaters," Will said. "It's okay. I checked it out from the air. The river looks good."

Trust a bush pilot's opinion of the rapids? Yeah, right. These guys spend most of their time half a mile or more above ground.

We flew up the valley. Heedless of the breathtaking mountains surrounding us, I stared down through the plane's tiny windows, straining to see signs of big water or obstacles that might create problems for us on the way down. There were fifteen miles of unfamiliar river between the headwaters and the mouth of the Chitistone. I noticed a few huge boulders and accompanying hydraulics, and absorbed a little shot of adrenaline.

We landed high on a rocky terrace just below the snout of the Nizina Glacier. Silty meltwater gushed from beneath it. Catherine was busy pumping up a raft and had frame pieces strewn over the ground. Another small plane landed, blowing sand over everything. It would soon be dark. I sorted through a pile of unfamiliar kitchen gear, then assisted Catherine with an equally unfamiliar mound of boat gear. At one point, I joked to Catherine, "So, just how far is the river from here? I can't even hear it."

"I don't know; I haven't even had time to think about that."

Finally, all six clients had arrived. The two pilots gathered everyone for a group photo. I was more concerned about our position—obviously distant from the river—than preserving a Kodak moment. I took Will aside and asked the ridiculous. "How far is the river?"

"It looked close from the air. It's just over that way," he said, pointing into the dimming light.

"Where's all the food for the trip?"

Will showed me the food bags and pulled out a couple of Tupperware containers. "This is the tomato sauce my wife made for tonight's dinner. And here's a premade tossed salad."

The pilots hopped in their small planes, lurched down the gravel terrace one after another, and lifted off, rising above the Nizina River Valley. Catherine and I fired up the stove, boiled whole-wheat pasta, heated the sauce, and served dinner. Gathered together for the first time, our group formally introduced themselves. Four of our party had attended Yale University together, several years back; this was a reunion for the young attorneys, who now lived scattered across the country. A sixty-some-year-old couple, friends of one of the attorneys, had joined the trip at the last minute.

In the embrace of silence and wild country, people either relax or become uneasy. The older couple, Jack and Liz, clearly fell into the latter category. They could not pitch their tent. At dinner, they complained about the meal. Jack commented on the "brown noodles," adding, "And I bet we're going to have some sort of hippie granola for breakfast!"

I noticed that Jack and Liz were tossing cigarette butts on the ground at regular intervals. I approached Jack. "Sir, I have a little metal can here, and it would be great if you would just toss your butts in here, instead of on the ground. After all, we're in the middle of a protected wilderness."

"You've got to be kidding," he said. "This is nothing but a godforsaken wasteland. It looks like a gravel pit!"

We polished off dinner and eventually, everyone turned in for the night. Any doubts I had about the conviviality of the group I kept to myself. The fol-

lowing morning, Catherine and I resumed rigging boats and served breakfast—granola! I took a walk down to the river with a couple of drybags. Multi-
leveled boulder terraces, three to seven feet high, stair-stepped down to the
water for half a mile. I returned with the bad news and rallied everyone to grab
a handle on one of the rafts. Liz refused to help. She sat on a boulder, wearing
a mosquito head net with a cigarette sticking through the mouth slit.

Jack piped up right away. "I thought this was going to be like one of those
Sobek trips, where the guides do everything!"

"Well, sir," I said, "if you want to run this river, everyone has to pitch in,
because there's no way Catherine and I are going to carry two sixteen-foot
rafts, oar frames, and all this gear by ourselves."

By late afternoon, we'd made multiple trips to the river; finally, all the gear
was beside the Nizina. On one of the many carries, I discovered that our
clients had brought along a case of beer and an apple box full of liquor bottles—enough for a fifth for each of us, and then some.

Catherine and I rigged the boats. She wore running shoes. "Did you bring
any rubber boots?" I said.

"Nah, I figure I'll just hop in and out from the boat to shore. That's what
we do on the Colorado."

"But this is Alaska. The river is frigid," I said, staring at the churning water.
"And what if it rains?"

"I heard it doesn't rain much in the interior of Alaska."

The clients waited. I gave a safety talk. Then we loaded up and launched.
The boats bucked and bounced through lively rapids, while convoluted limestone cliffs rose above us, crowned by jagged peaks. Glacial silt ground against
raft hulls, shushing the chattering and soothing the nervous passengers. I felt
good. Our journey had finally begun.

SEVERAL HOURS LATER, we made camp for the night on a long
broad beach. Tents went up on a bluff above the river, and I built a fire near
the water. The top of the apple box came off, and booze began to flow. We ate
supper; everyone relaxed, absorbing the fire's warmth. Alpenglow lit up the
rugged Wrangell Mountains surrounding us. Long after Catherine and I

turned in for the night, the fire blazed, and the singing grew more slurred. Fiery embers greeted the new day; at 4 A.M., the group finally went to bed.

I heard the first drops of rain at 5 A.M., and turned over for a few more hours of sleep. When I rose, it was raining hard. The river already threatened to take our boats. Catherine and I pulled them higher onto the beach, used the oars to erect a tarp, and dug into the breakfast bag. There were eight small packets of instant oatmeal clustered into a bag, along with several tea bags, packets of hot chocolate, and a small supply of instant coffee. "Oh, boy," I said, "this is barely enough food for four hungry people, let alone eight."

I pawed through the rest of the food bags and discovered similar portions of food allotted for each meal. Catherine and I made hot drinks and delivered them to the tents. Liz and John reported that their tent—a tiny A-frame, single-walled pup tent—was leaking and Liz's down sleeping bag had a wet spot. John, a young attorney from North Carolina, emerged in a snug Gore-Tex running suit. "Is that your raingear?" I asked.

John nodded. One by one, everyone emerged from their tents and squeezed under the tiny tarp. I glanced at ponchos and other flimsy raingear. At least most of the group had rubber boots. After breakfast, we moved the boats again, pulling them tight up against the high bluff where the tents stood. By lunch, the water had eaten up the campfire ashes.

Every few hours, we checked the boats, watching the water rise ominously. Catherine was already on her second set of Gore-Tex raingear. Turns out, she'd come to Alaska with a friend who was photographing gear for a catalog; he'd given her a slew of brand-new, expensive raingear. Water had soaked through the first set; it lay balled up in a corner of the tent, along with a pair of soaked running shoes.

By evening, water lapped at the boats and we pulled them up again—this time to the top of the bluff. We served an embarrassingly meager dinner, as damp campers tipped the liquor bottles repeatedly and began to ask the proverbial questions: "When is the rain going to stop and when are we going back on the river?" Reasonable queries, no doubt, but how could I possibly answer them? So we waited. And waited.

THE RAIN CONTINUED for two more days. We ran out of hot drinks, and food supplies grew desperately low. Everyone complained of being wet, and several clients wanted to know what was going to happen, since they had to be back at work in a couple of days. I had no radio. It wouldn't have helped anyway; no planes had flown over us. Catherine's Gore-Tex was soaked—all three sets of top-of-the-line North Face gear. "Gore-Tex doesn't work in a hard rainfall," I told her. "And in this weather, there's no way to dry it out." My rubberized Helly Hansen fishing raingear was holding out. Still, I knew everyone else was miserable. Catherine and I had the only truly rain-proof tent. Catherine said, "I think we should just pack up and go for it."

"Are you kidding?" I said. "I bet the Nizina Canyon is treacherous right now! I say we wait for the rain to stop."

Tension in camp was palpable. We had more than twenty-five miles of swift, braided river to go before reaching the head of a narrow, twisting canyon that provides plenty of excitement even under normal Class III conditions. Beyond that, other tributaries feed into the Nizina. At flood stage, there would be dangerous boils, eddies, and whirlpools in the hairpin turns. Once we put into the river again, we might not be able to stop. The gravel bars were sub-merged, the eddies washed out.

IT'S NOON ON day five and I'm crouched by the river in my raingear, staring at the water, and visualizing a rescue. Everyone is hunkered down in the tents, and I haven't seen a soul yet today. Suddenly, I hear the low droning *whup-whup* of a helicopter rotor. A Bell Jet Ranger roars overhead. I can only stare, arms slack at my sides. What I really want to do is wave my arms fran-tically. But we are not in trouble. I cannot ask for a rescue simply because it's raining, people are poorly equipped for the weather, and they want out of here. We're basically safe if we stay put. The helicopter disappears up the valley. Heads emerge from tents, and I take a poll. "If there was a possibility that we could be picked up, does anyone here want to leave?" Unhesitatingly, all vote to leave; they want me to flag down the chopper.

Nearly an hour later, I hear the helicopter again. Suddenly, it appears, swooping down the valley, flying low. Before I can even raise an arm, it's on the ground. The pilot motions me over to the cockpit. Stooping low to avoid the rotor blades, hands over my ears, I run over. "What the hell are you people doing out in the middle of the river?" he shouts.

I explain our situation. He tells me he's part of a search-and-rescue mission organized by the National Park Service. They've been searching for two missing people and a plane for the past two days. A party on horseback discovered that one of their riders was missing, apparently swept away during a stream crossing. "A Supercub pilot dropped his wife off on a gravel bar in the middle of the Chitina River and never returned for her," he said. "Must've crashed. She was stranded out there with the water rising. We got her out, but we haven't found him or the plane yet. You're not planning on running this river are you? It's wall-to-wall water out there. We don't need another tragedy on our hands."

"Actually, I was hoping not to have to," I say. "We've been sitting here for a few days, waiting to see if the river might go down a bit."

"The May Creek Ranger Station is five minutes from here. I'm going over there to get permission to sling you guys over. I'll be right back. Get your stuff packed up." With that, he lifts off. I poll everyone again; the decision is unanimous. They want off the river.

A mad scramble to pack up gear ensues; the helicopter returns, landing on what's left of our bluff. The engine winds down, chopper blades twirling to a stop. "Don't deflate the rafts; takes too long," says the pilot, jumping out of his cockpit as the engine dies. He pulls out a big net and helps us wrap it around the fully inflated boats loaded with our soggy gear. Liz and Jack climb into the cockpit with their duffels. The pilot hooks one end of a cable to the net, the other to the helicopter, and hops back on. Minutes later, the metal bird whines, revs up, and pulls straight off the ground, hoisting the bulky net. It hovers briefly, our gear dangling below its belly, then roars across the river and disappears. Less than an hour later, after three chopper-hauls, everyone is sipping hot coffee by the potbellied stove in a spacious log building. "I think we should have gone for it," says one of the young attorneys. "That would have been an exciting ride."

"Yeah, I was ready," says another. "We should get our money back, since we didn't float the whole river."

Will flies over from McCarthy Lodge and ferries us back. It's raining there, too. People are throwing sandbags along the riverbanks to protect their cabins. The Kennicott River is in flood; two vehicles have already been swept away. With a hot meal and dry beds, the clients' grumbling slowly subsides. Now they drink vodka and tell war stories to anyone in the lodge who will listen.

PERHAPS WE SHOULD have stayed out there a few days longer, waiting for the river to crest; maybe that would have humbled them. All I knew was—come hell or high water—the next time I guided a river trip I'd be the one in charge.

As a child, Maryland-born **Karen Jettmar** rowed skiffs and paddled surfboards near Annapolis. She left for the Alaskan wilderness after college in 1973, and spent four summers paddling solo throughout Glacier Bay National Park before breaking the gender stereotype to work as a backcountry ranger in several Alaska parks. Naturalist, conservation activist, photographer, and wilderness guide, she is the author of two guidebooks—*The Alaska River Guide* and *Alaska's Glacier Bay*—and the forthcoming *Arctic Refuge*, a book of photography and essays. After her misadventure on the Nizina River in 1985, she started her own adventure company, offering extended journeys to wild rivers in Alaska and Canada.

the mother of all takeouts

Vince Welch

IT ALL STARTED a few years ago. The phone calls that is. Usually late at night, and usually in the heart of winter. The conversations always began with small talk. But the caller's true intentions were soon revealed by those three inevitable words, "Remember the time . . ." I confess to making such calls myself. This is what old-timers do a lot of: tell stories. I had become one, for better or worse. And so I was obliged to listen to my fellow tale-spinners. *Of course*, I remembered the times we all ran Crystal Rapid and made it into the upper eddy. Yes, *I had been* on the trip with four flips and a midnight flash flood that obliterated the kitchen and washed away a copulating pair of late-night tent scratchers. Even if I hadn't. What about those memorable passengers like "Uno Con Ma" Bob and Don "de la Boca," or seventy-year-old Ruth who was sleeping out for the first time in her life? Even if I don't remember them, I'd never admit it to the storyteller. I'd dare not let on. After all, these were stories from the river, and the truth—I knew—lay in the telling. So two boats flipped instead of three; Unkar beach was washed away in '83, not '80. So what! To examine these stories too closely was to lose them. So I let them be.

Except for one. In the beginning, I didn't pay too much attention to it. It sounded like just another river story, with the usual variations. But it came up, again and again. In the plain light of day or the dead of the night, in letters, on postcards and shredded cocktail napkins, in bathrooms and bars and moving cars, on epic hikes or casual strolls, in The Canyon, or on the road, people were talking about an apparently historical takeout. This seemed strange to me. A story about a takeout? And when I finally realized that large numbers of storytellers (thirty-four at last count) claimed vehemently to have been on this takeout, my curiosity got the better of me. Obviously all these people could not have been in the vehicle in question on that fateful day. As anyone who has ridden the Grey Ghost knows, it can hold six, perhaps eight boatmen and their gear in some degree of comfort. Add a dependable driver—if you can find one—and that's all, folks. I also knew, from personal experience, that the Ghost was not always the vehicle of first choice for a tired, sunbaked crew. A converted, previously Mormon-owned milk delivery van, it was hell on wheels. So why all the claims to have been there?

As my research progressed, I learned to live with the numerous inconsistencies, stunning as they were. One individual was adamant that the takeout occurred in early July of 1981. Another confident soul assured me that it all came down in late August of 1983. I had heard that the river trip itself had been great; that it had been horrible. The water was high; no, it was very low. Four boats flipped; no, it was a golden trip. And from one cynic, who admitted that she was never tired of telling what she called "The Mother of All Takeouts," I recorded this conspiracy tale: that this takeout never really took place; that it was the ultimate river concoction, brewed by a few deliberately and many unintentionally for consumption by the ever-growing, ever-gullible river masses.

Over the years, however, I was able to identify a few uncontestable facts from the bird's nest of rumor, hearsay, and wishful storytelling. These facts ran like shimmering threads through all the versions I had heard of this so-called magical takeout. You, of course, must decide where the truth rests.

The BIG RIDE actually took place sometime in the early '80s. Beyond a doubt, the vehicle involved was the boxy monstrosity called the GREY GHOST. All parties agreed that HOOVER DAM was crossed sometime in the afternoon. And every storyteller insisted that OFFICER NOLAN was a prince of a guy, given the situation. There was unanimous agreement that a stop was made at CIRCUS CIRCUS, the notorious Las Vegas casino, though the details of this particular episode vary tremendously. And every tale-spinner mentions, with a variety of embellishments, an encounter in a field outside of Glendale involving A CREW MEMBER, A CAMEL, and A BANANA. Finally, and perhaps most peculiar of all, each and every narrator insists that the occupants of the Grey Ghost (which most people claim to have been) wore CHICKEN SUITS. An improbable set of facts you are saying to yourself. I heartily agree. But this is where my search led me. And so it is with much humility that I now attempt to re-create what happened in the hot stinking desert on that memorable day.

LONG AGO AND far away, when The Canyon and I were much younger . . .

"We can't just go straight back to the warehouse," said Haircut absentmindedly. His locks recently shorn, Haircut's amorous life had improved to the point where he was grinning constantly.

"No good reason to," replied Ishitonka, adjusting his skirt as he climbed on the bumper of the Ghost to adjust the carburetor. The rest of the crew waved good-bye, as two vans stuffed with passengers pulled away from Pierce Ferry. A chant exploded simultaneously from both vehicles. *"Dories! Dories! Dories!"* Applause followed. It had been a good trip, even a great trip. The river had been large and translucent, bouncy, but kind and forgiving. There had been communions at dawn; dances in the moonlight. Stories with endings and food with flavor—shared well. Sand castles and fireworks and tag-team mud wrestling with park rangers had been leavened with stubbed toes, lost hikers, and an all-night rip of a storm.

Of course, there had also been a flip in Lava Falls. But exciting rescues always escalate the customary Alive-Below-Lava celebration into a pagan survivors' ball. In short, a good time was had by all. Still, it was a relief to watch the vans disappear over the hill.

"We've got twelve dozen eggs that are rotting in the hot stinking sun," said Amanda Crumpecker, twelve-year veteran of the river. "What are we gonna do with 'em?"

"I *need* to do some *trundling*. Right now, before anything happens!" shouted Sparrow.

"How about some cold Utah brew?" asked Leland Stone.

"Let's do it all," whispered Eyebrow Bob to no one at all.

Haircut surveyed his ragged crew. Yikes! Maybe this bunch should go straight home, he thought. No detours, no off-ramps, no nonsense. It wasn't easy being a trip leader on the river, or just off it. Haircut tucked his Hawaiian shirt in. The ends came dripping out the crotch of his red Patagonia shorts. He said in a firm voice, "We'll have to take the long way home if you guys want to do everything!"

"What?" sputtered Leland Stone.

"*Get in the car!*" screamed Sparrow.

And so it began.

Ishitonka had driven only a few miles up the empty road when Sparrow said, "This is the place." Ishitonka pulled the Ghost over and the crew tumbled out of the van in search of large boulders. On that Sunday morning, the earth trembled and many rocks that had previously led unexciting lives at the top of arroyos suddenly found themselves at the bottom. Small scabs of earth peeled off and red plumes veiled the sky. And the sounds of trundling filled the air, and Sparrow and Ishitonka knew this was good. After much dust and noise had been created, they drove on.

An hour down the road, the eggs—putrid, garbage-bound eggs—were pulled from their protective cardboard cocoons and given new purpose in their rather short span of earthly existence. Who threw them first, and at what, remains an unanswered question. They were hurtled at fence posts, trees, and abandoned cars, at road signs of all sizes and shapes. *Especially* at road signs. The *clang* of direct hits reverberated through the barren lands. And the lesser creatures of this apparently godforsaken country were thankful for this flying roadkill, for this manna from heaven. For a hit or a miss still meant a meal. SLOW AT CROSSING and APPROACH AT YOUR OWN RISK and NARROW CURVE—BEWARE were soon dripping with the essence of chicken life.

Amanda Crumpecker smiled at this sacred manifestation of resource utilization. And she sang: "You can break my yolk, but never my heart; I ain't just another road sign on your way to another woman's womanly parts."

In the midst of her bliss, she raised a hot stinking egg high over the bald-headed Leland and brought it down, ever so easy. The sticky substance began to spread over the smooth surface. It quickly invaded the ears and short hairs on the neck of a stunned Stone, before free-falling onto his shirt. His eyes glazed over and he let out a short bark. And it was good (for Amanda anyway).

And it is said to this day that Leland will only order his *huevos* scrambled.

A FEW MILES before Hoover Dam, a battered, foreign-made pickup snuck up behind the Grey Ghost. Like the tail of a wayward kite, it hung frantically on its bumper. Ishitonka, driver extraordinaire and perennially cool head, surveyed the orange Toyota for signs of malice or intelligent life. Suddenly the vehicle began to weave in and out of its lane, as if it were trying to signal for help. Ishitonka slowed to fifteen miles per hour. Horn honking and lights blinking, the renegade truck drew parallel with the Ghost. Two smiling idiots leaned out and waved excitedly. Then they sped off. A bumper sticker on the back of their pickup read ALICE'S CHICKENS—GROWN TO SUIT YOU—MESQUITE, NEVADA.

"Strange," murmured Ishitonka.

"Indeed," Eyebrow agreed.

As the Ghost approached Hoover Dam, Eyebrow Bob spied the unmistakable back end of an eighteen-wheeler parked in front of the Squirrel's Rest Diner. On the back of the truck, in large, bloodred letters, sprawled the words ENGLAND and TRUCKING. In his mind, this was the largest road sign he had ever seen. As if in a trance, Eyebrow slid into firing position in the front of the Ghost. He hung out the open door, with the wind in his face. Delicately, nay, almost lovingly, he cupped three white orbs in his hands. And with the serenity of a born-again assassin, he took aim and fired.

He managed three direct hits.

Officer Nolan, black coffee in one hand, had just lit a cigarette for Shorty McVeigh. Years ago, Nolan had given Shorty his first speeding ticket—and they had been friends ever since. It is like that, in the desert. When the three nutritional missiles struck Shorty's rig, both men felt the ignominy simultaneously. Nolan gulped his coffee down and charged toward his patrol car.

"Crazy sons of bitches!" he yelled, without realizing it. "On a Sunday of all days. I'll bring 'em in, Shorty." Shorty jumped up and down on the simmering blacktop. A tour group of retired teachers simply stared in disbelief. Meanwhile, the egg yolk began to sizzle on the pavement.

Halfway across the Great American Plug that stoppers a premier southwestern river, Ishitonka noticed flashing red lights reflected in his rearview mirror.

"Guys, we are being pursued," he said.

"No way," replied Bob.

"No shit," added Sparrow.

"Not again!" sighed Amanda.

By the time the Ghost pulled over, the sea of root beer cans and chip bags and cigarette butts had been deposited in the two Big Boy coolers in the rear of the van. All contraband had been stashed under the seats. The crew had straightened their hair, belongings, and attitudes in preparation for Officer Nolan's visit. As Ishitonka veered off the road, the Sunday traffic slowed noticeably. Heads turned, tongues wagged, and the occasional middle finger was thrust upward, inserted into sultry summer air.

Moments later the police car pulled in behind them. A strange, liquid calm filled the interior of the van. The crew floated in a communal vision of a single dory poised on the brink above Lava Falls. Eyebrow Bob—Catholic by birth—just knew what he had to do. A good sheep, no matter how far it has strayed from the fold, always remembers the formidable lessons of lambhood: better to ask forgiveness than permission. This was not the time to think too hard about consequences.

He leaped out of the door of the van into the sun-glassed stare of The Law. A shiny badge on the starched uniform shirt revealed his antagonist's name. Eyebrow drew a deep breath of desert air and began his confession.

"I'm sorry, Officer Nolan. I threw those eggs. I don't know what possessed me. It was a very, very, very inappropriate thing to do. I hope that rig wasn't damaged . . ."

"Inappropriate? Let's just call it 'dumb,'" said Nolan.

"Yes, sir. Dumb. Divinely dumb," replied Eyebrow.

"You could have hit somebody. Look at all these folks from the bus, just enjoying themselves!" Nolan continued his lecture. "And what about the children? What do you think *they* think when they see grown-ups throwing eggs?"

"You're absolutely right, sir," mumbled Eyebrow. "Poor timing on my part. We're just off the river and I guess I forgot how to act."

"Who's that?" asked Officer Nolan, indicating the be-skirted Ishitonka who was clicking photos in Nolan's direction. "What's he doing?"

"Oh, that's our driver, Ishitonka."

"I take pictures of everything," Ishitonka offered, by way of explanation.

"Everything, huh? You licensed to drive this rig, sir?" inquired Officer Nolan, stepping toward the open door of the van. He peered in and found—four passengers in a slumber.

"Tired puppies," said Ishitonka, as he opened his ammo can. Out came a dog-eared, paper-thin certificate of highway mastery. Officer Nolan stepped back with the paper in his hand. He examined it carefully.

"Everything appears to be in order, Mister . . . Gerhart."

Suddenly a roar of laughter peeled off Officer Nolan's pursed leather lips. "Hurricane! You folks from Hurricane, Utah? Hell, I should have known. Say, you know Clarissa Beauregard?"

"Oh yeah. We're old friends," rejoiced Eyebrow, sensing the channel of opportunity that opened before him, as it sometimes does at the head of a nasty rapid.

"We've been running rivers together for years. We're on our way home right now."

"Goin' home the long way, aren't you?"

"It was necessary, sir," replied Eyebrow.

"I see." Both Officer Nolan and Eyebrow Bob watched an eighteen-wheeler slide to a stop.

"Uh-oh, here comes Shorty," said Officer Nolan. Eyebrow noticed his escape route blocked by boulders and the big truck.

"Listen up," said Nolan. "Since you're from Hurricane and you know Clarissa, I'm gonna cut you some slack here. I'll handle Shorty. Just say you're sorry and offer to pay for a wash for his rig. He's been meaning to get one anyhow, okay?"

"Right. Yes, sir. Thank you, Officer Nolan. Sir. We won't let this happen again." Eyebrow Bob looked sincerely contrite.

"Sure thing," said Officer Nolan.

It was all settled quickly. Shorty and Eyebrow shook hands. Ishitonka took one last picture.

Five minutes later the Grey Ghost merged again with the current of traffic. Shorty and Officer Nolan waved good-bye. Then they both leaned against the side of the patrol car, like two old redwood trees resting against one another after a freak storm. Eyebrow Bob sunk into his seat, exhausted by success. Home was still a long way off.

LATER THAT AFTERNOON, in the parking lot of Circus Circus, in a city that had once been nothing but a pit stop for weary pioneers, Haircut issued a rare command to the crew.

"Stick together! This could be dangerous."

"Then why enter this neon hellhole?" asked Amanda Crumpecker.

"Because it is there," sang Sparrow." And besides, we need food and drink after our ordeal."

"And entertainment," added Leland Stone.

"I know just the spot for us," said Haircut."I scouted it once, and am fairly confident of the run. Trust me!"

And so it came to pass that the weary travelers left the furnace heat of the desert parking lot and entered into what some have referred to as an "air-conditioned nightmare." They marched as one through the carpeted alley watched by security guards, until they arrived at the Merry-Go-Round, a revolving bar with a circus theme and expansive view.

Thereupon they sat and rested on ridiculous, painted ponies. And thus Leland Stone spake: "Six martinis, please. Bombay, and very dry." And round and round went the watering hole, while they swapped lies with absolutely perfect strangers. And the lights danced and the music thumped to a pedestrian beat. And lions roared, seals barked, and handsome men in red leotards ate fire and swallowed swords, and brave women in sequins and feathers cascaded through the air, while the multitudes below ooohed and aaahed, and spent their disposable income on fluffy, stuffed animals and tall, colorful drinks with pastel swizzle sticks and platters of food that could have fed a Third World country—or starving boat crew—for months. Amanda Crumpecker's stomach was growling so loudly that the bartender looked concerned.

And thus it came to pass in this place that the doors of perception, momentarily flung open by the spirits from India, slammed shut again. And the crew of the Grey Ghost descended into Emma Lee's Home-cooking Cafeteria, located somewhere in the netherworld of Circus Circus, for dinner. It was cheap. And for a while, it was good.

But not for long. Ishitonka had been first to notice security guards moving into strategic positions throughout the dining room: four or five thickset, well-dressed, no-neck types with pencil-thin mustaches and shiny shoes, foaming at the mouth. Their point man was quickly advancing toward our heroes' table.

"I think we have attracted some attention," Ishitonka informed the rest of the crew. "Could be my plaid skirt they're curious about."

"Did we do something wrong?" Leland, who had ordered pasta à la Bombay, wanted to know.

"Not yet," answered Haircut. "But we look like we might. And they can't stand that. That's for sure. I propose a graceful exit."

"Where is Sparrow?" wondered Eyebrow Bob.

"I, for one, haven't a clue," Amanda responded between bites of cheesecake. "But if we aren't normal, I should like to know the definition of the word. Certainly the majority of people in this establishment don't qualify. I feel overwhelmingly normal." Everyone at the table nodded in agreement. She then turned toward the security guards, flickered her tongue, and blew them a kiss.

"We oughta get outta here pronto," urged Haircut.

"Perhaps I could have a word or two with them and explain the situation," Eyebrow suggested.

But by then the crew had already begun to weave their way through the maze of tables and chairs. They zigzagged between screaming kids and overfed gamblers, blue-haired little grannies and slouching teenagers, instantly absorbed by the amorphous mass of indoor thrill-seekers. The security guards trailed them at a safe distance, walkie-talkies in hand. Eventually the wandering tribe found a revolving glass door labeled THANKS FOR COMING.

From the roof of the Grey Ghost, the stray Sparrow watched the crew spill into the parking lot, which was now filled to capacity. They seemed to linger there on the curb, unnecessarily and on the edge of disaster, searching the horizon. Haircut was scratching his head; Ishitonka was scratching his crotch. Sparrow could almost hear the words, "*Where* did we put that damn thing?" He could clearly see the security guards bolting through the revolving door like unleashed, underfed pit bulls on Thorazine. It was then that Sparrow grabbed the conch, puckered his twisted lips, and blew for all he was worth.

"*Get in the Boat!*" he screamed. Then he dove off the roof into the driver's seat in one fluid move and brought the Ghost to life. He circled the parking lot, picking up one boatman here, snatching another one there, till all were safely aboard.

"Home, Sparrow. Straight home!" Haircut's voice rang from the back of the van.

And they nearly made it straight home, except for a stop in Glendale later that night, where, in a field near a Mini-Mart, Leland Stone discovered a camel named Clyde.

During the course of his Bombay-fueled conversation with the humped creature, it became apparent to Leland that it was delirious with hunger. Being a generous soul by nature, he ran back to the Mini-mart and purchased a large, ripe banana.

Back at the fence, he peeled it and placed one end in his mouth, as was camel custom. In a magnificent gesture of friendship and trust, Leland leaned over the fence, so Clyde could reach his end of the banana. Soon, man and beast began to nibble toward a common understanding. But before these two had a chance to exchange phone numbers, Haircut pulled Leland away from the fence and into the waiting van.

"I think we've done it all," said Haircut to no one in particular. "Hit it, Ishitonka."

The Grey Ghost swerved out onto the highway and before long, disappeared into the warm, velvety night.

Epilogue

DURING THAT INFAMOUS season, takeouts went from bad to worse. Naturally, other crews seized upon this novel, recreational approach to trip ends. In the commissary, trip leaders were heard to ask for "extra eggs," in case they ran short. There are some accounts of shortages on the river, due to hoarding. Stationary targets, like signposts, quickly became passé; moving targets, albeit slow-moving ones—mostly cows—became fashionable until calmer minds prevailed. Stops at Circus Circus reached a nadir when one beer-addled crew member, wearing nothing but his loincloth and a dumb-founded expression, was left stranded at a gas station next to a strip club at 1 A.M.

It was only a matter of time before management put an end to these activities. Gradually things returned to normal, and The Mother of All Takeouts entered the realm of myth and legend.

Having nearly drowned at the ages of ten, twenty-one, and thirty-four, **Vince Welch** has been a water lover all his life. A swimmer, sailor, abalone diver, and ex-boatman—he is presently surfing with his son in New Zealand. Vince co-authored *The Doing of the Thing*, which won the 1998 National Outdoor Book Award. He is also an ordained minister in The Church of the Flowing Water. Come all ye faithful!

tales of the motley crew

Deidre Elliott

AT LAST TWO of my boating buddies and I finally had enough money to buy our own raft. No more hitching a ride as passengers on someone else's boat, no more begging to borrow an ancient Yampa-model from a friend. Besides, that borrowed boat had become so worn-out that, on our last trip, on Utah's Green River, someone constantly had had to operate the air pump just to keep the boat's leaking chambers partway inflated. For most of that last day on the water, the rest of us had had to paddle and pray—and then, as we pulled into the takeout in Dinosaur National Monument, try to ignore the guffaws of people on shore who pointed and snickered at our ancient, collapsing, and not-so-river-worthy craft. Even though we had patched and prodded, this borrowed boat would travel no farther.

But now we could buy our own, brand-new, fourteen-foot, fully functioning, four-chambered neoprene beauty. This baby would carry six paddlers or one person at the oars with a few passengers. Never again would we be the objects of ridicule.

Except. Except that the three of us—and, it seems, everyone we ever asked to come along on our river trips—were second-stringers. You know what I mean. In high school we'd been the presidents of clubs (but not of the really cool clubs), the editors of yearbooks (but not the stars profiled in their pages), or the athletes who occasionally caught a pop fly but never actually scored the winning run. We were the kids who knew everyone, but who weren't known by everyone. Not that I'm complaining. If you needed someone competent and dependable, congenial but not too competitive . . . yes, that described my friends and me. We'd been that way through college and on into adulthood. And as for running rivers, well . . . would a really cool kid ever have had to borrow a sagging raft?

On that last trip, the one just before we bought our new boat, there on the banks of the Green River in Dinosaur National Monument, someone who had seen us frantically paddling toward shore called us "motley." We'd just come off a wild and thrilling ride through the Gates of Lodore. We'd navigated whitewater that had challenged the great explorer John Wesley Powell himself, and yet our crew had been christened—by total strangers—"motley."

The name stuck. We tried to make it a source of pride, but a series of misadventures both on and off the water confirmed to us and to everyone else that, indeed, we were a motley crew. (And not in that really cool rock star Crüe-with-a-fancy-umlaut way either.) Here's what I mean.

IT WAS THE start of a new boating season. Pam, Elaine, and I had been enjoying our fancy new raft for a full year when we received word that we'd been issued a permit to run Idaho's Salmon River in July. Pam and I both lived on the eastern slope of the Rockies; she in Longmont, Colorado, and me in Boulder. Elaine, our other partner, lived in Grand Junction on the western slope. We'd decided that a trip through Westwater Canyon's rollicking whitewater was just the thing we needed to double-check the raft and polish our river skills.

Westwater is sometimes called the "Little Grand Canyon." Even though it is nowhere near as long or as deep as the actual Grand, it *is* on the Colorado River, it *does* contain stunningly gorgeous scenery, and *it boasts kick-ass rapids.* Rafters and kayakers look forward to the dark beauty of narrow passages through black schist topped with red slickrock as well as to the challenge of rapids with names like Funnel Falls, Sock-it-to-me, and Surprise. But the biggest rapid on Westwater is Skull, where the level of the river suddenly drops. Here, a huge diagonal wave aims to force boaters directly into a hole resembling the entrance of hell. I've seen unlucky rafts hit Skull wrong and circle and circle, almost to the point of exhaustion, as the boaters try to power away from that hole.

But hey. That year the Motley boat didn't even get to the water, much less to Skull Rapid, before we had confirmed our reputation as the un-coolest raft ever. Since I had the biggest garage, it had fallen to me to store the raft at the end of the previous season. Elaine had been the last to use the raft and she'd winterized it, but hadn't remembered to tell me. Pam had picked up the raft from Elaine and transported it over the spine of the Rockies from the western slope to the eastern slope. She'd also winterized the raft, but, again, hadn't told me. So, in an effort to make sure that no leftover moisture remained between the rubber seams and folds, I'd followed the manufacturer's instructions and sprinkled the raft with cornstarch.

When it was time to unroll the big bundle of flaccid rubber for the Westwater trip at the water's edge at the Loma put-in, the winterizing efforts of the three Motley owners became obvious. I untied the carrying ropes, unfolded the boat, and voilà! Instant blizzard! Kayakers began to laugh. Other rafters stepped back in order to avoid being coated with cornstarch. Elaine shook her head; Pam sighed. The red dirt around us began to pale. All three of us had emptied a box of cornstarch to the curves and corners of the raft. In fact, being a conscientious boat owner, I'd added two, one for good measure. The boat had stayed dry all right; so dry that it could now create its own mini-climate. Criminy. I'm sure people still get to the Loma put-in and recall the day when it "snowed" there in the middle of June.

A MONTH LATER we headed north and west to Idaho and the Main Salmon. With 425 miles, the Salmon is the longest free-flowing river in the U.S., outside of Alaska. Its water is so clear that you can pick out patterns on the rocks of the riverbed. The current is cold too. No warm desert water here. No moderate ambient air temperatures either. For Coloradoans come north for an adventure, the chilly daytimes and downright cold nighttimes of central Idaho were more than invigorating. They demanded our attention and got it. So did the rock-studded channel of the Salmon River itself. Each of our—still motley—paddlers had a chance to have his or her legs scraped by boulders as we pinballed our way downstream.

Off the water other challenges existed. Hornets circled dinner's fruit salad, black widow spiders sought the warmth of sleeping bags, forest fires (one or two ridges over, but still close enough) turned the skies red, and the occasional rattlesnake angrily sent us the message to leave the rocky trails alone.

All of us tried to be more attentive than usual to our surroundings. Sometimes we were rewarded as when we caught glimpses of deer or bighorn sheep, but sometimes we forgot to pay attention and were punished. A twisted ankle, a slip on a wet rock that produced a sore hand . . . these were manageable errors, but Camille, poor Camille. She paid the highest price for inattention.

It was supposed to be a quick riverbank pit stop, just before another big rapid that had everyone on edge. The women went upstream; the men went downstream. We scrambled over rocks, pushed aside small bushes, did what needed to be done, and scrambled back down to the rafts. Camille was the last to arrive.

"Hey! I found these great big leaves. They work even better than toilet paper," she said.

"Say, Camille," I asked. "You didn't by any chance pick up some poison ivy, did you?"

"I dunno. What's it look like?"

Yep. Basic mistake. Luckily, we had some surgical-grade soap and disinfectant in our first-aid kit. Regardless, by day's end, Camille was miserable. Unfortunately, we were two days into a multiday trip on "The River of No Return." By the time we got off the water and Camille could get to a doctor, she was unashamedly scratching herself at every opportunity. She didn't care who saw her or what they thought. Poison ivy made her itch, and so she scratched.

Actually, she was pretty lucky that she had been able to wash off most of the irritating substances. The doctor said that she could have become seriously ill. Yes. It was a big mistake, a really big mistake. But that's something that could happen to anyone, right? You don't have to be a member of the Motley Crew to mistake one plant for another. But burning a raft? That's something else again. That's pure Motley.

PAM AND QUENTIN had been dating for a while. And like any serious boater, she wanted to check out her new guy's boating potential before the relationship got any more serious. She'd planned a trip on the Dolores River in southwestern Colorado. Quentin seemed like a natural for river running.

He was a teacher with a special interest in outdoors education and had a great gift for working with troubled teens. In fact that was how Pam and Quentin had met, when both were part of a summertime backpacking trip for high school students.

El Río de Nuestra Señora de los Dolores was named by the Spanish explorers Dominguez and Escalante as they searched for a more northern route to connect far-flung Spanish missions. The river tumbles down from above 10,000 feet in the Colorado Rockies near Lizard Head Pass and winds 250 miles to join the Colorado River near Moab, Utah. It passes through sub-alpine terrain, ponderosa pine forests, and red sandstone canyons. Slickrock Canyon on the desert section of the river reminds some old-timers of Glen Canyon before it was flooded by Lake Powell. There are Indian ruins up side creeks; great blue herons nesting in cottonwoods; an amazing "hanging flume," a remnant from mining days; and rapids along the way, big enough to kick-start your adrenaline flow.

The Motley and its companion boats had passed the worst of the rapids, including the ominously named Snaggletooth, and everyone was relaxing during a rather placid stretch of river.

One of the positive things about the Motley Crew was that we believed in democracy. Each paddler or passenger (if they rode in an oar rig) had an opportunity to captain the boat. You got the chance to be in charge of the other paddlers and you got the chance to row the boat, especially during calm stretches where beginners could learn to "read" the river.

That day on the Dolores the other boats also had placed their less experienced passengers at the helm. Now here's a math problem for you: What do you get when you put several inexperienced boaters on a narrow stretch of river, bunch them together, add a dose of inattentiveness, and then multiply by one very large surprise rock at midstream? Factor in a sudden surge in water speed and volume and you get bumper boats. You get collisions. You get passengers knocked overboard. And you get one raft, the Motley, on its side and firmly wrapped against the rock.

After that, on the Motley raft, you get a midriver scramble from the boat up onto the rock. As for the other boaters, you get experienced folks jumping for command of their crafts and rushing to pick up the accidental swimmers. You get everyone else shouting and thrashing about, and finally pulling in to shore to assess the situation.

At this point, it's important to note that several of the people in the group were engineers. And whether or not they were familiar with ropes and pulleys—whether or not they had ever used a rope or a pulley in their particular field of engineering—each engineer was sure that it would take a rope and a pulley to unwedge the Motley from the rock. Just *how* to set up the rope-and-pulley system was the question.

Meanwhile, gallant kayakers began ferrying stranded Motley rafters from the big rock to shore. It was at this point that Quentin's pluck—and Pam's affection for him—began to become apparent.

"Jump into the water!" a kayaker shouted to Quentin, the last boater remaining on the rock. "Grab hold of the back of my kayak and I'll take you to shore."

"I can't swim!" Quentin called back, still sitting on the rock. "And . . ." He hesitated.

"What?"

"And . . . I'm a little bit . . . I'm a little bit afraid of water."

Ah, the things we do for love. Quentin had agreed to go on a river trip with Pam, all the while concealing the fact that water terrified him and also that, mountain boy that he was, he couldn't swim a stroke.

Regardless, he managed to plunge into the roiling water of the Dolores River and grab the loop on the back of the kayak. Once on shore, he joined the others as they tried to figure out how to loosen the raft, still loaded with most of the gear, and maneuver it to safety.

The upshot of too many engineers trying to figure out a system of ropes and pulleys was that one brave—nonengineering—kayaker finally got disgusted, felt for the river knife at his belt, paddled out to the raft, and slit two tubes of the Motley in order to unlock the river's hold on the boat. Sure enough, the raft popped free and floated to shore.

But how did the raft get *burned*? That was Quentin's contribution. He graciously had offered to patch the raft while Pam collected gear that had floated downriver during the accident. Since the slashes in the tubes were each several inches long, Quentin patched well into the night. As a final gesture—no doubt wanting to impress his girlfriend with his attention to detail—he decided to touch up the scraggly ends of the polypropylene rope that was attached to the back of the raft. He took out his lighter, flicked it open, and ever so carefully melted the ends of the rope. He finished by tying the rope with a piece of parachute cord so that the rope rested on the top of raft's stern.

Everyone crawled into their sleeping bags that night grateful that, on a river named after Our Lady of Sorrows, no genuine sorrows had befallen our group that day.

But, during the night, Our Lady was working overtime.

THE NEXT MORNING Pam and Quentin discovered a hole the size of a small backpack in the rear of the raft. The ragged edges of rubber still felt warm. Evidently, when Quentin had heated the polypropylene rope, heat had remained in its core and wicked its way up through the center of the rope. It finally met the neoprene of the raft, only to smolder and melt rubber throughout the night, creating The Hole.

Quentin apologized. And apologized. And apologized. Of course, Pam wasn't mad. Neither was Elaine or I. We all thought it was hilarious. I mean, who burns a raft? Scrape a raft against the occasional rock? Certainly. Send an unsuspecting paddler for a swim through a big rapid? Probably. Even flip a raft? Eventually. But who gets to say they've burned a raft? Not many people. It takes someone special to burn a raft. Only a true member of the Motley Crew could do that. Quentin fit in just fine.

THE REST OF the trip went smoothly. Another season passed, and Quentin and Pam got married. Elaine moved on to kayaking. I stuck with rafting for a while, then passed the boat on to my daughters. The raft is looking even more ragged now. Its neoprene is patched and scraped, and the frame dented in more than a few places. But its crews no longer shrink from the nickname "motley." They now wear the term like a badge of honor.

Cool!

Deidre Elliott is a traitor to the West. She now teaches creative writing at Western Carolina University in North Carolina. That's *Deliverance* territory, where kudzu vines tangle riverbanks, boaters swap recipes for barbecue sauce, and—some say—Elvis still goes skinny-dipping in the "crick" every Saturday. Her work has been published in a southwestern anthology, *Getting Over the Color Green*, and in magazines like *Crazyhorse*, *South Dakota Review*, *Puerto del Sol*, and *North Dakota Quarterly*. Currently, she is completing a book on natural history—*Broken Country*. In the near future, Deidre plans on taking a motley crew of her students rafting on the Tuckaseegee River.

the best "true tourist tale" ever

Barry Smith

HAVING LIVED IN a tourist town for nearly ten years, I have become a fan of the "True Tourist Tale."

I don't mean those dubious tourist anecdotes, either, like people asking what time the Maroon Bells ring or at what altitude the deer become elk. No, the *true* is the most important part of the "True Tourist Tale," as the details of reality are the crux of the biscuit when it comes to the moments of silliness, oversight, confusion, and oftentimes downright stupidity that can possess people when they leave the confines of home.

However, as rich a breeding ground as my hometown is for such stories, I had to travel to another tourist town, Moab, in order to hear what has to be the best True Tourist Tale ever. And I don't use *ever* lightly.

Here's how everything is *supposed* to work: In Moab, Utah, there exists a no-frills, family-owned outfitting company called Tex's Riverways. One of the services that they offer is the Green River float trip. This excursion involves them driving you and your newly rented canoe to Mineral Bottom on the Green River. Once there, you fill up your canoe with all of your gear and float the fifty-two miles down to where the Green joins the Colorado River. The guys from Tex's meet you there with a big jet boat, whereupon they load your canoe, your camping gear, and you on the boat and motor you back up the Colorado to Moab.

Pretty simple, right? All you have to do is fend for yourself for about a week (it's generally a four- or five-day minimum trip) in the desert wilderness, a task that isn't necessarily all that hard, given the fact that a canoe will hold a whole lot of gear, including coolers.

All right, then. Enter a middle-aged couple from the fine state of

Washington. He is a medical doctor. She is a teacher. One of the things she teaches is outdoors education, with an emphasis on canoeing. Down the river head two successful, professional, competent people with outdoor experience. What could go wrong?

Well, in all fairness, a lot of things could go wrong. You could slip and break your leg getting out of the canoe. Your appendix could rupture. You could choke on a chicken bone. You could get a really bad ice cream headache from drinking that cold beer too fast. Or you could . . . and I know this will be hard to believe . . . get *really, really* lost.

Now, I've done this very trip a few times myself, and there were moments when my estimated position and my actual location were out of sync by a twist or a bend. However, since the river only flows one way, it's hard to screw up too badly, for eventually you come to a distinctive landmark and are able to orient yourself. This couple had three maps with them, two of which actually contained photographs of some very distinct rock formations that one sees over the course of the trip. The other was a topographic map with river miles listed on it.

Despite all this planning, though, our heroes soon became incredibly lost. So lost, in fact, that when they came upon some ripples in the otherwise smooth river, the ones that the outfitter had told them about, even pointed out specifically on one of their many maps, they thought that they were at least twenty miles upriver from the spot where they actually were.

Their reaction, however, was not, "Damn! We're way down here already? Boy, were we confused." It was more like, "Hey, here's some water ripples that those jerks who have been doing this for ten years neglected to tell us about."

I suppose that, in the interest of foreshadowing, I should point out that about four miles below the confluence of the Green and Colorado Rivers there is a long series of very dangerous rapids.

But hey, that's still days away, and there's a big warning sign before you hit the rapids. Certainly once they get to The Confluence—an impossible-to-mistake landmark—everything will fall into place, right? Right?

So you'd think. The junction of the Green and Colorado Rivers is the sort of geographic occurrence that Stevie Wonder couldn't miss.

It is clearly and distinctly the joining of forces of two very large rivers. You're floating down one river (and have been for days), you look to your left and, damn! A whole other river, with a whole other set of towering rock walls, separate and distinct. Look, you can see way up the other canyon. Another river. This must be The Confluence we've heard so much about. Yep . . . there's even a photograph of this spot right here on the map.

That is what you would assume would happen, but lest we forget, our adventurers, a medical doctor and an outdoors educator, are shaping up to be the kind of people who wouldn't know the Colorado River if it dumped twenty thousand cubic feet of water per second on them. Which, for the most part, it did.

They, for reasons possibly never to be understood, and despite the fact that the woman has done this trip before, think that they are merely witnessing the "abandoned meander" listed on the map, a geographic anomaly that they passed a good three days and thirty miles earlier.

Okay, okay, let's not nitpick about the fact that an *abandoned* meander is a place where a river once flowed but no longer does, hence the whole *abandoned* thing, meaning that there's, you know, not water in it anymore. And let's not keep bringing up the fact that this woman teaches canoeing to children, yet has just mistaken the mighty Colorado River, the one that carved out the Grand Canyon, for a riverbed that's been water-free for tens of hundreds of thousands of years. There's no time for the trivial, because it gets better.

For you see, about four miles below the confluence are some rapids. Some real, big, hairy rapids. So hairy, in fact, that there is a sign on the riverbank. A sign that, without bringing Stevie Wonder into it again (though they really should consider the benefits of including him in their next outdoor adventure), is about the size of your average side of a barn, reading, in big red letters:

DANGER

CATARACT CANYON

HAZARDOUS RAPIDS 2½ MILES

"Aha," thought our intrepid boatpersons. "We have in fact just passed the abandoned meander [exactly thirty miles upriver from where they *actually* were], and this sign is warning us of the dangerous rapids that exist thirty-two and a half miles downriver. It's just that the sign has been vandalized.

Some punk scraped off the 3 from the 32. Great! Once again we know exactly where we are! We must paddle fast, for we need to make up those long, lost miles so that we can make it to the confluence in time for our jet boat pickup tomorrow."

(As a short note, these thought processes are not purely inventions of mine, but paraphrases of the actual explanations given by the couple after they were rescued. But I'm getting ahead of myself.)

Now, I have never run these rapids, which our white-collar boaters are fast approaching. But those who have tell me that even a good hundred yards away they sound like a freight train. The drifters, still locating themselves on the map way up at Mile 30, assumed that this ominous, frothy, tornado-like sound was a sure sign that they were fast approaching the "ripples" that they had been told about.

Have I mentioned that this man was a doctor? You know, like, making life-and-death decisions every day? Well, he made one on this trip, too. Just before they hit the rapids, he mentioned to his wife that maybe they should put on their life jackets, just in case these ripples are more than they can handle. You know, maybe these Utah boys have a different definition of ripples than we do. Apparently it never occurred to them to just kinda pull over and maybe take a stroll down the riverbank and have a gander at what was making this huge, heart-stopping noise.

They hit the rapids and, predictably, their canoe dumped and they lost everything except the clothes they had on, a paddle, and the metal, airtight toilet, which the woman clung to because it was the only thing floating. They ended up on opposite sides of the bank, separated by rapids. Had it not been a warm, sunny day, they would likely have died of hypothermia. (That noise you hear is me resisting the urge to make tasteless comments about the failure of natural selection.)

They hiked to where the jet boat was picking up some other canoes and got the attention of the outfitter, the very same outfitter who relayed this story to me a few weeks ago. He motored them back up to Moab, and straight into the pages of True Tourist Tales history.

Now I can only assume that they are safely back to their daily routines: him carefully writing out prescriptions and her filling impressionable young minds with the nuances of how to competently maneuver in the outdoors.

Barry Smith writes the syndicated column "Irrelativity" for *The Aspen Times* in Aspen, Colorado, and has done so for a good number of years now. He has floated the Green River five times, and still finds the ripples quite challenging. In addition to maintaining his website, he writes poetry, radio comedy, short film and TV scripts (which he has been known to actually produce), little to-do lists, and the occasional phone number on his hand. Lately he's been writing "I can do it!" in tiny letters, over and over again, on a large piece of poster board.

marble canyon, the back door

Scott Thybony

A PAIR OF broken oars hung on the side of the ranch house in Indian Flat, a reminder of a few seasons on the Colorado. My last trip had ended three years before, and I had moved on to other things. Or so I thought.

Around Halloween some friends had gathered and a bottle of rum came out. Scott Milzer paced back and forth relating a sea kayaking tale, when suddenly he noticed our yellow rez dog curled by the woodstove. Storm had been rescued as a stray after being injured and dumped by the side of the highway.

"What tricks does she know?" Milzer asked.

"None," I told him. "She's still half wild."

"None? Every dog needs to know a trick."

He positioned himself in front of the dog, who was eyeing him suspiciously, and called out her name. "Storm!" She jumped up and stood there wondering what she had done wrong. He pointed at the floor, and gave the dog his best hypnotic stare. "Crawl like a cur," he shouted, "crawl like a cur!"

Immediately the dog dropped to her belly and began crawling across the floor. None of us had ever seen such a sorry display of canine humiliation before. We couldn't believe it, and between the groans and laughs we told our friend to cut it out. He ended the session with a smile, little realizing he would soon be learning the same trick himself.

The bottle passed around, and the river stories began. Terry Brian, who had just returned from Venezuela, talked about an epic portage where he had thrashed his way from one green-hell river to the next, crossing high passes slick with mud. He liked that sort of thing but missed the Colorado. Until this year he had an unbroken record of having run it every season. He began telling us about the time he went through Lava Falls on an air mattress to win a bet, when suddenly Milzer had an idea.

"Let's run the river!" he said. "I've never been on the Colorado." Terry agreed in a flash, but at this stage of the evening it was hard to tell if he was serious. I hesitated, believing the idea would run its course in a few minutes, as these things do, and then we could settle down to planning something practical. "I can't go back to Seattle," Milzer added, "without a story." The rest of the conversation unfolded this way:

"Correct me if I'm wrong," he said. "Your mescal has got its worm, and your wormwood has got its twig, but inside every bottle of rum is . . ."

"A plan, Mr. Milzer."

"A plan, Mr. Thybony. Inside every bottle is a plan. Too little and it's missed; too much and it's forgotten. We have hit the right balance."

Before anyone realized, the three of us were laughing at the sheer improbability of it. Milzer was under the impression we did this sort of thing all the time, and to bolster his own credentials told us about his last adventure on a big river. After drinking Pabst beer to excess during a tour of duty in Vietnam, he found himself swimming across the Mekong on a dare. He admitted it was one of the dumber things he had done, but his only punishment was getting sent to Bangkok, instead of Australia, for R&R. Now he wanted to take on the Colorado.

"Okay," I said, "I'll do it on one condition—we don't get caught." Of the three stealth trips I knew about that evening in 1979, all parties had ended up getting busted. I was more concerned about embarrassing friends who still worked for the park than about the fine. And Terry had the most to lose. Guiding was his profession, and he couldn't risk getting blackballed. But his need to get back on the home river overrode any cautionary thoughts. Sometimes, you act first and worry about the justifications for it later.

The immediate problem we faced was the time frame. Milzer had to be back in Seattle in about a week, so we had to act fast—one day to gather supplies and pack gear, then on our way the following day. The next problem was choosing the route. The put-in and takeout were the places most vulnerable to interdiction, so I gave some thought to their selection. We soon decided to stay within Marble Canyon, in the upper reaches of the Grand Canyon, and use the Navajo reservation for access. This might let us exploit a turf war between the Park Service and the Navajos. The park claimed everything below the rim, while the tribe said their land extended to the river's high-water line. We could argue, probably unsuccessfully, that the park had no authority over parties operating from the reservation side. This jurisdictional gray area let us view our actions as rule avoiding, not breaking. We could think of ourselves simply as undocumented boatmen about to enjoy an off-season excursion.

Harvey Butchart, who had spent years piecing together obscure routes, told me about one leading down a side canyon to a dryfall. It then follows the main gorge and reaches the river through a break in the Redwall cliffs. That would get us in; getting out was more problematic. We would need to leave the river at the confluence of the Little Colorado River and main Colorado, ascend an outrageously steep route, and climb the outer walls to reach the rim. A Navajo had told a friend of Butchart's about this route, predicting white men wouldn't like it.

A river trip resembles a floating circus with its daily routine of striking camp, packing all the gear onboard, and off-loading each evening. Even going as light as possible we couldn't avoid carrying heavy loads. Our craft of choice was a twelve-foot Avon Redshank, capable of handling the rapids on this stretch if we made half-decent runs. The drawback was it weighed a good seventy pounds dry, and with a pack frame, life jackets, and other odds and ends, I would be carrying about ninety pounds. The other loads ended up being almost as heavy. Everything for a multiday trip—boat, paddles, and all the normal dross and duffel—had to be packed in, and then carried out.

Any pack over forty pounds I consider excessive, but now had little choice. On portages, Canadian voyageurs were known to routinely hump loads weighing up to four hundred pounds using tumplines. This convinced me to try one. In theory the head strap, placed high on the forehead, transfers the bulk of the weight to the spine. The tumpline did this, I found, only with the generous assistance of certain neck muscles last put to use in America sometime back in the nineteenth century.

The three of us hit Flagstaff the next day, each with a list of things to buy. Milzer returned with all his items checked off and one extra purchase. He bought three Halloween masks, those Lone-Ranger-style half-masks. His think-ing went like this: If we passed anybody on the river, we could don our masks and float by without being recognized. None of us really thought this would work, but we also knew you couldn't run a clandestine trip without masks.

By early morning we were off. My wife, Sandy, and Nancy Brian volun-teered to drop us at the rim and pick us up five days later. The first challenge, it turned out, was finding the descent route. Dirt roads spidered across the high desert with few landmarks to guide them. We weren't exactly lost, but took the wrong fork enough times to lose track of where we were. It's a com-mon experience. A man once restored a vintage car and decided to take it on a test drive across the reservation. After making endless false turns, he came to a fork in the road where he noticed a Navajo man sitting by himself. The driv-er pulled up looking for directions and admitted he was lost. The Indian sat there staring at the old car for a moment before looking up. "You been lost a long time," he said.

When the terrain out the windshield finally fit the map, the sun was straight up. The women watched us disappear over the rim, staggering under Sherpa-sized loads and trying to see through our masks. In about thirty sec-onds these came off when the trail began hugging the cliff face. To our sur-prise, it turned out to be an old horse trail in fairly decent condition, last improved in the 1950s for pack trains. It had its share of washouts and disap-peared for long stretches in the bottom of the drainage, but suited our pur-poses.

The full realization of what we were about to do finally hit when we reached the river. Our deflated boat looked pathetically small next to the big Colorado, running fast and cold. But there was no going back. The three of us took turns working the foot pump until we had resuscitated the Redshank. Even fully inflated, it still resembled the type of raft that comes with a tag on the side reading, FOR AGES 8 AND UP.

When all was ready, Captain Terry took the stern with a pipe in his mouth and an ARIZONA FEEDS cap on his head. I settled onto the thwart, and Milzer, bundled in his Seattle rain gear, manned the bow. The raft broke through the eddy, and we let the current swing us downriver. The Redshank handled well even fully loaded, and Terry steered it smoothly through a couple of riffles. It's always a release of spirit to be on the water, but our enthusiasm was tempered by having to keep looking over our shoulders. Any moment we might run into another river party.

For the next two days we made a leisurely float through Marble Canyon, pulling in whenever the impulse hit. The three of us crisscrossed the cliffs at Vaseys Paradise, explored the Bridge of Sighs and Eminence Break areas, and poked into side canyons. We whooped and hollered our way down several rapids, and saw no one. Each night the boat was pulled high out of the water and hidden behind a screen of willows. Each morning we pushed into the current. By the third day the weather had turned cold, and snow had fallen on the rim. Soon the growl of a motor sounded from upriver, piercing the illusion of having the canyon to ourselves. We knew this could be it, the end of the cruise. A single boat churned around the bend, bearing down on us. We watched in silence as it got closer, unable to identify it. Finally Terry broke the tension by announcing it was only a commercial trip.

The three of us scrambled to open our drybags and pulled out the masks. In a moment the motor rig shot past without throttling down, the passengers poncho-wrapped and bent forward against the cold. A wave or two, and they were gone. We never knew if those on the other boat had noticed anything strange, and did not encounter another party for the rest of the trip.

In camp that night, Terry told us about his first run down the Colorado. "There I was . . . ," he began with a laugh. "June, 1972. I was in college and had no idea what I was getting into, absolutely none. I came from the East Coast in a beat-up VW bus that broke down over Wolf Creek Pass in Colorado, and I coasted it down all the way to Cortez." He left his vehicle and started hitch-hiking.

"I got a ride with a Navajo, and he says, 'Where you go?' And I said, 'Grand Canyon.' 'Oh, Grand Canyon, I drop you off there.' And he drops me off in Teec Nos Pos. I am standing out there in the middle of nowhere, absolutely frittered. I'm standing with my thumb out, pack on, and a van with hippies pulls up." It turned out they were also on their way to the Grand Canyon, and Terry convinced them the best place to see it was from Lees Ferry.

"I should have missed the trip," he continued. "It was supposed to take off that morning, and I got there at noon. I'm thinking I'm toast. So I pull up to the loading ramp in this hippie van and see gear everywhere, all this dead rubber splayed out on the ground. These are army surplus rescue rafts, and one even has an inflatable roll bar. The trip leader had only done two trips. Nobody knows what's happening, and I'm clueless." Terry had been hired to run a baggage boat, but they were short a boatman so he ended up running a passenger raft on his first trip. "Five boats flipped, I was the only one who didn't, but we made it. And by the end of the trip we had twenty-four broken oars."

Approaching Kwagunt Rapid the next day, we took the precaution of lashing down gear and tightening life jackets. We had known from the start this one might take us for a swim, and by the time we drifted to the entry, the raft was rigged to flip. Rated a 6 on the Grand Canyon's 10 scale, it was the most serious whitewater we would meet. No sense scouting it; we knew what had to be done. Breaking waves tossed spray into the air at the top of the rapid, a phenomenon known as "slavering." The beast was anxious to be fed. A moment later Terry dropped in, angling left to dodge a boat-swallowing pour-off. Then it was paddle like hell, make a cut or two, and ride out the wave train. The Redshank seesawed through the waves, getting slapped by a few laterals and taking on enough splash to remind us we had been through a rapid. "Well," Terry said as we floated out the bottom drenched, "I guess we cheated death again."

During my boatman days, I only ran into a single party trying to sneak the Grand. One evening two guys walked into our camp above Soap Creek Rapid asking directions. It's not often you get asked for directions on the river; most people are heading only one way. They soon confessed to having slipped in by a side canyon with only a rubber ducky, a road map, and no clue about running rivers or reading maps. The leader traced the blue line of the river on the unfolded map until it joined another blue line marking the Little Colorado. He was under the impression they could take a left at the Confluence and float out to the nearest highway at the Cameron Trading Post. Unfortunately water doesn't run uphill. I gently broke the news, and suggested they might want to consider hiking back the way they came. They thanked me for the advice, but early the next morning I saw them float past camp. Luckily, they flipped in House Rock Rapid just as a river patrol appeared on the scene. The rangers fished them out and gave them a safe, but not inexpensive, ride to the helipad at Phantom Ranch.

Reaching the Confluence, we paddled a few boat lengths up the Little Colorado before landing. By then the river had worked its magic, and Milzer lobbied hard for continuing downstream. In addition to an increased risk of getting caught, I pointed out we had no way of getting word to the women who were meeting us the next day. On top of that, we were out of food. "We could eat moss and drink back-eddy beers," Milzer insisted, "or raid the trash cans at Phantom Ranch."

We spread out the gear to dry until it was time to pack up. The rim towered 3300 feet above, and we wanted to be in position to reach it tomorrow. Bent under spine-compressing loads once again, we headed up the Little Colorado and made camp in a rock shelter. That night Milzer tossed and turned until dawn in what he called the "Cave of the Bad Dreams."

As the sky lightened, we began the climb, moving slower than we had on the way in. Milzer was coming down with the flu as we slogged up a series of talus slopes and traversed the headwalls of steep ravines. The route resembled the child's board game of Chutes and Ladders. Hit the wrong square, and you could find yourself sliding back to the geological layer below. "It's a great route," Terry said, "but you'd never want to take a boat out here." Nobody disagreed.

Even when traveling light this terrain makes for a rough scramble, but with heavy loads we resembled three penitents crawling their final, tortuous mile. On some stretches each step had to be carefully planted, testing to see if the loose talus would hold before shifting weight to the next. And Terry did it without boots. For as long as I had known him, he always scrambled about in flip-flops. He once sent his friends a photo taken on a 20,000-foot summit in South America, showing him standing in the snow with a pair of crampons strapped to his flip-flops. Only a joke, we figured, but no one was certain.

Near the top, we entered a ravine notched from the rim cliffs. The angle of the route now approached the vertical, requiring several hand-and-toe climbs.

Trailing a rope, I climbed a pitch and hauled up my pack, repeating this at the next level. But Terry refused to take off his pack on principle. Milzer and I were wrestling with our loads on a lower rock face and could hear Terry struggling above us on the last, overhanging pitch. Unable to see him, we could gauge his progress by the grunts alone. Suddenly we heard a guttural cry and waited to see if he would zip past. But it was only a final, determined effort to pull himself over the lip, and it worked.

We soon heard the voices of Nancy and Sandy high above and knew our ride was waiting. The women had spotted us from the rim and watched our slow progress. As Milzer stopped to rest, Sandy couldn't resist. "Hey, Milzer!" she shouted down. "Crawl like a cur, crawl like a cur!"

"I'm crawling like a cur," he said to himself, "because I'm as sick as a dog."

Finally at the rim, we shuffled over to the truck, glad to be back on level ground.

Before the trip, I had quickly scanned a classic book on portaging by Dixon Wallace. The section on using a tumpline ended with a warning to the novice, which I had overlooked. "His first portage," Wallace wrote, "will not be what he can conscientiously term an experience of unalloyed joy." As it turned out, my only moment of unalloyed joy was letting the pack drop with a thud for the last time on reaching the top.

Scott Thybony, a former river guide, travels through North America on assignments for major magazines, including *National Geographic*, *Smithsonian*, and *Outside*. His book *Burntwater* was chosen as a PEN Center West finalist for creative nonfiction and selected for the "Original Voices" series by Border Books. Thybony's interviews have ranged from astronauts to medicine men. At various times he has found himself eating raw caribou with Inuit hunters, hors d'oeuvres with World Cup ski champions, and Dutch oven beer biscuits with river runners.

first date

Michael Engelhard

WITH EACH PADDLE stroke, muscles play across her tanned, well-rounded shoulders. Straight, chestnut-colored hair falls to the nape of her neck, barely concealing the swanlike curve.

"Such a beautiful day, non?"

It is indeed. I cannot believe my luck. Here I am, with an exotic woman, on a remote northern river, a blue sky smiling above everything.

What more could a man want?

IT ALL BEGAN with an ad.

Or rather, with the idea—after so many years of romantic shipwrecks, of forever stumbling into the pits of physical attraction and carnal confusion—that a soul mate could perhaps better be found by comparing souls. So I decided to have my profile printed in *Alaska Men*, the pathbreaking periodical that has been "bringing you Alaska bachelors since 1987." *You* meaning the female half of the Lower 48. *Bachelors* meaning "husband material," in the words of the magazine editor herself. This illustrious and illustrated gem also gave the world a T-shirt with the slogan ALASKA MEN—THE ODDS ARE GOOD, BUT THE GOODS ARE ODD! and the Firefighter Calendar, a long-overdue male equivalent of the swimsuit calendar and Playboy centerfold. Actually, the odds in places like Fairbanks or Anchorage seem about even, and as for oddity . . . judge for yourself. I certainly qualified for the honorific "Alaska Man." Although of German extraction, I had been a resident of the Big Dipper state for almost four years.

So, undaunted by the commodification of my body, I sent in a filled-out questionnaire, together with a picture of my expressive, clean-cut features

against the backdrop of a bush plane. (Not my own—the plane, that is.) Asked
to describe my ideal first date to the readers, I did not hesitate for a second: *My
ideal first date would be a weeklong wilderness trip together, because I believe that's where
your compatibility and true colors show quickly.* They ran a full page in the magazine,
and I was happy with the way I looked and sounded on glossy paper.

I was hoping for the mother lode, this time around.

As a safety precaution against love-crazed stalkers, crank calls, or bomb
threats from jealous ex-boyfriends, I had my phone number unlisted and rented a mailbox at the post office in town. (*Paranoid* was not one of the character
traits I had cared to mention in my sales pitch.) As it turned out, the magazine's readership was rather diverse, and not at all limited to the continental
U.S.: I received fan mail from England; one letter—in broken English—
arrived from Quebec; another came from a black nurse in Kotzebue. A lone-
ly-sounding fisherwoman trawling off the coast of South Africa wrote me on
yellow legal pad paper. One of my female pen pals had grown up in a light-
house. She admitted she talked a lot to dead people. I received notes from
female prison inmates, which made me blush, although I pride myself on not
being prudish. Some epistles contained locks of hair. (Fortunately no other
body parts.) Others were smudged with lipstick kisses, or steeped in mysterious perfumes.

Quite a few women were suspicious. They wanted to know why I had used
a portrait shot for a photo. Was I obese? Or missing a limb? Foolishly, I had
believed in the old saw that "eyes are the windows to the soul."

I quickly became an expert graphologist, a reader-between-lines. At times,
the colorful stamps intrigued more than the enclosed words. But every time I
peered into the dark hole of my mailbox and spotted the white or pink flash
of envelopes, I trembled with the prospect of having hit pay dirt. Letters and
pictures of women in various poses and stages of life lay scattered all over my
fourteen-by-fourteen-foot plywood palace without running water. (Hence the
self-described *rustic minimalist* in the magazine.) I bought a folder and organized my correspondence alphabetically, and felt like a little boy locked into the
candy store overnight.

A frantic flurry of letter writing ensued with a few fortunate candidates.

And bit by bit, as I got to meet their souls—and they mine—the choice became clear.

Monique was a French woman living in Albuquerque, a lover of literature and a painter. I personally prefer Ed Abbey's rants to Simone de Beauvoir, and much of photographic realism strikes me as uninspired. But I felt I had to make some concessions. Monique had also divorced her husband—a former salvage diver—when he turned into a couch potato. *My kind of woman exactly!* We swapped phone numbers, and the first time her sweet, melodious lilt bridged the distance between us, I could have eaten the receiver of my phone.

When she finally walked through the gate at the Fairbanks airport, my heart danced a little jig: She looked like a French version of Audrey-the-doe-eyed Hepburn. Except, with her delicate five-foot-four frame, she was shorter than I expected—about half the size of the glass-encased grizzly bear flanking the Alaska Airlines counter. Monique had told me her height, but it had never quite registered, and I am bad with numbers anyway. (In my self-portrait that translated into *concerned with quality rather than quantity*.)

She knew, however, that the way into the heart of a Taurus is through his belly. In my cramped kitchen nook, she went straight to work, preparing a dish of braised scallops, green asparagus, potatoes "au gratin," smothered in a killer sauce of heavy cream and Cognac (no cheap brandy for her)—something with a nasal-sounding name I can't quite remember. That first night, we slept chastely apart: myself in the stuffy loft reached via ladder and hatch and Monique on the floor of my domicile, which tilts slightly, because I live on permafrost in the muskeg that encircles town.

We spent our first full day together doing touristy things. Aboard the sternwheeler *Discovery* we plowed the silty flood of the Chena River, while the theme music of *Love Boat* kept playing in my head. We stopped at Susan Butcher's place, and the famous musher welcomed us from her backyard. Leaning on the rails of the big white riverboat, we watched Susan's handler race her Iditarod-winning team. The huskies looked a little hot on this blistering subarctic July day, as they pulled a sled around the yard, their driver barely visible behind clouds of dust.

"But there is no snow," observed my lovely companion.

"We Alaskans do things differently," I reassured her.

A pleasant-enough evening was spent at the Malemute Saloon of the old Ester Gold Camp. Monique got her first glimpse of Alaskan manhood and mores from the player of the upright piano—a token Sourdough dressed in turn-of-the-century-garb—who kept spitting with great relish into the sawdust that covered the floor.

The day after, a small plane delivered us to the banks of the Koyukuk River, north of the Arctic Circle, where its turbid waters skirt the village of Allakaket. Our great adventure was about to begin.

Surrounded by piles of gear, I wrestled with the Klepper, the collapsible double kayak made-in-the-old-country that was to be our craft. I remembered that the brand name is a Teutonic term for an old nag ready to be sent to the slaughter. Out of their packsack, the canvas deck and rubberized bottom, the keel, ribs, thwarts, gunwales and rudder parts rather resembled the remains of a butchered seal on shore. I could not make sense of the gibberish of the German instructions, even though I am normally fluent in that language. (*Manually challenged* was another trait that never made it into print, because it clashed with *self-reliant* and *down-to-earth*.) With the help of my fine-featured visitor from the high desert and advice from a number of Eskimo and Athabaskan spectators, I eventually figured out where all the Flügelmuttern and Keuzschlitzschrauben needed to go. We assembled The Thing and shoved off.

"SHOULD WE LOOK for a camp, Mai-kel?" Monique now warbles from the bow of the boat.

I just *love* the way she pronounces my name.

"Biensure." I flaunt my command of the Gallic tongue and contemplate adding a *cherie* for good measure.

We make camp in a clearing overlooking the river. Humping the contents of our craft up the steep bank, I realize I forgot a minor piece of equipment—the cooking pot. (It was all there, out in the open, black on white in *Alaska Men*: . . . *not obsessing about the mundane details of life* . . .) I prove my resourcefulness and worth as a paramour by emptying the can of Coleman fuel for the stove into our water bottles. We will have to dip drinking water with our cups, straight from the river. So what, a little sediment never hurt anybody. With the saw of my penknife, I cut the one-gallon tin can in half. The upper part, hammered flat with a rock, makes a nice lid, the bottom a beautiful, if sharp-lipped, pot.

"Voilà!" I beam.

I can see admiration in Monique's eyes, and her radiant smile reveals a chipped front tooth cute enough to die for. My knees feel like the green Jell-O I keep hidden as a surprise dessert. Our pasta-and-tomato-sauce dinner is slightly compromised by an aftertaste of gasoline, which—I feel confident—will be gone in a day or two. And anyway, this is robust bush fare, not some kind of "frou-frou cuisine."

After we have cleaned dishes in a low impact style, with gravel and sand, we set up our shelter. I left the roomy three-person dome tent at home and brought the doghouse instead. We are snug in the tent, lying on top of an unzipped sleeping bag. A shared sleeping bag!

"Tell me about your life in Alaska," she demands.

"Great," I think, "time for some pillow talk." And proceed to recount the adventures of one spring, working for big-game hunting outfits on Kodiak Island and near Katmai's volcanoes.

"I hauled supplies from sea level up into the mountains, and forty-pound bearskins and skulls back to the boats. It was the perfect preparation for an ascent of Denali the following summer." I can tell she is impressed, by her snuggling closer. I go on to recount an episode in Glacier Bay National Park, failing to mention that I flew there to meet another blind date. (She turned out to be . . . but that's a different story.)

"I was out sea kayaking, trying to paddle close to a griz on a spit of land, to get a better picture of him. Next thing you know, he jumps into the drink and starts dog-paddling after me . . ."

The instant these words come out of my mouth, I realize they were a mistake.

"There are bears out here too, n'est-ce pas?" Her voice almost falters.

"Sure . . . I don't know, actually." What else is there to say?

"Ssssh! What was that?"

"What?"

"That sound. Like a splash."

"Probably just a piece of cutbank slumping into the river."

"No, lis-ten!"

And we both do, and her body is rigid, and I can sense tension coming off her like heat. The economy-sized can of bear repellent lying handily at the foot of our love nest probably does not help much to alleviate her fear. I stay quiet, but all I can hear before I drift off into sleep is an ominous rumbling in the distance.

SOON THE MIDSUMMER sun tilts upward on its low arc and light caresses the tops of black spruce trees on a bluff that resemble big bottle-brushes. I walk to the morning-still river, urged by my bladder. Water the color of milk coffee roils at the tips of my boots.

Something about its hue strikes me as odd. Scanning the beach, I cannot see our paddles.

"Monique."

"Yes?" comes her voice from the tent, still heavy with sleep.

"Did you put the kayak paddles away last night?"

"No. Pourquoi?"

"They must be here, somewhere."

I look inside the boat, behind the tent, behind bushes . . . nothing. Suddenly the truth hits me in hot and cold flashes: The river has come up. It must have been raining hard last night, and only upstream. Unloading the boat, I had just dropped the damned paddles, left them lying on the beach. And the flood took them away like so much driftwood.

"Merde alors!" Monique's words, not mine. She stands by the tent, wrapped in her sleeping bag, sculpted collarbones exposed to the new day, which all of a sudden promises to be bleak.

I just stand there, *six feet tall, blond, blue-eyed, confident and comfortable in the outdoors.* God's gift to womanhood.

After a quick and tense breakfast, we are back on the water. I guess we could have lined the kayak downstream, skirting the brushy fringe of the Koyukuk. But I decide to pass on a bushwhacking ordeal. Not easily browbeaten by the weather's antics, we are poling downriver instead, using unwieldy lengths of driftwood. This is very awkward to do from a sitting position. When I try it kneeling, the kayak threatens to capsize. The current is sluggish; at this pace it could take us weeks to get to Hughes, and the poles only help with propulsion where the river is shallow enough.

THE NEXT FEW days are best forgotten. They stretch before us endlessly, an impression that can only in part be credited to the untiring Arctic sun.

The poles break frequently and need to be replaced. When they do, the Klepper truly behaves like a horse carcass. It turns sideways, spins, grinds into gravel bars, or drifts helplessly toward dangerous "strainers"—fallen trees skimming the surface. They vibrate in the stream's passing, potential death-traps, with the power to puncture or pin and flip boats, to keep swimmers' heads underwater. Whenever Monique lowers herself to the point of looking at me, I can see deep lines furrowing her once-comely brow. At some point I try to cheer her up: "This could be Venice, and I could be your gondoliere." (Did I mention *great sense of humor?*) More frosty frowns are my only reward, and I wonder if it could be a cultural thing. Perhaps the French don't like Italians.

In the evenings I lie in my sleeping bag by myself, with sore shoulders and blistered hands, too tired and raw to even think about touching this attractive woman next to me. Instead, I calculate food rations and distances in my head.

Six days out, we pitch the tent on a sweep of gravel lining a river meander. By now, I wear boxing gloves made of bandages from the first-aid kit. But nevertheless: Tonight is the night. Tonight, I will make my move. Tonight, I will check my soul mate's compatibility. Over dinner, Monique had talked to me again, even laughed at some halfhearted jokes. (I had served her pea soup "au cretin," with a flourish: a filthy bandanna draped over my arm.) I start by removing the wraps around my fists, flexing stiff joints. This will be bare knuckles. Last man standing.

Just as I roll over, crunching footfalls approach the tent. They stop abruptly.

Silence. In one fluid move I reach for the bear spray, roll out of the sleeping bag, and poke my head through the tent flap. (. . . *athletic* . . .) I am determined to protect this babe in the woods, if necessary, at the price of my life.

"Hi guys. This is tribal land. Part of the village of Hughes."

"Why? How close are we?" I ask the young man with slightly Asiatic features, who waits respectfully ten feet from the tent.

"'Bout half a mile."

"I didn't know we were that close," I apologize. Knowing that the river would get us where we needed to go, I had not brought maps.

"There is a camping fee, if you guys spend the night here."

I look for my wallet, which I *did* bring. You never know, even the bush is getting expensive these days. I pay; our Koyukon host nods and leaves. Back inside, I realize that the spark of desire has been snuffed out. It could have been the interruption, but more likely forking out fifteen bucks for a campsite without showers, picnic tables, or even a barbecue pit has cooled my ardor.

Next morning, we land at the village. Observant hunters, who have been experts with small watercraft for thousands of years, have gathered on the riverbank to take in our deft maneuvering. On the improvised boat slip, I busy myself with the load, trying to avoid eye contact with the elders. With their tanned, leathery faces, their quiet demeanor and equipoise, these are true Alaska Men, the genuine article.

"You know, they make real nice kickers now," one of them volunteers.

"I know, and goddamn paddles, too," I curse under my breath.

BACK IN FAIRBANKS, we are saying our good-byes at the airport.

"Will you call me when you get to Albuquerque?"

"Perhaps."

A quick hug, a French peck on both cheeks that makes me feel like a European head of state, and Audrey Hepburn disappears through the gate— a mirage.

(I did not know it then, but she never called. Not even collect.)

As soon as I got back to my bachelor pad, I built a bonfire and torched my file of letters in the yard: *given to histrionics*. From the bench on my rickety porch, I watched as fat flakes of ash rose above tangles of fireweed that were already beginning to turn. I contemplated the possibility of another long winter holed up in my cabin, baking twelve kinds of Christmas cookies. For myself. To hell with it! With a sigh, I fed my complimentary copy of *Alaska Men* to the flames.

After his debacle on the Koyukuk River, **Michael Engelhard** moved to Moab, Utah, where he still lives with an unlisted phone number. When he is not soliciting river yarns he writes incendiary natural history and book reviews for *ISLE*, *Wild Earth*, and *Plateau Journal*. He is the author of an essay collection, *Where the Rain Children Sleep*, and wrote the text for a German coffee table book, for which he has not yet seen a dime in royalties. Due to the recent low-water years in the Southwest, he currently scrapes to make a living as a river guide and outdoors instructor.

glossary

ammo can cross between attaché briefcase and a boatman's lunchbox, containing assorted tidbits, bric-a-brac, or thigamajings; caution!—*not* to be confused with **groover**

boatmen / river runners (even when they take their time) includes: boatboys, boatdudes, and boatwomen; *synonyms:* **guide(s)**, goofball(s)

bottleneck where the **river** gets pinched; musical instrument for campfire entertainment

camstrap strap with patented cinch-buckle (that never locks) to fasten load; short for "camera strap"; *not* to be confused with "camp strip"

cataraft raft with twin pontoons, resembling a catamaran sans mast

cfs measure of river—or beer—flow; *acronym* and frequent answer given by **river rangers**: check for yourself

chute polite alternative for popular *expletive* (similar to "heck"–"hell")

dam artificial obstacle (erected with taxpayers' money) between fun stretches of **river**; *not* to be confused with popular *expletive*

deck roof or floor of a **dory** (depending on where you find yourself); a set of playing cards, used to determine the **running order** in scary **rapids**

de-rig one of numerous confusing D-words (and a similarly confusing activity) in river lingo: de-brief, de-bauch, D-ring, de-relict, de-fault; unloading the boats and cleaning the damn gear

dory classically proportioned, easily damaged—often wooden—boat, rowed by strapping lasses and lads—hence "hunky-dory"

downstream toward **takeout**, civilization

drybag bag of spare clothing before it falls into **river**; *not* to be confused with "dirtbag"

ducky also "rubber ducky"; **boatman's** toy; a means to get clients out of your boat for a while; a craft—small, inflatable, often yellow, and always uncomfortable

eddy short for Eddy Mc Stiff's—a notorious bar in Moab, Utah; an area of calm water, or **upstream** current (I kid you not)

eddying out / catching an eddy parking a boat, or **swimmer** in calm water; *euphemism* for "taking a break"

endo / endover   variation of the **flip**, also known as "heels-over-head"; bad situation—*more* than a crisis; *not* to be confused with **hangover** (although side effects may be similar)

entrance slot   first gambling machine as you enter a casino

flatwater   bottled sparkling mineral water (Evian) that has lost its carbonation in **rapids**

flip   elegant turnover of omelets or pancakes on a griddle; inelegant turnover of watercraft in a **rapid**

gratuity   a *derivative* of, but not *synonym* with, "gratitude"

grease bomb   form of evening entertainment entailing the utilization of rancid bacon grease

groover   standard, required receptacle for human waste (*not* wasted humans —those are to be stored *above* **deck**); *derivatives*: groovy, grooving

guests   together with **rapids**, one of the most-discussed topics in any river **outfit**; the people who are always right; raison d'être for **guides**; *synonyms*: customers, passengers, clients, city slickers, babes in the woods, pains in the neck; often used ironically, or threateningly, as in "be my guest"

guide   a person who knows (or is supposed to know) the way . . . and just about everything else; a book that shows where the *really bad* **rapids** are; *synonyms*: maid, cook, entertainer, nurse, babysitter, therapist, slave

guide license   license to **flip** commercially

hangover   a person (passenger or **boatman**) half in, half out of the boat, in danger of becoming a **swimmer**

hatch   intentional **hole** (*no*, a different kind) in the **deck** of a **dory**; a Grand Canyon **outfit**

haystack   big wave; place **guide** looks for a lost client, paddle, or potato peeler

headdrop   drop at the head of a **rapid**; somebody's fall from a boat, headfirst

highside   final stage of an unbalanced boat before a **flip**; the tube of a raft *opposite* the one over which water is pouring in; a *command* to throw your butt onto selfsame tube

hole   the place you want to hide in after a **flip**; where you should *not* be (at least not sideways); **warehouse**

house rock   musical entertainment, often with **guides** as performers (as in "house blend" or "rocking the house")

hydraulic   *not* a car part; the swirly, pushy part of the **river** (see: **rapid**)

J-rig   big raft, equipped with outboard motor(s), consisting of two or three bent, silvery pontoons; rather resembles (and handles like) a zeppelin

kayaking   **river** running in a nutshell

kitchen   nonenclosed beach space where **guides** hang out (also refers to utensils, equipment, and furniture therein); scene of meals and other crimes

Lake Mead   ("Lake Merde") misnomer; a man-made reservoir—crime of the century

Lake Powell   ("Lake Foul") ditto; proper: Glen Canyon Reservoir

lateral   wave from the wrong direction; a muscle easily pulled while rowing

oarlock   the instant a **river runner** freezes, failing to row away from a **hole**

outfit / outfitter   modern slaveholder; person or business providing services, gear, clothing, and **boatmen**, none of which fit or work

permit   piece of paper the land-managing bureaucracy requires you to obtain (for a king's ransom) in order to have fun; *not* to be confused with, but similar to, **guide license**

pour-over   rock in the current, over which water flows, frequently hiding or causing a **hole** on the **downstream** side; *not* to be confused with "pull over!"

put-in, putting in   beginning (of) a river trip, where boats are *put in* the water; *not* to be confused with "putting out"

rapid   hydraulic commotion; raison d'être of many, if not most, **river runners**

rig-to-flip   putting your ship in shape (whatever works for *you*); bribing a **guide** to **flip**

river   heaven-on-earth; where **river runners** go to Be; *synonyms*: Home, Nirvana, Out There, Promised Land, The Real World, Elysian Fields

river ranger   The Law; occasionally ranges outside the office; often former **boatman**; checks **permits**, **guide licenses**, **groover**, and illegal substances

river runner   read the book!

run   attempted or actual course through a **rapid**; **guide's** thought upon seeing passengers show up at **put-in**

running order   order in which **river runners** get to use **groover** after extremely foul meal; *not* to be confused with "standing order" (for beer during **de-rig**) or "pending warrant"

sarong   colorful, imported combination of loincloth and kilt, preferred evening attire of fashion-conscious **boatmen** of both sexes (together with toenail polish and **Tevas**)

shuttle   rickety vehicle, often **outfitter**-owned (but occasionally requisitioned), on which gear and boats and food and **river runners** and clients are transported between **warehouse** and **river** (riding one makes you feel as if you were on a mission to outer space)

sleeper   a rock barely covered with water; **boatman** asnore at the oar, or late riser

snout rig   cataraft on steroids

Sportyak   small type of watercraft; *not* a recreational pack animal

standing wave   stationary wave, caused as the **river** flows over a bump in its bed; a wave so high, the **boatman** has to stand up to look over it

strainer   forced joke or bad pun; a half-submerged **swimmer** stuck in the current

surfing (a **hole**)   *not* a sport requiring a board; rather, a sort of crisis

surfing (a **wave**)   a sport (sort of) requiring a kayak; going nowhere against the mainstream

swimmer   person out of the boat, or without a boat to begin with; another form of crisis; as an *exclamation*, it replaced the archaic "Man overboard!"; often result of a **hangover**

takeout   a kind of fast food; end of river trip, where boats are *taken out* of the water; *not* to be confused with "intake" (see: **kitchen**)

Tevas   the *only* brand of river sandals to wear if you want to be cool— "Chacos" (also: "Chuck 'ems") are second-rate; *not* to be confused with "divas," or **dory guides**

throwbag   coiled-rope-in-a-bag, thrown to assist **swimmer** (tip: hold on to the end!); *not* to be confused with "throw-up bag"

TL   *acronym*: trip leader, head **guide**—one who keeps his or her head (most of the time), who can read and write and tell **upstream** from **downstream**

tongue   body part involved in kissing (hopefully); the smooth, glassy place at the top of a **rapid** where you *should* be

tracking   ability of a boat to maintain a straight course; ability of a **guide** to find lost gear or people

upstream   toward **put-in**, civilization

warehouse   hell-on-earth, chaos; repository of unspeakable and uncountable things; where **guides** go to die

wetsuit   set of spare clothing after it fell into **river**

whirlpool   **river** Jacuzzi-cum-Merry-Go-Round (cannot be turned off)

whitewater   **river** between stretches of **flatwater**; related to "whiteout"; *synonyms*: redwater, greenwater, brownwater, underwater, full of water

yakker   kayak pilot; talkative passenger; a yak herder or Tibetan client

Z-drag   German passenger's term for a **flatwater** stretch, or for **boatmen's** working costumes (as in "luk at zee drag kweens!")